W9-DCD-226

THE PLAYS AND POEMS

OF RICHARD BRINSLEY SHERIDAN

MR. YOUNG AS ROLLA IN "PIZARRO"
FROM A TINSELLED PRINT 1834, SHOWING THE TRADITIONAL COSTUME

The PLAYS & POEMS *of*
RICHARD BRINSLEY
SHERIDAN

Edited with Introductions, Appendices
and Bibliographies by

R. CROMPTON RHODES

Author of The Stagery of Shakespeare
Shakespeare's First Folio
The Theatre Royal, Birmingham, 1774-1824
Black Sheep: a Comedy
Editor of Sheridan's Ode to Scandal

VOLUME III

NEW YORK
RUSSELL & RUSSELL · INC
1962

PR
3680
.A5
.R4
1962
v.3

36004l

PUBLISHED, 1962, BY RUSSELL & RUSSELL, INC.

L. C. CATALOG CARD NO: 62-13850

PRINTED IN THE UNITED STATES OF AMERICA

TO SIR CHARLES HYDE, BART.

Cabrini College Library
21117
Radnor, Pa.

CONTENTS

Pizarro, A Tragedy

Note

"PIZARRO, A Tragedy in Five Acts . . . Adapted to the English Stage by RICHARD BRINSLEY SHERIDAN," was printed in 1799 from the text as revised after the first performance. The songs in *Pizarro* omitted (with one exception) in that Edition were printed with the music in *The Music of Pizarro* by Michael Kelly [1799?]. They are now for the first time restored (in brackets) in full to the text, which otherwise follows the First Edition.

R.C.R.

CONTENTS

Introduction

IT was not Sheridan the dramatist who adapted *Pizarro* to the English Stage : it was Sheridan the politician, the orator. "Never," wrote George Daniel a quarter century afterwards in his Edition of the play, "was a piece better *timed* than *Pizarro*. The English nation, viewing revolutionary France with horror and dread, threatened, too, with an incursion on their own shores, were excited to a high pitch of loyal enthusiasm, and rallied round their monarch, as one man, to preserve inviolate *his* rights, and consequently *their own*. At this eventful crisis, *Pizarro* made its appearance at Drury Lane, and was hailed with rapture by a long succession of as brilliant audiences as ever graced a theatre. Every allusion that bore, however remotely, upon public feeling, was seized with the utmost avidity, while the more direct and palpable appeals were applauded to the very echo."

Nevertheless, the Tories professed to see a menace in the doctrines of *Pizarro*. *The Anti-Jacobin Review* for June, 1799—the play was acted at Drury Lane on May 24th—discerned in the piece a revolutionary tractate. It began by saying that "in *Pizarro* we have a chief or general painted in the most infamous characters, being only meant as a malevolent portrait of men in high stations, although it be disguised with the cloak of history." It ended by declaring that *Pizarro* "has no other appearance than that the author has thrown together a jumble of characters, somewhat in the performance of a dramatic piece, in order the more successfully to foist his sapping principles on the undiscerning multitude: nor can we wonder that Sheridan should exert his abilities, when the main tendency is to promote the views of his party, by a gradual dissolution of the most sacred ties of society."

A saner and more searching criticism, which appeared at the

end of the year in the annual of *Public Characters* of 1799, may be taken to represent the concensus of contemporary considered and educated opinion. It contains, of course, the inevitable allusion of *The Critic*.

"After a retirement of twenty years from the stage, Mr. Sheridan came forward, at the end of last season, in the humble situation of the editor of Kotzebue, the celebrated German dramatist, and appears, in that instance, to have been more actuated by his interest as a manager, than by the generous feelings of a writer, emulous of lasting fame. To gratify the public taste for scenes of exquisite sensibility, supported by incidents, sometimes impossible, and, in almost every case, improbable; and to strengthen the exhibition by the attractions of striking machinery, scenic grandeur, and appropriate music, was evidently the object which he had in view in that strange degradation of superior talents. The pressing wants of the theatre, and of those dependent upon its success, called for instantaneous relief, and the most likely mode of procuring it was an unqualified compliance with popular absurdity.

" 'For we who live to please, must please to live,'

is the only apology he can make, for the prostitution of his muse.

"It would seem, that Mr. Sheridan had altogether forgotten he had written *The Critic*; for there are very few scenes or passages in *Pizarro*, which can escape the just satire and humorous ridicule contained in that production. He has, indeed, condescended, in his alteration of *The Death of Rolla*, to revive the character of the ingenious Mr. *Puff*; for the most prejudiced mind must feel how very pointedly Mr. Sheridan's observations in *The Critic* apply to the favourite tragedy of *Pizarro*:—'Now then for my magnificence! my battle! my noise! and my procession!—Smaller things must give way to a striking scene at the opening; that's the rule:—A play is not to show occurrences that happen every day, but things just so strange, that though they never did, they might happen.' But the criticisms of Mr. Sheridan were no longer remembered;

sound and show triumphed over commonsense; thenumerous
admirers of sensibility, tortured to excess, were gratified; the
votaries of pompous exhibition and romance were indulged in
their favourite passion; and *Pizarro*, with all its defeᵈs, re-
commended by the joint reputation of Kotzebue and Sheridan, attraᵈtedmore numerous and fashionable audiences than
have ever attended an English theatre.

"The speech of Rolla, exhorting the Peruvians to defend
their king and country, their civil and religious inſtitutions,
againſt a ferocious band of lawless invaders, was highly inſtru-
mental to the success of the piece, and it is the only passage of
the play to which Mr. Sheridan has an exclusive claim. The
appeal to the people in support of their rights and national independence, is bold and animating. The ſtriking image of the
vulture and the lamb, is, however, used with more effeᵈt in his
speech on the impeachment of Mr. Haſtings;[1] but his right to
borrow from himself cannot be queſtioned.

"The genius of the German dramatiſt is unqueſtionably of
the firſt order. In conduᵈting a passion through its moſt intri-
cate mazes, he is, perhaps, unequalled, and he seldom fails to
produce emotions of the moſt agonizing kind. Butprobability,
the genuine source of concern and dramatic feeling, is too frequently violated. An inſtant's refleᵈtion is sufficient to expose
the delusion of the scene, and deſtroy the intereſt which the
skill of the poet creates.

"Mr. Sheridan muſt be convinced, that, with the exceptions of Rolla's patriotic harangue, *Pizarro* is more indebted
for its popularity to the merits of the original, to the aᵈtor, the

[1]"It is well known that the simile of the vulture and the lamb, which occurs in the
address of Rolla to the Peruvians, had been previously employed by Mr. Sheridan; and
it showed a degree of indifference to criticism—which criticism, it must be owned, not
unfrequently deserves—to reproduce before the public an image, so notorious both
from its application and its success. But, called upon, as he was, to levy, for the use of
that Drama, a hasty conscription of phrases and images, all of a certain altitude and
pomp, this veteran simile, he thought, might be pressed into the service among the rest.
The passage of the Speech in which it occurs is left imperfect in the Report:—
" 'This is the character of all the protection ever afforded to the allies of Britain under
the government of Mr. Hastings. They send their troops to drain the produce of industry, to seize all the treasures, wealth, and prosperity of the country, and then they call
it Protection!—it is the protection of the vulture to the lamb'."—Moore *Sheridan*, p. 366.

machinist, the painter, and the composer, than to any alterations he has made, or to any judgment he has evinced in adapting it to the English stage. It is to be lamented, that he has, by
this motley exhibition, degraded his reputation as the first
dramatic writer of the country, and sunk himself to a level with
the play-wrights of the day; to whom profit is every thing, and
fame nothing. It remains for him to shake off that indolence,
which appears to have become constitutional, and make a
satisfactory atonement, by some work of genius, for his mer-
cenary conduct in confirming the vitiated state of public taste,
against which he contended, in 1779, with so much energy
and success."

Pizarro was adapted from *Die Spanier in Peru, oder Rolla's
Tod*, a sequel by Augustus von Kotzebue to his own play *Die
Sonnen-Jungfrau* (translated in 1799 by Anna Plumptre as *The
Virgin of the Sun*). Both plays were dramatized from a novel by
Marmontel *The Incas of Peru*. Moore explains that Sheridan de-
parted but little from *The Spaniards in Peru*:

"In the plot, and the arrangement of the scenes, it is well
known, there is but little alteration from the German original.
The omission of the comic scene of Diego, which Kotzebue
himself intended to omit,—the judicious suppression of Elvira's love for Alonzo,—the introduction, so striking in representation, of Rolla's passage across the bridge, and the re-
appearance of Elvira in the habit of a nun, form, I believe, the
only important points in which the play of Mr. Sheridan's devi-
ates from the structure of the original drama."

But Moore overlooked the introduction into *Pizarro* of what
may be termed the operatic element, the ideas of which Sheridan
derived from *The Virgin of the Sun*. It is true that this makes no
show from the printed book, from which all the songs but one
were omitted, but the operatic solemnities in the Temple of the
Sun, for instance, were an essential part of the production, and
made (at the time, at least) impressive by Michael Kelly's music.
It was this "pomp and pride and circumstance" which as much
as any other element, ensured the theatrical *effect* of *Pizarro*.

Sheridan used a translation of *The Spaniards in Peru* by one whom Moore calls "an unknown paraphraſt." She who is identified by Sichel as a Miss Phillips and by Boaden as Maria Geisweiler—the married and single names (I believe) of the same writer. Moore would blame the translator and not Sheridan for the florid ſtyle of his 'Pizarro—"So convenient was it to his indolence to take the ſtyle as he found it, that, except in a few scenes and passages, he adopted with scarcely any alteration the exaćt words of the translator." However, he adds, "Sheridan's own contributions to the dialogue are not of a much higher or purer order. He seems to have written down to the model before him, and been inspired by nothing but an emulation of its faults. His ſtyle, accordingly is kept hovering in the same sort of limbo, between blank verse and prose—while his thoughts and images, however shining and effećtive on the ſtage, are like the diamonds of theatrical royalty, and will not bear inspećtion off it." Sheridan in publishing Pizarro, invited his readers to form "a judgment on its merits and defećts" by comparing it with one of the literal translations.[1] Accordingly, it will be found that Kotzebue had no responsibility for this characteriſtic extravagance. Alonzo and Cora are discussing their child:

Cora. I am sure he will speak soon: then will be the laſt of the three holidays allowed by Nature's sanćtion to the fond anxious mother's heart.

Alonzo. What are those three?

Cota. The ecſtasy of his birth I pass; that in part is selfish; but when firſt the white blossoms of his teeth appear, breaking the crimson buds that did encase them; that is a day of joy; next, when from his father's arms he runs without support, and clings, laughing and delighted, to his mother's knee; that is the mother's heart's next holiday; and sweeter ſtill the third, whene'er his little ſtammering tongue shall utter the grateful sound of Father, Mother!—Oh! that is the deareſt joy of all!

Alonzo. Beloved Cora!

Cora. Oh! my Alonzo! daily, hourly, do I pour thanks to Heaven for the dear blessing I possess in him and thee.

Moore would blame the translator for this, but I am not so sure.

[1]See, for instance, Pizarro, or the Death of Rolla, Edinburgh [1804?].

In his anxiety to dispossess Sheridan of as much responsibility for it as he could, he was ready to believe anything to the purpose. *Pizarro* is bombastic, extravagant, hysterical, but it is homogeneous. On Moore's own showing, Sheridan almost entirely re-wrote the scene between Alonzo and Pizarro (Act III, scene iii) in which occurs one of his famous similes:—

To him I should not need to urge the foul barbarities which drove me from your side; but I would gently lead him by the hand through all the lovely fields of Quito; there, in many a spot where late was barrenness and waste, I would show him how now the opening blossom, blade, or perfumed bud, sweet bashful pledges of delicious harvest, wafting their incense to the ripening sun, give cheerful promise to the hope of industry. This, I would say, is my work! Next I should tell how hurtful customs and superstitions, strange and sullen, would often scatter and dismay the credulous minds of these deluded innocents; and then would I point out to him where now, in clustered villages, they live like brethren, social and confiding, while through the burning day Content sits basking on the cheek of Toil,[1] till laughing Pastime leads them to the hour of rest—this too is mine! And prouder yet, at that still pause between exertion and repose, belonging not to pastime, labour, or to rest, but unto Him who sanctions and ordains them all, I would show him many an eye, and many a hand, by gentleness from error won, raised in pure devotion to the true and only God!—this too I could tell him is Alonzo's work! Then would Las-Casas clasp me in his aged arms; from his uplifted eyes a tear of gracious thankfulness would fall upon my head, and that one blessed drop would be to me at once this world's best proof, that I had acted rightly here, and surest hope of my Creator's mercy and reward hereafter.

It seems to me that Sheridan had a much larger share in *Pizarro* than Moore will allow: I feel that what he took for the

[1] "His line in *Pizarro*—his own not Kotzebue's—'Content sits basking in the cheek of toil ' (a line quoted with applause by John Bright sixty years after) was not bombast. He approached the Irish problem entirely from the cottager's standpoint [etc.]—" Sichel, *Sheridan*, Vol. I, p. 81 [The literal translation gives "content smiling on the countenance of innocence."].

translator's original manuscript was nothing of the sort, but the
transcript of an intermediate version by Sheridan before he had
completed his plan of reconstruction.¹ There is no doubt whatever that he was immensely pleased with the style. On the third
night, he sat in his box and "repeated every syllable after each
performer, counting poetically the measure upon his fingers, and
sounding with his voice like a music-master, with a degree of
earnestness that is beyond my power to describe," is the testi-
mony of one who sat with him.²

Sheridan certainly "put oratory on" *The Spaniards in Peru*.
Pitt, having been to see *Pizarro*, was asked by a friend his
opinion of it. "If you mean," he replied, "what Sheridan has
written, there is nothing new in it, for I heard it all long ago at
Hasting's trial."³ It was not merely the famous simile of the
Vulture and the Lamb; in Alonzo's denunciations of Pizarro in
Peru they heard the repetition of Sheridan's denunciations of
Warren Hastings in India. And Sheridan was as proud of Rolla's
address to the Peruvians as he was of his Begum speech. He
actually used it in an "Address to the Surrey Volunteers" in
1803. Here is the speech of Rolla:—

My brave associates! partners of my toil, my feelings, and
my fame! Can Rolla's words add vigour to the virtuous energies which inspire your hearts? No! *you* have judged as I have,
the foulness of the crafty plea by which these bold invaders
would delude you. Your generous spirit has compared, as mine
has, the motives which, in a war like this, can animate *their*
minds, and *ours*. *They*, by a strange frenzy driven, fight for
power, for plunder, and extended rule. *We*, for our country,

¹Boaden says (no doubt on Kemble's authority) that Sheridan worked on his version
for months, which must mean more than that he added the oratorical ornamentation.
If the literal translation is to be trusted, the introduction of Diego was not Kotzebue's :
it was meant to provide a part for Suett, which points to the manager, not the translator.
If Moore is correct, the idea of Cora's song came from Lewis's translation: it probably
suggested to Sheridan the operatic element, including the finale, and caused a revision
of his plan. The performers, according to Boaden, had already received their parts with
Kotzebue's ending, which implies (I take it) Sheridan's draft. It was his afterthoughts
that caused the delay. These conjectures lead me to suggest that the style was Sheridan's.
But it needs much closer investigation than is possible in a footnote.

²Daniel Stuart, quoted in Boaden's *Life of Mrs. Jordan*.

³Quoted in Oxberry's edition of *Pizarro* (1824).

our altars, and our homes. *They* follow an adventurer whom they fear, and obey a power which they hate. *We* serve a monarch whom we love—a God whom we adore. Whene'er they move in anger, desolation tracks their progress! Whene'er they pause in amity, affliction mourns their friendship. They boast, they come but to improve our state, enlarge our thoughts, and free us from the yoke of error! Yes—*they* will give enlightened freedom to *our* minds, who are themselves the slaves of passion, avarice, and pride. They offer us their protection—yes, such protection as vultures give to lambs— covering and devouring them! They call on us to barter all of good we have inherited and proved, for the desperate chance of something better which they promise. Be our own plain answer this:—The throne *we* honour is the *people's choice*— the laws we reverence are our brave fathers' legacy—the faith we follow teaches us to live in bonds of charity with all mankind, and die with hope of bliss beyond the grave. Tell your invaders this, and tell them, too, we seek no change; and, least of all, such change as they would bring us.

An Editor of 1824 asserted that he borrowed this celebrated harangue from this passage in Cowper's *Task*:

> "We love
> The King who loves the law, respects his bounds,
> And reigns content within them; him we serve,
> Freely and with delight, who leaves us free.
> We love the man, the paltry pageant you:
> We, the chief patron of the commonwealth,
> You, the regardless author of its woes:
> We, for the sake of liberty a king:
> You, chains and bondage for a tyrant's sake
> Our love is principle, and has its root
> In reason—is judicious, manly, free:
> Yours, a blind instinct, crouches to the rod
> And licks the foot that treads it in the dust."

Be that as it may, there are anticipations of this harangue in the speeches at the trial of Hastings, and the substance of it is to be found (as Moore says) in the speeches on the threatened invasion by Bonaparte in the previous year. To this address, into which Kemble infused so heroic a dignity, *Pizarro* owed much of its popular success.

It would be expected from these various accounts that the first night of *Pizarro* was an unprecedented success. But its fate hung in the balance—"Despite the just and genuine applause it had excited in many scenes, at the end it encountered so much violent opposition as then to give but little presage of its future triumphant career." Thus Frederick Reynolds the playwright, who was present. The acting was by no means uniformly good. Suett was outrageously bad as the "comic relief" of Diego, Alonzo's servant, a character borrowed from Kotzebue's *Virgin of the Sun*, to which *Pizarro* is virtually a sequel. Mrs. Jordan was also a failure, and Sheridan was, even on the third night "in the utmost ill-humour, shocked, almost stamping with anger" at everything she said as Cora. Palmer as Valverde was ridiculed by the audience, but then, as Thomas Leman Rede said in *The Road to the Stage* (1827) "the part is a bugbear to most performers." Even Mrs. Siddons was met with laughter, although "by her fine taste and majestic manner," as Reynolds said, echoing Kemble, "she made, in a great degree, a heroine of a soldier's trull." But it was John Philip Kemble as Rolla who determined the success of the play: his noble and dignified bearing, his measured cadences, elevated it to an heroic plane. Kemble, said Boaden, "in fact had all that was really worth anything in the play"—Rolla, he argued, was not merely Kotzebue's hero, but that hero enriched "by the great orator" with spoils captured from Carl Moor in Schiller's *Robbers* and from his own patriotic speeches. On the second night, Diego was suppressed, never to appear again, and other small alterations were made, so that the piece was then acted in the form that it was printed. In sixty nights it brought £30,000 to the treasury, in despite of the fact that it was put aside for three months in the second season through the illness of Mrs. Siddons.

There were reasons, however, for the inadequacy of Mrs. Siddons and Palmer on the first night. At the last rehearsal neither they nor Kemble had received their complete parts, which Sheridan was writing in the prompter's room while the rehearsal was in progress, and they did not see some of their speeches for the laſt aƈt until they were at the end of the fourth. This rehearsal took place on the day of the performance, and was ſtill in progress while the audience was packing the house for the firſt night to overflowing. Michael Kelly, who wrote the music for *Pizarro*, tells the ſtory in his *Reminiscences*; it has often been disputed, largely because he has been misunderſtood as saying that Sheridan brought the aƈtors their parts piece-meal during the aƈtual firſt performance. There is reason, however, to accept it as absolutely true since Boaden, who got much of his information from Kemble, told the same ſtory in his *Life of Mrs. Siddons*.

It is easy to recount the faults of *Pizarro*, but it is not so easy to discern the reasons for its success. As a tragedy it proved to be no *pièce d'occasion*, soaring on the wings of a faƈtious patriotism; it was permanently in the repertory of the English Stage for sixty years and more, until the days of Phelps and Charles Kean.[1] Therefore, one may without prejudice, and ſtill knowing that it gliſtens, but is not gold, regard it *en homme du théâtre*. Its speeches are the sort which were commended by the old aƈtor in Pinero's *Trelawney of the Wells*, the sort that " you can get your teeth into." They are full of "guff," patriotic and sentimental, rich and full-blooded. The charaƈters are bold and highly-coloured; they are not merely "one penny plain," nor yet "two pence coloured," to echo the simile that Stevenson borrowed from the theatrical prints of his boyhood, they are ornamented in profusion, like the *éditions de luxe* of that forgotten art, with silk and tinsel. If one has a sense of the theatre, it is impossible not to recognize the triumphant effeƈtiveness of the rescue by Rolla, that "noble savage," of Cora's child—of his single-handed fight with the Spaniards—of his escape across the bridge with the child in his arms—of the pathos ("sublime" they called it in Kemble's day) of his death. Dr. Johnson used to say that the moſt pathetic line in the language is Jane Shore's dying speech in Rowe's tragedy:

"Forgive me, *but* forgive me."

[1] Kean revived it at the Princess's in 1856; Phelp's at Sadler's Wells in 1862.

Frederick Reynolds said this was surpassed by Rolla's dying reply, as he places the child in her arms, to Cora's "Oh God, there's
blood upon him!—"

"'Tis *my* blood, Cora."

Of course, the whole argument becomes ridiculous at the
whisper of, say, Lear's grief at the death of Cordelia. Yet there is
no doubt that *Pizarro* was, in its day, "good theatre." To recon-
struct it in its fullness one must imagine the great stage of old
Drury; the picturesque scenery of ancient Peru; the striking
costumes with armour and plumes and skins of wild beasts; the
solemn ceremonies in the Temple of the Sun; the throb of the
music ; the lights ; and through all and above all, the heroic,
defiant figure of John Philip Kemble, subduing it all to a splendid, tumultuous monodrama.

All this, of course, *en homme du théâtre* . . .

And, however one may wish to minimize the share that Sheridan had in the making of this *Pizarro*, whatever one may deduce
from his dilatory methods in completing his work, there can be
no doubt that his heart was in its sentiments, in its situations, in
its style. When he printed it, he dedicated it to his second wife,
"to her, whose approbation of this Drama, and whose peculiar
delight in the applause it has received from the public, have been
to me the highest gratification derived from its success." He invited the public to compare it with the two previous translations
of Kotzebue's *Spaniards in Peru*. Surely, no other evidence is
needed that the author of *The Critic* had great pride in *Pizarro*.

Dramatis Personae

ATALIBA, King of Quito	Mr. Powell
ROLLA, } Commanders of his Army	{ Mr. Kemble
ALONZO, }	{ Mr. C. Kemble
CORA, Alonzo's Wife	Mrs. Jordan
PIZARRO, Leader of the Spaniards	Mr. Barrymore
ELVIRA, Pizarro's Mistress	Mrs. Siddons
ALMAGRO	Mr. Caulfield
GONZALO, }	(Mr. Wentworth
DAVILLA, } Pizarro's Associates	{ Mr. Trueman
GOMEZ, }	(Mr. Surmont
VALVERDE, Pizarro's Secretary	Mr. R. Palmer
LAS-CASAS, a Spanish Ecclesiastic	Mr. Aickin
AN OLD BLIND MAN	Mr. Cory
OROZEMBO, an old Cacique	Mr. Dowton
A BOY	Master Chatterley
A CENTINEL	Mr. Holland
ATTENDANT	Mr. Maddocks
PERUVIAN OFFICER	Mr. Archer

SOLDIERS, *Messrs.* FISHER, EVANS, CHIPPENDALE, WEBB, &c.

The Vocal Parts by

Messrs. KELLY, SEDGWICK, DIGNUM, DANBY, &c.—Mrs. CROUCH, Miss DE CAMP, Miss STEPHENS, Miss LEAK, Miss DUFOUR, &c.

17

III. C

Advertisement

AS the two translations which have been published of Kotzebue's Spaniards in Peru have, I understand, been very generally read, the Public are in possession of all the materials necessary to form a judgment on the merits and defects of the Play performed at Drury Lane Theatre.

Dedication

TO HER, whose approbation of this Drama, and whose peculiar delight in the applause it has received from the Public, have been to me the highest gratification its success has produced—I dedicate this Play.

RICHARD BRINSLEY SHERIDAN.

Prologue

Written by Richard Brinsley Sheridan, Esq.

Spoken by Mr. King.

CHILL'D by rude gales, while yet reluctant May
Withholds the beauties of the vernal day;
As some fond maid, whom matron frowns reprove,
Suspends the smile her heart devotes to love;
The season's pleasures too delay their hour,
And winter revels with protracted power:
Then blame not, Critics, if, thus late, we bring
A Winter Drama—but reproach—the spring.
What prudent Cit dares yet the season trust,
Bask in his whisky, and enjoy the dust?
Hors'd in Cheapside, scarce yet the gayer spark
Achieves the Sunday triumph of the Park;
Scarce yet you see him, dreading to be late,
Scour the New Road, and dash thro' Grosvenor-gate:—
Anxious—yet timorous too!—his steed to show,
The hack Bucephalus of Rotten-row.
Careless he seems, yet, vigilantly sly,
Woos the stray glance of Ladies passing by,
While his off heel, insidiously aside,
Provokes the caper which he seems to chide.
Scarce rural Kensington due honour gains;
The vulgar verdure of her walk remains!
Where white-rob'd misses amble two by two,
Nodding to booted beaux—'How'do, how'do?"
With gen'rous questions that no answer wait,
"How vastly full! A'n't you come vastly late?
I'n't it quite charming? When do you leave town?

19

A'n't you quite tir'd? Pray can we set you down?"
These suburb pleasures of a London May,
Imperfect yet, we hail the cold delay;
Should our Play please—and you're indulgent ever—
Be your decree—"'Tis better late than never."

Act the First

SCENE I

A magnificent Pavilion near PIZARRO'*s Tent—a View of the Spanish Camp in the back Ground.—*ELVIRA *is discovered sleeping under a canopy on one side of the Pavilion.—*VALVERDE *enters, gazes on* ELVIRA, *kneels, and attempts to kiss her hand;* ELVIRA, *awakened, rises and looks at him with indignation.*

Elvira. AUDACIOUS! Whence is thy privilege to interrupt the few moments of repose my harassed mind can snatch amid the tumults of this noisy camp? Shall I inform your master of this presumptuous treachery? shall I disclose thee to Pizarro? Hey!

Valverde. I am his servant, it is true—trusted by him—and I know him well; and therefore 'tis I ask, by what magic could Pizarro gain your heart, by what fatality still holds he your affection?

Elvira. Hold! thou trusty SECRETARY!

Valverde. Ignobly born! in mind and manners rude, ferocious, and unpolished, though cool and crafty if occasion need—in youth audacious—ill his first manhood—a licensed pirate—treating men as brutes, the world as booty; yet now the Spanish hero is he styled—the first of Spanish conquerors! and for a warrior so accomplished, 'tis fit Elvira should leave her noble family, her fame, her home, to share the dangers, humours, and the crimes of such a lover as Pizarro!

Elvira. What! Valverde moralizing! But grant I am in error, what is my incentive? Passion, infatuation, call it as you will; but what attaches *thee* to this despised, unworthy leader?—Base lucre is thy object, mean fraud thy means. Could you gain me,

21

Cabrini College Library
21117
Radnor, Pa.

you only hope to win a higher interest in Pizarro—I know you.

Valverde. On my soul, you wrong me; what else my faults, I have none towards you: but indulge the scorn and levity of your nature; do it while yet the time permits; the gloomy hour, I fear, too soon approaches.

Elvira. Valverde, a prophet too!

Valverde. Hear me, Elvira—Shame from his late defeat, and burning wishes for revenge, again have brought Pizarro to Peru; but trust me, he over-rates his strength, nor measures well the foe. Encamped in a strange country, where terror cannot force or corruption buy a single friend, what have we to hope? The army murmuring at increasing hardships, while Pizarro decorates with gaudy spoil the gay pavilion of his luxury! each day diminishes our force.

Elvira. But are you not the heirs of those that fall?

Valverde. Are gain and plunder then our only purpose? Is this Elvira's heroism?

Elvira. No, so save me Heaven! I abhor the motive, means, and end of your pursuits; but I will trust none of you:—in your whole army there is not one of you that has a heart, or speaks ingenuously—aged Las-Casas, and he alone, excepted.

Valverde. He! an enthusiast in the opposite and worse extreme!

Elvira. Oh! had I earlier known that virtuous man, how different might my lot have been!

Valverde. I will grant, Pizarro could not then so easily have duped me; forgive me, but at that event I still must wonder.

Elvira. Hear me, Valverde.—When first my virgin fancy waked to love, Pizarro was my country's idol. Self-taught, self-raised, and self-supported, he became a hero; and I was formed to be won by glory and renown. 'Tis known that when he left Panama in a slight vessel, his force was not an hundred men. Arrived in the island of Gallo, with his sword he drew a line upon the sands, and said, "Pass those who fear to die or conquer with their leader." Thirteen alone remained, and at the head of these the warrior stood his ground. Even at the moment when my ears firſt caught this tale, my heart exclaimed, "Pizarro is its lord!" What since I have perceived, or thought, or felt! you muſt have more worth to win the knowledge of.

Valverde. I press no further; ſtill assured that while Alonzo de Molina, our General's former friend and pupil, leads the enemy Pizarro never more will be a conqueror. [*Trumpets without.*

Elvira. Silence! I hear him coming; look not perplexed.— How myſtery and fraud confound the countenance! Quick, put on an honeſt face, if thou canſt.

Pizarro [*speaking without*]. Chain and secure him; I will examine him myself.

Pizarro *enters.*

(Valverde *bows*—Elvira *laughs.*)

Pizarro. Why doſt thou smile, Elvira?

Elvira. To laugh or weep without a reason, is one of the few privileges we women have.

Pizarro. Elvira, I will know the cause, I am resolved!

Elvira. I am glad of that, because I love resolution, and am resolved not to tell you. Now my resolution, I take it, is the better of the two, because it depends upon myself, and yours does not.

Pizarro. Psha! trifler!

Valverde. Elvira was laughing at my apprehensions that——

Pizarro. Apprehensions!

Valverde. Yes—that Alonzo's skill and genius should so have disciplined and informed the enemy, as to——

Pizarro. Alonzo! the traitor! How I once loved that man! His noble mother entruſted him, a boy, to my proteƈtion. At my table did he feaſt—in my tent did he repose. I had marked his early genius and the valorous spirit that grew with it. Often I had talked to him of our firſt adventures—what ſtorms we ſtruggled with—what perils we surmounted. When landed with a slender hoſt upon an unknown land— then, when I told how famine and fatigue, discord and toil, day by day, did thin our ranks; amid close-pressing enemies, how ſtill undaunted I endured and dared—maintained my purpose and my power in despite of growling mutiny or bold revolt, till with my faithful few remaining I became at laſt victorious!—When, I say, of these things I spoke, the youth Alonzo, with tears of wonder and delight, would throw him on my neck, and swear, his soul's ambition owned no other leader.

Valverde. What could subdue attachment so begun?

Pizarro. Las-Casas—he it was, with fascinating craft and canting precepts of humanity, raised in Alonzo's mind a new enthusiasm, which forced him, as the ſtripling termed it, to forgo his country's claims for those of human nature.

Valverde. Yes, the traitor left you, joined the Peruvians, and became thy enemy and Spain's.

Pizarro. But firſt with weariless remonſtrance he sued to win me from my purpose, and untwine the sword from my determined grasp. Much he spoke of right, of juſtice and humanity, calling the Peruvians our innocent and unoffending brethren.

Valverde. They!—Obdurate heathens!—They our brethren!

Pizarro. But when he found that the soft folly of the pleading tears he dropt upon my bosom fell on marble, he flew and joined the foe: then, profiting by the lessons he had gain'd in wrong'd Pizarro's school, the youth so disciplined and led his new allies, that soon he forc'd me—Ha! I burn with shame and fury while I own it! in base retreat and foul discomfiture to quit the shore.

Valverde. But the hour of revenge is come.

Pizarro. It is; I am returned—my force is ſtrengthened, and the audacious Boy shall soon know that Pizarro lives, and has—a grateful recollection of the thanks he owes him.

Valverde. 'Tis doubted whether ſtill Alonzo lives.

Pizarro. 'Tis certain that he does; one of his armour-bearers is juſt made prisoner: twelve thousand is their force, as he reports, led by Alonzo and Peruvian Rolla. This day they make a solemn sacrifice on their ungodly altars. We must profit by their security, and attack them unprepared—the sacrificers shall become the victims.

Elvira [*aside*]. Wretched innocents! And their own blood shall bedew their altars!

Pizarro. Right! [*Trumpets without.*] Elvira, retire!

Elvira. Why should I retire?

Pizarro. Because men are to meet here, and on manly business.

Elvira. O, men! men! ungrateful and perverse! O, woman! still affectionate though wrong'd! The Beings to whose eyes you turn for animation, hope, and rapture, through the days of mirth and revelry; and on whose bosoms in the hour of sore calamity you seek for rest and consolation; THEM, when the pompous follies of your mean ambition are the question, you treat as playthings or as slaves!——I shall not retire.

Pizarro. Remain then—and, if thou canst, be silent.

Elvira. They only babble who practise not reflection. I shall think—and thought is silence.

Pizarro. Ha!—there's somewhat in her manner lately——

PIZARRO *looks sternly and suspiciously towards* ELVIRA, *who meets him with a commanding and unaltered eye.*

Enter LAS-CASAS, ALMAGRO, GONZALO, DAVILLA, OFFICERS *and* SOLDIERS.—*Trumpets without.*

Las-Casas. Pizarro, we attend your summons.

Pizarro. Welcome, venerable father—my friends, most welcome. Friends and fellow-soldiers, at length the hour is arrived, which to Pizarro's hopes presents the full reward of our undaunted enterprise and long-enduring toils. Confident in security, this day the foe devotes to solemn sacrifice: if with bold surprise we strike on their solemnity—trust to your leader's word—we shall not fail.

Almagro. Too long inactive have we been mouldering on the coast—our stores exhausted, and our soldiers murmuring—Battle! Battle!—then death to the arm'd, and chains for the defenceless.

Davilla. Death to the whole Peruvian race!

Las-Casas. Merciful Heaven!

Almagro. Yes, General, the attack, and instantly! Then shall Alonzo, basking at his ease, soon cease to scoff our suffering and scorn our force.

Las-Casas. Alonzo!—scorn and presumption are not in his nature.

Almagro. 'Tis fit Las-Casas should defend his pupil.

Pizarro. Speak not of the traitor—or hear his name but as the bloody summons to assault and vengeance. It appears we are agreed?

Almagro and *Davilla.* We are.

Gonzalo. All!—Battle! Battle!

Las-Casas. Is then the dreadful measure of your cruelty not yet compleat?—Battle!—gracious Heaven! Against whom?—Against a King, in whose mild bosom your atrocious injuries even yet have not excited hate! but who, insulted or victorious, still sues for peace. Against a People who never wronged the living Being their Creator formed: a People, who, children of innocence! received you as cherish'd guests with eager hospitality and confiding kindness. Generously and freely did they share with you their comforts, their treasures, and their homes: you repaid them by fraud, oppression, and dishonour. These eyes have witnessed all I speak—as Gods you were received; as Fiends have you acted.

Pizarro. Las-Casas.

Las-Casas. Pizarro, hear me!—Hear me, chieftains!—And thou, All-powerful! whose thunders can shiver into sand the adamantine rock—whose lightnings can pierce to the core of the rived and quaking earth—Oh! let thy power give effect to thy servant's words, as thy spirit gives courage to his Will! Do not, I implore you, Chieftains—Countrymen—Do not, I implore you, renew the foul barbarities which your insatiate avarice has inflicted on this wretched, unoffending race!—But hush, my sighs —fall not, drops of useless sorrow!—heart-breaking anguish, choke not my utterance—All I entreat is, send me once more to those you *call* your enemies—Oh! let me be the messenger of penitence from you, I shall return with blessings and with peace from them.—Elvira, you weep!—Alas! and does this dreadful crisis move no heart but thine?

Almagro. Because there are no women here but she and thou.

Pizarro. Close this idle war of words: time flies, and our opportunity will be lost. Chieftains, are ye for instant battle?

All. We are.

Las-Casas. Oh, men of blood!—[*Kneels.*] God! thou haſt anointed me thy servant—not to curse, but to bless my country-men: yet now my blessing on their force were blasphemy againſt thy goodness.—[*Rises.*] No! I curse your purpose, homicides! I curse the bond of blood by which you are united. May fell divi-sion, infamy, and rout, defeat your projeĉts and rebuke your hopes! On you, and on your children, be the peril of the innocent blood which shall be shed this day! I leave you, and for ever! No longer shall these aged eyes be seared by the horrors they have witnessed. In caves, in foreſts, will I hide myself; with Tigers and with savage beaſts will I commune: and when at length we meet again before the bless'd tribunal of that Deity, whose mild doĉtrines and whose mercies ye have this day renounced, then shall you feel the agony and grief of soul which tear the bosom of your accuser now! [*Going.*]

Elvira. Las-Casas! Oh! take me with thee, Las-Casas.

Las-Casas. Stay! loſt, abused lady! I alone am useless here. Perhaps thy loveliness may persuade to pity, where reason and religion plead in vain. Oh! save thy innocent fellow-creatures if thou canſt: then shall thy frailty be redeemed, and thou wilt share the mercy thou beſtoweſt. [*Exit.*

Pizarro. How, Elvira! wouldſt thou leave me?

Elvira. I am bewildered, grown terrified!—Your inhumanity —and that good Las-Casas—oh! he appeared to me juſt now something more than heavenly: and you! ye all looked worse than earthly.

Pizarro. Compassion sometimes becomes a beauty.

Elvira. Humanity always becomes a conqueror.

Almagro. Well! Heaven be praised, we are rid of the old moraliſt.

Gonzalo. I hope he'll join his preaching pupil, Alonzo.

Pizarro. Now to prepare our muſter and our march. At mid-day is the hour of the sacrifice. Consulting with our guides, the route of your divisions shall be given to each commander. If we surprise, we conquer; and if we conquer, the gates of Quito will be open to us.

Almagro. And Pizarro then be monarch of Peru.

Pizarro. Not so fast—ambition for a time must take counsel from discretion. Ataliba still must hold the shadow of a sceptre in his hand—Pizarro still appear dependant upon Spain: while the pledge of future peace, his daughter's hand, secures the proud succession to the crown I seek.

Almagro. This is best. In Pizarro's plans observe the statesman's wisdom guides the warrior's valour.

Valverde [aside to ELVIRA]. You mark, Elvira?

Elvira. O, yes—this is best—this is excellent.

Pizarro. You seem offended. Elvira still retains my heart. Think—a sceptre waves me on.

Elvira. Offended?—No!—Thou know'st thy glory is my idol; and this will be most glorious, most just and honourable.

Pizarro. What mean you?

Elvira. Oh! nothing—mere woman's prattle—a jealous whim, perhaps: but let it not impede the royal hero's course.— [*Trumpets without.*] The call of arms invites you—Away! away! you, his brave, his worthy fellow-warriors.

Pizarro. And go you not with me?

Elvira. Undoubtedly! I needs must be the first to hail the future monarch of Peru.

Enter GOMEZ.

Almagro. How, Gomez! what bring'st thou?

Gomez. On yonder hill among the palm-trees we have surprised an old cacique; escape by flight he could not, and we seized him and his attendant unresisting; yet his lips breathe nought but bitterness and scorn.

Pizarro. Drag him before us.

[GOMEZ *leaves the tent, and returns conducting* OROZEMBO *and* ATTENDANT, *in chains, guarded.*

What art thou, stranger?

Orozembo. First tell me which among you is the captain of this band of robbers.

Pizarro. Ha!

Almagro. Madman!—Tear out his tongue, or else——

Orozembo. Thou'lt hear some truth.

Davilla [*showing his poniard*]. Shall I not plunge this into his heart?

Orozembo [*to* PIZARRO]. Does your army boaſt many such heroes as this?

Pizarro. Audacious!—This insolence has sealed thy doom. Die thou shalt, grey-headed ruffian. But firſt confess what thou knoweſt.

Orozembo. I know that which thou haſt juſt assured me of—that I shall die.

Pizarro. Less audacity perhaps might have preserved thy life.

Orozembo. My life is as a withered tree—it is not worth preserving.

Pizarro. Hear me, old man. Even now we march againſt the Peruvian army. We know there is a secret path that leads to your ſtrong-hold among the rocks; guide us to that, and name thy reward. If wealth be thy wish——

Orozembo. Ha! ha! ha! ha!

Pizarro. Doſt thou despise my offer?

Orozembo. Thee and thy offer!—Wealth!—I have the wealth of two dear gallant sons—I have ſtored in heaven the riches which repay good aċtions here—and ſtill my chiefeſt treasure do I bear about me.

Pizarro. What is that? Inform me.

Orozembo. I will; for it never can be thine—the treasure of a pure, unsullied conscience.

Pizarro. I believe there is no other Peruvian who dares speak as thou doſt.

Orozembo. Would I could believe there is no other Spaniard who dares aċt as thou doſt!

Gonzalo [*aside*]. Obdurate Pagan!—How numerous is your army?

Orozembo. Count the leaves of yonder foreſt.

Almagro. Which is the weakeſt part of your camp?

Orozembo. It has no weak part—on every side 'tis fortified by juſtice.

Pizarro. Where have you concealed your wives and your children?

Orozembo. In the hearts of their husbands and their fathers.

Pizarro. Know'st thou Alonzo?

Orozembo. Know him!—Alonzo!—Know him!—Our nation's benefactor!—The guardian angel of Peru!

Pizarro. By what has he merited that title?

Orozembo. By not resembling thee.

Almagro. Who is this Rolla, joined with Alonzo in command?

Orozembo. I will answer that; for I love to hear and to repeat the hero's name. Rolla, the kinsman of the King, is the idol of our army; in war a tiger, chafed by the hunter's spear; in peace as gentle as the unweaned lamb. CORA was once betrothed to him; but finding she preferred Alonzo, he resigned his claim, and, I fear, his peace, to friendship and to CORA's happiness; yet still he loves her with a pure and holy fire.

Pizarro. Romantic savage!—I shall meet this Rolla soon.

Orozembo. Thou hadst better not! The terrors of his noble eye would strike thee dead.

Davilla. Silence, or tremble!

Orozembo. Beardless robber! I never yet have trembled before God—why should I tremble before man?—Why before thee, thou less than man!

Davilla. Another word, audacious heathen, and I strike!

Orozembo. Strike, Christian! Then boast among thy fellows —I too have murdered a Peruvian!

Davilla. Hell and vengeance seize thee! [*Stabs him.*]

Pizarro. Hold!

Davilla. Couldst thou longer have endured his insults?

Pizarro. And therefore should he die untortured?

Orozembo. True! Observe, young man—your unthinking rashness has saved me from the rack; and you yourself have lost the opportunity of a useful lesson; you might have seen with what cruelty vengeance would have inflicted torments, and with what patience virtue would have borne them.

Elvira [*supporting* OROZEMBO's *head upon her bosom*]. Oh! ye are monsters all. Look up, thou martyr'd innocent—Look up once more, and bless me ere thou diest. God! how I pity thee!

Orozembo. Pity me!—Me! so near my happiness! Bless thee,

lady!—Spaniards—Heaven turn your hearts, and pardon you as
I do. [OROZEMBO *is borne off dying.*
Pizarro. Away!—Davilla! If thus rash a second time——
Davilla. Forgive the hasty indignation which——
Pizarro. No more—unbind that trembling wretch—let him
depart; 'tis well he should report the mercy which we show to in-
solent defiance.—Hark!—our troops are moving.
Attendant [*on passing* ELVIRA]. If through your gentle means
my master's poor remains might be preserved from insult——
Elvira. I understand you.
Attendant. His sons may yet thank your charity, if not avenge
their father's fate. [*Exit.*
Pizarro. What says the slave?
Elvira. A parting word to thank you for your mercy.
Pizarro. Our guard and guides approach. [*Soldiers march
through the tents.*] Follow me, friends—each shall have his post
assigned, and ere Peruvia's God shall sink beneath the main, the
Spanish banner, bathed in blood, shall float above the walls of
vanquish'd Quito. [*Exeunt.*

Manent ELVIRA *and* VALVERDE.

Valverde. Is it now presumption that my hopes gain strength
with the increasing horrors which I see appal Elvira's soul?
Elvira. I am mad with terror and remorse! Would I could fly
these dreadful scenes!
Valverde. Might not Valverde's true attachment be thy refuge.
Elvira. What wouldst thou do to save or to avenge me?
Valverde. I dare do all thy injuries may demand—a word—
and he lies bleeding at your feet.
Elvira. Perhaps we will speak again of this. Now leave me.
[*Exit* VALVERDE.
Elvira [*alone*]. No! not this revenge—no! not this instrument.
Fie, Elvira! even for a moment to counsel with this unworthy
traitor!—Can a wretch, false to a confiding master, be true to
any pledge of love or honour?—Pizarro will abandon me—yes;
me—who, for his sake, have sacrificed—Oh, God!—What have
I not sacrificed for him; yet, curbing the avenging pride that

swells this bosom, I still will further try him. Oh, men! ye who, wearied by the fond fidelity of virtuous love, seek in the wanton's flattery a new delight, oh, ye may insult and leave the hearts to which your faith was pledged, and, stifling self-reproach, may fear no other peril; because such hearts, howe'er you injure and desert them, have yet the proud retreat of an unspotted fame—of unreproaching conscience. But beware the desperate libertine who forsakes the creature whom his arts have first deprived of all natural protection—of all self-consolation! What has he left her? —Despair and vengeance!   [*Exit.*

END OF THE FIRST ACT

Act the Second

SCENE I

A Bank surrounded by a wild Wood, and Rocks.—CORA, *sitting on the root of a tree, is playing with her Child.*—ALONZO *looks over them with delight and chearfulness.*

Cora. NOW confess, does he resemble thee, or not?

Alonzo. Indeed he is liker thee—thy rosy softness, thy smiling gentleness.

Cora. But his auburn hair, the colour of his eyes, Alonzo.—O! my lord's image, and my heart's adored! [*Pressing the Child to her bosom.*]

Alonzo. The little darling urchin robs me, I doubt, of some portion of thy love, my Cora. At least, he shares caresses, which till his birth were only mine.

Cora. Oh no, Alonzo! a mother's love for her dear babe is not a ſtealth, or taken from the father's ſtore; it is a new delight that turns with quicken'd gratitude to HIM, the author of her augmented bliss.

Alonzo. Could Cora think me serious?

Cora. I am sure he will speak soon: then will be the laſt of the three holydays allowed by Nature's sanction to the fond anxious mother's heart.

Alonzo. What are those three?

Cora. The ecſtasy of his birth I pass; that in part is selfish: but when firſt the white blossoms of his teeth appear, breaking the crimson buds that did incase them; that is a day of joy: next, when from his father's arms he runs without support, and clings, laughing and delighted, to his mother's knee; that is the mother's heart's next holyday: and sweeter ſtill the third, whene'er his little ſtammering tongue shall utter the grateful sound of, Father, Mother!—O! that is the deareſt joy of all!

33

Alonzo. Beloved Cora!

Cora. Oh! my Alonzo! daily, hourly, do I pour thanks to Heaven for the dear blessing I possess in him and thee.

Alonzo. To Heaven and Rolla.

Cora. Yes, to Heaven and Rolla: and art thou not grateful to them too, Alonzo? art thou not happy?

Alonza. Can Cora ask that question?

Cora. Why then of late so restless on thy couch? Why to my waking, watching ear so often does the stillness of the night betray thy struggling sighs?

Alonzo. Must not I fight against my country, against my brethren?

Cora. Do they not seek our destruction, and are not all men brethren?

Alonzo. Should they prove victorious?

Cora. I will fly, and meet thee in the mountains.

Alonzo. Fly, with thy infant, Cora?

Cora. What! think you a mother, when she runs from danger, can feel the weight of her child?

Alonzo. Cora, my beloved, do you wish to set my heart at rest?

Cora. Oh yes! yes! yes!

Alonzo. Hasten then now to the concealment in the mountains; there dwells your father, and there all our matrons and virgins, and our warriors' offspring, are allotted to await the issue of the war. Cora will not alone resist her husband's, her sisters', and her monarch's wish.

Cora. Alonzo, I cannot leave you: Oh! how in every moment's absence would my fancy paint you, wounded, alone, abandon'd! No, no, I cannot leave you.

Alonzo. Rolla will be with me.

Cora. Yes, while the battle rages, and where it rages most, brave Rolla will be found. He may revenge, but cannot save thee. To follow danger, he will leave even thee. But I have sworn never to forsake thee but with life. Dear, dear Alonzo! can you wish that I should break my vow?

Alonzo. Then be it so. Oh! excellence in all that's great and lovely, in courage, gentleness, and truth; my pride, my content, my all! Can there on this earth be fools who seek for happiness, and pass by love in the pursuit?

Cora. Alonzo, I cannot thank you: silence is the gratitude of true affection: who seeks to follow it by sound will miss the track. [*Shout without.*] Does the King approach?

Alonzo. No, 'tis the General placing the guard that will surround the temple during the sacrifice .'Tis Rolla comes, the first and best of heroes. [*Trumpets sound.*]

Enter ROLLA.

Rolla [*as entering*]. Then place them on the hill fronting the Spanish camp. [*Enters,*]

Cora. Rolla! my friend, my brother!

Alonzo. Rolla! my friend, my benefactor! how can our lives repay the obligations which we owe you?

Rolla. Pass them in peace and bliss.—Let Rolla witness it, he is overpaid.

Cora. Look on this child—He is the life-blood of my heart; but if ever he loves or reveres thee less than his own father, his mother's hate fall on him!

Rolla. Oh, no more!—What sacrifice have I made to merit gratitude? The object of my love was Cora's happiness.—I see her happy.—Is not my object gain'd, and am I not rewarded? Now, Cora, listen to a friend's advice. You must away; you must seek the sacred caverns, the unprofan'd recess, whither, after this day's sacrifice, our matrons, and e'en the Virgins of the Sun, retire.

Cora. Not secure with Alonzo and with thee, Rolla?

Rolla. We have heard Pizarro's plan is to surprise us.—Thy presence, Cora, cannot aid, but may impede our efforts.

Cora. Impede!

Rolla. Yes, yes. Thou know'st how tenderly we love thee; we, thy husband and thy friend. Art thou near us? our thoughts, our valour—vengeance will not be our own.—No advantage will be pursued that leads us from the spot where thou art placed; no succour will be given but for thy protection. The faithful lover dares not be all himself amid the war, until he knows that the beloved of his soul is absent from the peril of the fight.

Alonzo. Thanks to my friend! 'tis this I would have urged.

Cora. This timid excess of love, producing fear instead of valour, flatters, but does not convince me: the wife is incredulous.

Rolla. And is the mother unbelieving too?

Cora. No more—Do with me as you please. My friend, my husband! place me where you will.

Alonzo. My adored! we thank you both. (*March without.*) Hark! the King approaches to the sacrifice. You, Rolla, spoke of rumours of surprise.—A servant of mine, I hear, is missing; whether surprised or treacherous, I know not.

Rolla. It matters not. We are everywhere prepared. Come, Cora, upon the altar 'mid the rocks thou'lt implore a blessing on our cause. The pious supplication of the trembling wife, and mother's heart, rises to the throne of mercy, the most resistless prayer of human homage. [*Exeunt.*

SCENE II

*The Temple of the Sun: it represents the magnificence of Peruvian idolatry: in the centre is the altar.—A solemn march.—The Warriors and King enter on one side of the Temple.—*ROLLA, ALONZO, *and* CORA, *on the other.*

Ataliba. Welcome, Alonzo!—(*To* ROLLA.) Kinsman, thy hand.—(*To* CORA.) Bless'd be the object of the happy mother's love.

Cora. May the sun bless the father of his people!

Ataliba. In the welfare of his children lives the happiness of their King. Friends, what is the temper of our soldiers?

Rollo. Such as becomes the cause which they support; their cry is, Victory or death! our King! our Country! and our God!

Ataliba. Thou, Rolla, in the hour of peril, hast been wont to animate the spirit of their leaders, ere we proceed to consecrate the banners which thy valour knows so well to guard.

Rolla. Yet never was the hour of peril near, when to inspire them words were so little needed. My brave associates—partners of my toil, my feelings and my fame!—can Rolla's words add vigour to the virtuous energies which inspire your hearts?——No—you have judged as I have, the foulness of the crafty plea by which these bold invaders would delude you—Your generous spirit has compared as mine has, the motives, which, in a war like this, can animate *their* minds, and ours.—They, by a strange frenzy driven, fight for power, for plunder, and extended rule—we, for our country, our altars, and our homes.— They follow an Adventurer whom they fear—and obey a power which they hate—we serve a Monarch whom we love—a God whom we adore.—Whene'er they move in anger, desolation tracks their progress!—Where'er they pause in amity, affliction mourns their friendship!—They boast, they come but to improve our state, enlarge our thoughts, and free us from the yoke of error!—Yes—they will give enlightened freedom to *our* minds, who are themselves the slaves of passion, avarice, and pride.—They offer us their protection—Yes, such protection as vultures give to lambs—covering and devouring them!—They call on us to barter all of good we have inherited and proved, for the desperate chance of something better which they promise. —Be our plain answer this: The throne we honour is the people's choice—the laws we reverence are our brave Fathers' legacy—the faith we follow teaches us to live in bonds of charity with all mankind, and die with hope of bliss beyond the grave. Tell your invaders this, and tell them too, we seek no change; and, least of all, such change as they would bring us.

[*Trumpets sound.*

Ataliba (embracing Rolla). Now, holy friends, ever mindful of these sacred truths, begin the sacrifice. [*A solemn Procession commences from the recess of the Temple above the Altar—The Priests and Virgins of the Sun arrange themselves on either side— The High-Priest approaches the Altar, and the Solemnity begins. The Invocation of the*

HIGH-PRIEST
Oh Pow'r supreme! in mercy smile
With favour on thy servants' toil!
Our hearts from guileful passions free
Which here we render unto thee!

is followed by the [semi-] chorus of

[TWO] PRIESTS AND [FOUR] VIRGINS.
Oh Pow'r supreme! in mercy smile
With favour on thy servants' toil!
Our hearts from guileful passions free,
Which here we render unto thee!

CHORUS OF PRIESTS AND VIRGINS.

Thou Parent Light but deign to hear
The voices of our feeble choir;
And this, our sacrifice of fear,
Consume with thine own hallowed fire!

Fire from above lights upon the ALTAR—*The whole assembly rise
and join in the Thanksgiving.*

Give praise, give praise, the God has heard,
Our God most awfully revered!
The altar his own flames enwreathed!
Then be the conquering sword unsheathed,
And victory set on Rolla's brow,
His foes to crush—to overthrow!][1]

Ataliba. Our offering is accepted. [*Rise, and all close round, and
prostrate at the Altar.*] Now to arms, my friends, prepare for
battle!

Enter ORANO.

Orano. The enemy!
Ataliba. How near?
Orano. From the hill's brow, e'en now as I o'er-looked their

[1] These verses from Kelly's edition of the music are not in the early editions.

force, suddenly I perceived the whole in motion: with eager haste they march towards our deserted camp, as if apprised of this most solemn sacrifice.

Rolla. They must be met before they reach it.

Ataliba. And you, my daughters, with your dear children, away to the appointed place of safety.

Cora. Oh, Alonzo! [*Embracing him.*]

Alonzo. We shall meet again.

Cora. Bless us once more, ere you leave us.

Alonzo. Heaven protect and bless thee, my beloved; and thee, my innocent!

Ataliba. Haste, haste!—each moment is precious!

Cora. Farewell, Alonzo! Remember thy life is mine.

Rolla. Not one farewell to Rolla?

Cora [*giving him her hand*]. Farewell! The God of war be with you: but, bring me back Alonzo. [*Exit with the Child.*

Ataliba [*draws his sword*]. Now, my brethren, my sons, my friends, I know your valour.—Should ill success assail us, be despair the last feeling of your hearts.—If successful, let mercy be the first. Alonzo, to you I give to defend the narrow passage of the mountains. On the right of the wood be Rolla's station. For me, strait forwards will I march to meet them, and fight until I see my people saved, or they behold their Monarch fall. Be the word of battle—God! and our native land. [*A march.*]

[*Exeunt.*

SCENE III

The Wood between the Temple and the Camp.

Enter ROLLA *and* ALONZO.

Rolla. Here, my friend, we separate—soon, I trust, to meet again in triumph.

Alonzo. Or perhaps we part to meet no more. Rolla, a moment's pause; we are yet before our army's strength; one earnest word at parting.

Rolla. There is in language now no word but battle.

Alonzo. Yes, one word more—Cora!

Rolla. Cora! Speak!

Alonzo. The next hour brings us—

Rolla. Death or victory!

Alonzo. It may be victory to one—death to the other.

Rolla. Or both may fall.

Alonzo. If so, my wife and child I bequeath to the protection of Heaven and my King. But should I only fall, Rolla, be thou my heir.

Rolla. How?

Alonzo. Be Cora thy wife—be thou a father to my child.

Rolla. Rouse thee, Alonzo! Banish these timid fancies.

Alonzo. Rolla! I have tried in vain, and cannot fly from the foreboding which oppresses me: thou know'ſt it will not shake me in the fight: but give me your promise.

Rolla. If it be Cora's will—Yes—I promise—[*Gives his hand.*

Alonzo. Tell her it was my laſt wish! and bear to her and to my son, my laſt blessing.

Rolla. I will.—Now then to our poſts, and let our swords speak for us. [*They draw their swords.*]

Alonzo. For the King and Cora!

Rolla. For Cora and the King!

[*Exeunt different ways. Alarms without.*

SCENE IV

A View of the Peruvian Camp, with a diſtant View of a Peruvian Village. Trees growing from a rocky Eminence on one Side. Alarms continue.

Enter an OLD BLIND MAN *and a* BOY.

Old Man. Have none returned to the camp?

Boy. One messenger alone. From the temple they all march'd to meet the foe.

Old Man. Hark! I hear the din of battle. O! had I ſtill retain'd my sight, I might now have grasp'd a sword, and died a soldier's death! Are we quite alone?

Boy. Yes!—I hope my father will be safe!

Old Man. He will do his duty. I am more anxious for thee, my child.

Boy. I can ſtay with you, dear grandfather.

Old Man. But should the enemy come, they will drag thee from me, my boy.

Boy. Impossible, grandfather! for they will see at once that you are old and blind, and cannot do without me.

Old Man. Poor child! you little know the hearts of these inhuman men.—[*Discharge of cannon heard.*] Hark! the noise is near —I hear the dreadful roaring of the fiery engines of these cruel ſtrangers.—[*Shouts at a diſtance.*] At every shout, with involuntary haſte I clench my hand, and fancy ſtill it grasps a sword! Alas! I can only serve my country by my prayers. Heaven preserve the Inca and his gallant soldiers!

Boy. O father! there are soldiers running——

Old Man. Spaniards, boy?

Boy. No, Peruvians!

Old Man. How! and flying from the field!—It cannot be.

Enter two Peruvian Soldiers.

O speak to them, boy!—Whence come you? How goes the battle?

Soldier. We may not ſtop; we are sent for the reserve behind the hill. The day's againſt us.　　　　　　[*Exeunt Soldiers.*

Old Man. Quick, then, quick!

Boy. I see the points of lances glittering in the light.

Old Man. Those are Peruvians. Do they bend this way?

Enter a Peruvian Soldier.

Boy. Soldier, speak to my blind father.

Soldier. I'm sent to tell the helpless father to retreat among the rocks: all will be loſt, I fear. The King is wounded.

Old Man. Quick, boy! Lead me to the hill, where thou may'ſt view the plain. [*Alarms.*]

Enter ATALIBA, *wounded, with* ORANO, *Officers, and Soldiers.*

Ataliba. My wound is bound; believe me, the hurt is nothing: I may return to the fight.

Orano. Pardon your servant; but the allotted prieſt who attends the sacred banner has pronounced that the Inca's blood once shed, no blessing can await the day until he leave the field.

Ataliba. Hard reſtraint! O! my poor brave soldiers!—Hard that I may no longer be a witness of their valour. But haſte you; return to your comrades: I will not keep one soldier from his poſt. Go, and avenge your fallen brethren. [*Exeunt* ORANO, *Officers, and Soldiers*.] I will not repine; my own fàte is the laſt anxiety of my heart. It is for you, my people, that I feel and fear.

OLD MAN *and* BOY *advance*.

Old Man. Did I not hear the voice of an unfortunate?—Who is it complains thus?

Ataliba. One almoſt by hope forsaken.

Old Man. Is the King alive?

Ataliba. The King ſtill lives.

Old Man. Then thou art not forsaken! Ataliba proteĉts the meaneſt of his subjeĉts.

Ataliba. And who shall proteĉt Ataliba?

Old Man. The immortal Powers, that proteĉt the juſt. The virtues of our Monarch alike secure to him the affeĉtion of his people and the benign regard of Heaven.

Ataliba. How impious, had I murmured! How wondrous, thou supreme Disposer, are thy aĉts! Even in this moment, which I had thought the bittereſt trial of mortal suffering, thou haſt infused the sweeteſt sensation of my life—it is the assurance of my people's love.

Boy [*turning forward*].O, father!—Stranger, see those hideous men that rush upon us yonder!

Ataliba. Ha! Spaniards!—And I—Ataliba—ill-fated fugitive, without a sword even to try the ransom of a monarch life.

Enter DAVILLA, ALMAGRO, *and Spanish Soldiers*.

Davilla. 'Tis he—our hopes are answered—I know him well —it is the King!

Almagro. Away! Follow with your royal prize. Avoid those

Peruvians, though in flight. This way we may regain our line.

[*Exeunt* DAVILLA, ALMAGRO, *and Soldiers, with* ATALIBA *prisoner.*

Old Man. The King! Wretched old man, that could not see his gracious form!—Boy, would thou hadst led me to the reach of those ruffians' swords!

Boy. Father! all our countrymen are flying here for refuge.

Old Man. No—to the rescue of their King—they will never desert him. [*Alarms without.*]

Enter Peruvian Officers and Soldiers, flying across the stage;
ORANO *following.*

Orano. Hold, I charge you! Rolla calls you.

Officer. We cannot combat with their dreadful engines.

Enter ROLLA.

Rolla. Hold, recreants! cowards!—What, fear ye death, and fear not shame? By my soul's fury, I cleave to the earth the first of you that stirs, or plunge your dastard swords into your leader's heart, that he no more may witness your disgrace. Where is the King?

Orano. From this old man and boy I learn that the detachment of the enemy which you observed so suddenly to quit the field, have succeeded in surprising him; they are yet in sight.

Rolla. And bear the Inca off a prisoner?—Hear this, ye base, disloyal rout! Look there! The dust you see hangs on the bloody Spaniards' track, dragging with ruffian taunts your King, your father!—Ataliba in bondage. Now fly, and seek your own vile safety, if you can.

Old Man. Bless the voice of Rolla—and bless the stroke I once lamented, but which now spares these extinguished eyes the shame of seeing the pale trembling wretches who dare not follow Rolla though to save their King!

Rolla. Shrink ye from the thunder of the foe—and fall ye not at this rebuke? Oh! had ye each but one drop of the loyal blood which gushes to waste through the brave heart of this sightless veteran! Eternal shame pursue you, if you desert me now!—

But do—alone I go—alone—to die with glory by my monarch's side!

Soldiers. Rolla! we'll follow thee. [*Trumpets sound;* ROLLA *rushes out, followed by* ORANO, *Officers, and Soldiers.*]

Old Man. O godlike Rolla!—And thou sun, send from thy clouds avenging lightning to his aid!—Haste, my boy; ascend some height, and tell to my impatient terror what thou seest.

Boy. I can climb this rock, and the tree above. [*Ascends a rock, and from thence into the tree.*] O—now I see them—now—yes— and the Spaniards turning by the steep.

Old Man. Rolla follows them?

Boy. He does—he does—he moves like an arrow!—now he waves his arm to our soldiers—[*Report of cannon heard.*] Now there is fire and smoke.

Old Man. Yes, *fire* is the weapon of those fiends.

Boy. The wind blows off the smoke; they are all mixed together.

Old Man. Seest thou the King?

Boy. Yes—Rolla is near him! His sword sheds fire as he strikes!

Old Man. Bless thee, Rolla! Spare not the monsters.

Boy. Father! father! the Spaniards fly!—O—now I see the King embracing Rolla. [*Waving his cap for joy. Shouts of victory, flourish of trumpets, &c.*]

Old Man [*falls on his knees*]. Fountain of life! how can my exhausted breath bear to thee thanks for this one moment of my life! My boy, come down, and let me kiss thee—My strength is gone! [*The Boy having run to the Old Man.*]

Boy. Let me help you, father—You tremble so——

Old Man. 'Tis with transport, boy!

[BOY *leads the* OLD MAN *off.*

Shouts, Flourish, &c.

Enter ATALIBA, ROLLA, *and Peruvian Officers and Soldiers.*

Ataliba. In the name of my people, the saviour of whose sovereign you have this day been, accept this emblem of his gratitude. [*Giving* ROLLA *his sun of diamonds*.] The tear that falls upon it may for a moment dim its lustre, yet does it not impair the value of the gift.

Rolla. It was the hand of Heaven, not mine, that saved my King.

Enter ORANO, *and Soldiers.*

Rolla. Now, soldier, from Alonzo?

Orano. Alonzo's genius soon repaired the panic which early broke our ranks; but I fear we have to mourn Alonzo's loss; his eager spirit urged him too far in the pursuit!

Ataliba. How! Alonzo slain?

1st Soldier. I saw him fall.

2nd Soldier. Trust me I beheld him up again and fighting—he was then surrounded and disarmed.

Ataliba. O! victory, dearly purchased!

Rolla. O Cora! Who shall tell thee this?

Ataliba. Rolla, our friend is lost—our native country saved! Our private sorrows must yield to the public claim for triumph. Now go we to fulfil the first, the most sacred duty which belongs to victory—to dry the widowed and the orphaned tear of those whose brave protectors have perished in their country's cause.

[*Triumphant march, and exeunt.*

END OF THE SECOND ACT.

Act the Third

SCENE I

A wild Retreat among stupendous Rocks.—Cora *and her Child, with other Wives and Children of the Peruvian Warriors, are scattered about the scene in groups.*—[*Five women sing a song expressive of their situation.*][1]

FLY away, Time, nor be the anxious hour delay'd—
Fly away, Time, that soothes the heart by grief dismay'd;
Should ghastly death appear in view,
> We can dare it;
With friends we love, so brave, so true,
> We will share it.
Fly away, Time, nor be the anxious hour delay'd
Fly away, Time, that soothes the heart by grief dismay'd.]

1st Peruvian Woman. Zuluga, seest thou nothing yet?

Zuluga. Yes, two Peruvian soldiers, one on the hill; the other entering the thicket in the vale.

2nd Peruvian Woman. One more has pass'd.—He comes— but pale and terrified.

Cora. My heart will start from my bosom.

> *Enter a Peruvian Soldier, panting for breath.*

Woman. Well! joy or death?

Soldier. The battle is against us. The King is wounded, and a prisoner.

Woman. Despair and misery!

Cora [*in a faint voice*]. And Alonzo?

Soldier. I have not seen him.

[1] 1st Edition reads instead of this direction : *They sing alternatively stanzas expressive of their situation, with a chorus in which all join.* So all Ridgway's editions. The " Glee " as originally sung is taken from Kelly's edition of the music.

1st Woman. Oh! whither muſt we fly?
2nd Woman. Deeper into the foreſt.
Cora. I shall not move.
Another Peruvian Soldier [without]. Victory! victory!

       He enters haſtily.
Rejoice! Rejoice! We are victorious!
Woman [spring up]. Welcome! welcome! thou messenger of
joy: but the King!
Soldier. He leads the brave warriors, who approach.
   [*The triumphant march of the army is heard at a diſtance.*
     —The Women and Children join in a ſtrain expres-
     sive of anxiety and exultation.
[*Warriors.* Victory now has made us free;
   We haſte, we haſte, our friends to see!]¹
   The Warriors enter singing the Song of Victory, in which
    all join.
Women. Hush! hush! don't you hear?
   A diſtant march assails the ear;—
   Hark! louder ſtill from yonder hill
   Increasing sounds with terror fill—]²
   The King and ROLLA *follow, and are met with rapturous*
    and affectionate respect. CORA, *during this scene, with*
    her Child in her arms, runs through the ranks searching
    and inquiring for ALONZO.
Ataliba. Thanks, thanks, my children! I am well: believe it;
the blood once ſtopp'd, my wound was nothing. [CORA *at length*
approaches ROLLA, *who appears to have been mournfully avoiding*
her.] Where is Alonzo?
         [ROLLA *turns away in silence.*
Cora [falling at the King's feet]. Give me my husband, give
this child his father.
Ataliba. I grieve that Alonzo is not here.
Cora. Hop'd you to find him?
Ataliba. Moſt anxiously.

  ¹From Kelly's edition of the music.
  ²Ibid. (These songs were sung simultaneously in the manner of a glee.)

Cora. Ataliba! is he not dead?

Ataliba. No! the Gods will have heard our prayers.

Cora. Is he not dead, Ataliba?

Ataliba. He lives—in my heart.

Cora. Oh King! torture me not thus! speak out, is this child fatherless?

Ataliba. Dearest Cora! do not thus dash aside the little hope that still remains.

Cora. The little hope! yet still there *is* hope! Speak to me Rolla; *you* are the *friend of truth.*

Rolla. Alonzo has not been found.

Cora. Not found! What mean you? will not *you*, Rolla, tell me truth? Oh! let me not hear the thunder rolling at a distance; let the bolt fall and crush my brain at once.—Say not that he is not found: say at once that he is dead.

Rolla. Then should I say false.

Cora. False! Blessings on thee for that word! But snatch me from this terrible suspense. Lift up thy little hands, my child; perhaps thy ignorance may plead better than thy mother's agony.

Rolla. Alonzo is taken prisoner.

Cora. Prisoner! and by the Spaniards? Pizarro's prisoner? Then is he dead.

Ataliba. Hope better—the richest ransom which our realm can yield, a herald shall this instant bear.

Peruvian Women. Oh! for Alonzo's ransom—our gold, our gems!—all! all!—Here, dear Cora,—here! here!

> [*The Peruvian Women eagerly tear off all their ornaments, and run and take them from their children, to offer them to* CORA.

Ataliba. Yes, for Alonzo's ransom they would give all!—I thank thee, Father, who hast given me such hearts to rule over!

Cora. Now one boon more, beloved monarch. Let me go with the herald.

Ataliba. Remember, Cora, thou art not a wife only, but a mother too: hazard not your own honour, and the safety of your infant. Among these barbarians the sight of thy youth, thy loveliness, and innocence, would but rivet faster your Alonzo's chains, and rack his heart with added fears for thee.—Wait, Cora, the return of the herald.

Cora. Teach me how to live till then.

Ataliba. Now we go to offer to the Gods, thanks for our victory, and prayers for our Alonzo's safety.

[*March and procession. Exeunt omnes.*

SCENE II

The Wood.

Enter CORA *and Child.*

Cora. Mild innocence, what will become of thee?

Enter ROLLA.

Rolla. Cora, I attend thy summons at th' appointed spot.

Cora. Oh my child, my boy!—haſt thou ſtill a father?

Rolla. Cora, can thy child be fatherless, while Rolla lives?

Cora. Will he not soon want a mother too?—For canſt thou think I will survive Alonzo's loss?

Rolla. Yes! for his child's sake.—Yes, as thou didſt love Alonzo, Cora, liſten to Alonzo's friend.

Cora. You bid me liſten to the world.—Who was not Alonzo's friend?

Rolla. His parting words——

Cora. His parting words! [*Wildly.*] Oh, speak!

Rolla. Consign'd to me two precious truſts—his blessing to his son, and a laſt requeſt to thee.

Cora. His *laſt* requeſt! his *laſt*!—Oh, name it!

Rolla. If I fall, said he—(and sad forebodings shook him while he spoke)—promise to take my Cora for thy wife; be thou a father to my child.—I pledged my word to him, and we parted.—Observe me, Cora, I repeat this only, as my faith to do so was given to Alonzo—for myself, I neither cherish claim or hope.

Cora. Ha! does my reason fail me, or what is this horrid light that presses on my brain? Oh, Alonzo! It may be thou haſt fallen a victim to thy own guileless heart—hadſt thou been silent, hadſt thou not made a fatal legacy of these wretched charms——

Rolla. Cora! what hateful suspicion has possessed thy mind.

Cora. Yes, yes, 'tis clear—his spirit was ensnar'd; he was led to the fatal spot, where mortal valour could not front a hoſt of murderers—He fell—in vain did he exclaim for help to Rolla. At a diſtance you look'd on and smil'd—You could have saved him—could—but did not.

Rolla. Oh, glorious sun! can I have deserved this? Cora, rather bid me ſtrike this sword into my heart.

Cora. No! live! live for love! for that love thou seekeſt; whose blossoms are to shoot from the bleeding grave of thy betray'd and slaughter'd friend!—But thou haſt borne to me the *laſt words* of my *Alonzo!* Now hear *mine*—Sooner shall this boy draw poison from this tortured breaſt—sooner would I link me to the pallid corse of the meaneſt wretch that perish'd with Alonzo, than he call Rolla father—than I call Rolla husband!

Rolla. Yet call me what I am—thy friend, thy protector!

Cora [diſtractedly]. Away! I have no protector but my God!— With this child in my arms will I haſten to the field of slaughter —There with these hands will I turn up to the light every mangled body—seeking, howe'er by death disfigur'd, the sweet smile of my Alonzo:—with fearful cries I will shriek out his name till my veins snap! If the smalleſt spark of life remains, he will know the voice of his Cora, open for a moment his unshrouded eyes, and bless me with a laſt look: But if we find him not— Oh! then, my boy, we will to the Spanish camp—that look of thine will win me passage through a thousand swords—They too are men.—Is there a heart that could drive back the wife that seeks her bleeding husband; or the innocent babe that cries for his imprison'd father? No, no, my child, every where we shall be safe.—A wretched mother bearing a poor orphan in her arms, has Nature's passport through the world. Yes, yes, my son, we'll go and seek thy father.   [*Exit with the child.*

Rolla [after a pause of agitation]. Could I have merited one breath of thy reproaches, Cora, I should be the wretch—I think

I was not formed to be.—HER safety muſt be my present purpose—then to convince her she has wronged me!

[*Exit.*

SCENE III

PIZARRO'*s* *Tent.*

Pizarro [*traversing the scene in gloomy and furious agitation*]. Well, capricious idol, Fortune, be my ruin thy work and boaſt. To myself I will ſtill be true.—Yet ere I fall, grant me thy smile to prosper in one aƈt of vengeance, and be that smile Alonzo's death.

Enter ELVIRA.

Who's there? who dares intrude? Why does my guard negleƈt their duty?

Elvira. Your guard did what they could—but they knew theii duty better than to enforce authority, when I refused obedience.

Pizarro. And what is it you desire?

Elvira. To see how a hero bears misfortune. Thou, Pizarro, art now not colleƈted—not thyself.

Pizarro. Wouldſt thou I should rejoice that the spears of the enemy, led by accurs'd Alonzo, have pierced the braveſt hearts of my followers?

Elvira. No:—I would have thee cold and dark as the night that follows the departed ſtorm; and sullen as the ſtill awful pause that precedes Nature's convulsion: yet I would have thee feel assured that a new morning shall arise, when the warrior's spirit shall ſtalk forth—nor fear the future, nor lament the paſt.

Pizarro. Woman! Elvira!—Why had not all my men hearts like thine?

Elvira. Then would thy brows have this day worn the crown of Quito.

Pizarro. Oh! hope fails me while that scourge of my life and fame, Alonzo, leads the enemy.

Elvira. Pizarro, I am come to probe the hero farther: not now his courage, but his magnanimity—Alonzo is your prisoner.

Pizarro. How!

Elvira. 'Tis certain; Valverde saw him even now dragged in chains within your camp. I chose to bring you the intelligence myself.

Pizarro. Bless thee, Elvira, for the news!—Alonzo in my power!—then I am the conqueror—the victory is MINE!

Elvira. Pizarro, this is savage and unmanly triumph. Believe me, you raise impatience in my mind to see the man whose valour and whose genius, awe Pizarro; whose misfortunes are Pizarro's triumph; whose bondage is Pizarro's safety.

Pizarro. Guard!—[*Enter* GUARD.]—Drag here the Spanish prisoner, Alonzo!—Quick bring the traitor here.

[*Exit* GUARD.

Elvira. What shall be his fate?

Pizarro. Death! death! in lingering torments! protracted to the last stretch that burning vengeance can devise, and fainting life sustain.

Elvira. Shame on thee! Wilt thou have it said that the Peruvians found Pizarro could not conquer till Alonzo felt that he could murder?

Pizarro. Be it said—I care not. His fate is sealed.

Elvira. Follow then thy will: but mark me; if basely thou dost shed the blood of this brave youth, Elvira's lost to thee for ever.

Pizarro. Why this interest for a stranger? What is Alonzo's fate to thee?

Elvira. His fate!—nothing!—thy glory, every thing!— Think'st thou I could love thee stript of fame, of honour, and a just renown?—Know me better.

Pizarro. Thou shouldst have known ME better. Thou shouldst have known, that, once provoked to hate, I am for ever fixed in vengeance.—[ALONZO *is brought in, in chains, guarded.* ELVIRA *observes him with attention and admiration.*]—Welcome, welcome Don Alonzo de Molina; 'tis long since we have met: thy mended looks should speak a life of rural indolence. How is it that amid the toils and cares of war thou dost preserve the healthful bloom of careless ease? Tell me thy secret.

Alonzo. Thou will not profit by it. Whate'er the toils or cares of war, peace still is *here.* [*Putting his hand to his heart.*]

Pizarro. Sarcastic boy!

Elvira. Thou art answered rightly. Why sport with the unfortunate?

Pizarro. And thou art wedded too, I hear; aye, and the father of a lovely boy—the heir, no doubt, of all his father's loyalty; of all his mother's faith.

Alonzo. The heir, I trust, of all his father's scorn of fraud, oppression, and hypocrisy—the heir, I hope, of all his mother's virtue, gentleness, and truth—the heir, I am sure, to all Pizarro's hate.

Pizarro. Really! Now do I feel for this poor orphan; for fatherless to-morrow's sun shall see that child. Alonzo, thy hours are numbered.

Elvira. Pizarro—no!

Pizarro. Hence—or dread my anger.

Elvira. I will not hence; nor do I dread thy anger.

Alonzo. Generous loveliness! spare thy unavailing pity. Seek not to thwart the tiger with his prey beneath his fangs.

Pizarro. Audacious rebel! Thou, a renegado from thy monarch and thy God!

Alonzo. 'Tis false.

Pizarro. Art thou not, tell me, a deserter from thy country's legions—and, with vile heathens leagued, hast thou not warred against thy native land?

Alonzo. No! Deserter I am none! I was not born among robbers! pirates! murderers!—When those legions, lured by the abhorred lust of gold, and by thy foul ambition urged, forgot the honour of Castilians, and forsook the duties of humanity, THEY deserted ME. I have not warred against my native land, but against those who have usurped its power. The banners of my country, when first I followed arms beneath them, were Justice, Faith, and Mercy. If these are beaten down and trampled under foot—I have no country, nor exists the power entitled to reproach me with revolt.

Pizarro. The power to judge and punish thee at least exists.

Alonzo. Where are my judges?

Pizarro. Thou wouldst appeal to the war council?

Alonzo. If the good Las-Casas have yet a seat there, yes; if not, I appeal to Heaven!

Pizarro. And to impose upon the folly of Las-Casas, what would be the excuses of thy treason?

Elvira. The folly of Las-Casas!—Such, doubtless, his mild precepts seem to thy hard-hearted wisdom!—O! would I might have lived as I will die, a sharer in the follies of Las-Casas!

Alonzo. To him I should not need to urge the foul barbarities which drove me from your side; but I would gently lead him by the hand through all the lovely fields of Quito; there, in many a spot where late was barrenness and waste, I would show him now the opening blossom, blade, or perfumed bud, sweet bashful pledges of delicious harvest, wafting their incense to the ripening sun, give chearful promise to the hope of industry. This, I would say, is my work! Next I should tell how hurtful customs, and superstitions strange and sullen, would often scatter and dismay the credulous minds of these deluded innocents; and then would I point out to him where now, in clustered villages, they live like brethren, social and confiding, while through the burning day Content sits basking on the cheek of Toil, till laughing Pastime leads them to the hour of rest—this too is mine!—And prouder yet—at that still pause between exertion and repose, belonging not to pastime, labour, or to rest, but unto Him who sanctions and ordains them all, I would show him many an eye, and many a hand, by gentleness from error won, raised in pure devotion to the true and only God!—this too I could tell him is Alonzo's work!—Then would Las-Casas clasp me in his aged arms; from his uplifted eyes a tear of gracious thankfulness would fall upon my head, and that one blessed drop would be to me at once *this* world's best proof, that I had acted rightly *here*, and surest hope of my Creator's mercy and reward *hereafter*.

Elvira. Happy, virtuous Alonzo! And thou, Pizarro, wouldst appal with fear of death a man who thinks and acts as he does!

Pizarro. Daring, obstinate enthusiast! But know the pious blessing of thy preceptor's tears does not await thee here: he has fled like thee—like thee, no doubt, to join the foes of Spain. The perilous trial of the next reward you hope, is nearer than perhaps you've thought; for, by my country's wrongs, and by mine own, to-morrow's sun shall see thy death.

Elvira. Hold!—Pizarro—hear me!—If not always *justly*, at least act always *greatly*. Name not thy country's wrongs—'tis plain they have no share in thy resentment. Thy fury 'gainst this youth is private hate, and deadly personal revenge; if this be so— and even now thy detected conscience in that look avows it— profane not the name of justice or thy country's cause, but let him arm, and bid him to the field on equal terms.

Pizarro. Officious advocate for treason—peace!—Bear him hence—he knows his sentence.

Alonzo. Thy revenge is eager, and I'm thankful for it—to me thy haste is mercy. For thee, sweet pleader in misfortune's cause, accept my parting thanks. This camp is not thy proper sphere. Wert thou among yon *savages*, as they are called, thou-'dst find companions more congenial to thy heart.

Pizarro. Yes; she shall bear the tidings of thy death to Cora.

Alonzo. Inhuman man! that pang at least might have been spared me; but thy malice shall not shake my constancy. I go to death—many shall bless, and none will curse my memory. Thou still wilt live, and still wilt be—Pizarro. [*Exit, guarded.*

Elvira. Now by the indignant scorn that burns upon my cheek, my soul is shamed and sickened at the meanness of thy vengeance.

Pizarro. What has thy romantic folly aimed at? He is mine enemy, and in my power.

Elvira. He is in your power, and therefore is no more an enemy. Pizarro, I demand not of thee virtue—I ask not from thee nobleness of mind—I require only just dealing to the fame thou hast acquired; be not the assassin of thine own renown. How often have you sworn that the sacrifice which thy wondrous valour's high report had won you from subdued Elvira, was the proudest triumph of your fame? Thou knowest I bear a mind not cast in the common mould—not formed for tame sequestered love—content 'mid household care to prattle to an idle offspring, and wait the dull delight of an obscure lover's kindness—no! my heart was framed to look up with awe and homage to the object it adored; my ears to own no music but the thrilling records of his praise; my lips to scorn all babbling but the tales of his achievements; my brain to turn giddy with delight, reading the applauding tributes of his monarch's and his country's gratitude; my every faculty to throb with transport, while I heard the shouts of acclamation which announced the coming of my hero; my whole soul to love him with devotion! with enthusiasm! to see no other object—to own no other tie—but to make HIM my WORLD! Thus to love is at least no common weakness.—Pizarro!—was not such my love for thee?

Pizarro. It *was*, Elvira!

Elvira. Then do not make me hateful to myself, by tearing off the mask at once—baring the hideous imposture that has undone me!—Do not an act which, howe'er thy present power may gloss it to the world, will make thee hateful to all future ages—accursed and scorned by posterity.

Pizarro. And should posterity applaud my deeds, think'st thou my mouldering bones would rattle then with transport in my tomb?—This is renown for visionary boys to dream of—I understand it not. The fame I value shall uplift my living estimation—o'er bear with popular support the envy of my foes—advance my purposes, and aid my power.

Elvira. Each word thou speakest—each moment that I hear thee—dispels the fatal mist through which I've judged thee. Thou man of mighty name, but little soul, I see thou wert not born to feel what genuine fame and glory are—yes, prefer the flattery of thy own fleeting day to the bright circle of a deathless name—yes, prefer to stare upon the grain of sand on which you trample, to musing on the starred canopy above thee. Fame, the sovereign deity of proud ambition, is not to be worshipped so: who seeks alone for living homage, stands a mean canvasser in her temple's porch, wooing promiscuously from the fickle breath of every wretch that passes, the brittle tribute of his praise. He dares not approach the sacred altar—no noble sacrifice of his is placed there, nor ever shall his worship'd image, fix'd above, claim for his memory a glorious immortality.

Pizarro. Elvira, leave me.

Elvira. Pizarro, you no longer love me.

Pizarro. It is not so, Elvira. But what might I not suspect— this wondrous interest for a stranger!—Take back thy reproach.

Elvira. No, Pizarro; as yet I am not lost to you—one string still remains, and binds me to your fate. Do not, I conjure you— do not for thine own sake, tear it asunder—shed not Alonzo's blood!

Pizarro. My resolution's fixed.

Elvira. Even though that moment lost you Elvira for ever?

Pizarro. Even so.

Elvira. Pizarro, if not to honour, if not to humanity, yet listen to affection; bear some memory of the sacrifices I have made for thy sake. Have I not for thee quitted my parents, my friends, my fame, my native land? When escaping, did I not risk in rushing to thy arms to bury myself in the bosom of the deep? Have I not shared all thy perils, heavy storms at sea, and frightful 'scapes on shore? Even on this dreadful day, amid the rout of battle, who remained firm and constant at Pizarro's side? Who presented her bosom as his shield to the assailing foe?

Pizarro. 'Tis truly spoken all. In love thou art thy sex's miracle—in war the soldier's pattern—and therefore my whole heart and half my acquisitions are thy right.

Elvira. Convince me I possess the first—I exchange all title to the latter, for—mercy to Alonzo.

Pizarro. No more!—Had I intended to prolong his doom, each word thou utterest now would hasten on his fate.

Elvira. Alonzo then at morn will die?

Pizarro. Think'st thou yon sun will set?—As surely at his rising shall Alonzo die.

Elvira. Then be it done—the string is crack'd—sundered for ever.—But mark me—thou hast heretofore had cause, 'tis true, to doubt my resolution, howe'er offended—but mark me now —the lips which, cold and jeering, barbing revenge with rancorous mockery, can insult a fallen enemy, shall never more receive the pledge of love: the arm unshaken by its bloody purpose, which shall assign to needless torture the victim who avows his heart, never more shall press the hand of faith!—Pizarro, scorn not my words—beware you slight them not!—I feel how noble are the motives which now animate my thoughts—who *could* not feel as I do, I condemn —who, feeling so, yet *would* not act as I SHALL, I despise!

Pizarro [*after a pause, looking at her with an affected smile of contempt*]. I have heard thee, Elvira, and know well the *noble* motives which inspire thee—fit advocate in virtue's cause!—Believe me, I pity thy tender feelings for the youth Alonzo!—He dies at sunrise!   [*Exit.*

Elvira. 'Tis well! 'tis just I should be humbled—I had forgot myself, and in the cause of innocence assumed the tone of virtue. 'Twas fit I should be rebuked—and by Pizarro. Fall, fall, ye few reluctant drops of weakness—the last these eyes shall ever shed. How a woman can love Pizarro, thou hast known too well—how she can hate, thou hast yet to learn. Yes, thou undaunted! Thou, whom yet no mortal hazard has appalled! Thou, who on Panama's brow didst make alliance with the raving elements, that tore the silence of that horrid night—when thou didst follow, as thy pioneer, the crashing thunder's drift, and stalking o'er the trembling earth, didst plant thy banner by the red volcano's mouth! Thou, who when battling on the sea, and thy brave ship was blown to splinters, wast seen—as thou didst bestride a fragment of the smoking wreck—to wave thy glittering sword above thy head—as thou wouldst defy the world in that extremity!—Come, fearless man—now meet the last and fellest peril of thy life—meet! and survive—an injured woman's fury, if thou canst.
                                                      [*Exit.*

[SCENE IV[1]

The Temples of the Sun—Priests and Priestesses at Sacrifice.

CHORUS.

To thee be praise
O Glorious Sun:

[1]This scene, so essential a part of the original spectacular production, is omitted in all editions except Dolby's (1823) and Hughes's (1823). The words are from Kelly's edition of the music.

Beneath whose beams
The field was won!
Raise high the voice
With shouts rejoice.]

END OF THE THIRD ACT.

Act the Fourth

SCENE I

A Dungeon in the Rock, near the Spanish Camp.—ALONZO *in Chains.*—*A Centinel walking near the Entrance.*

Alonzo. FOR the laſt time, I have beheld the shadow'd ocean close upon the light.—For the laſt time, thro' my cleft dungeon's roof, I now behold the quivering luſtre of the ſtars.—For the laſt time, O sun! (and soon the hour) I shall behold thy rising, and thy level beams melting the pale miſts of morn to glittering dewdrops.—Then comes my death, and in the morning of my day, I fall, which—No, Alonzo, date not the life which thou haſt run, by the mean reck'ning of the hours and days, which thou haſt breath'd: A life spent worthily should be measured by a nobler line—by deeds—not years—Then would'ſt thou murmur not—but bless the Providence, which in so short a span, made THEE the inſtrument of wide and spreading blessings, to the helpless and oppress'd!—Tho' sinking in decrepid age—HE prematurely falls, whose memory records no benefit conferred by him on man: They only have lived long who have lived virtuously.

Enter a Soldier—shows the Centinel a Passport, who withdraws.

Alonzo. What bear you there?

Soldier. These refreshments I was order'd to leave in your dungeon.

Alonzo. By whom order'd?

Soldier. By the lady Elvira; she will be here herself before the dawn.

Alonzo. Bear back to her my humbleſt thanks; and take thou the refreshments, friend—I need them not.

Soldier. I have served under you, Don Alonzo.—Pardon my saying, that my heart pities you.   [*Exit.*

Alonzo. In Pizarro's camp, to pity the unfortunate, no doubt requires forgiveness.—[*Looking out.*] Surely, even now, thin streaks of glimmering light steal on the darkness of the East.—If so, my life is but one hour more.—I will not watch the coming dawn; but in the darkness of my cell, my last prayer to thee, Power Supreme! shall be for my wife and child!—Grant them to dwell in innocence and peace; grant health and purity of mind— all else is worthless. [*Enters the Cavern.*

Centinel. Who's there? answer quickly! who's there?

Rolla. A Friar, come to visit your prisoner.

ROLLA *enters, disguised as a Monk.*

Rolla. Inform me, friend—Is not Alonzo, the Spanish prisoner, confined in this dungeon?

Centinel. He is.

Rolla. I must speak with him.

Centinel. You must not.

Rolla. He is my friend.

Centinel. Not if he were your brother.

Rolla. What is to be his fate?

Centinel. He dies at sun-rise.

Rolla. Ha! —then I am come in time.

Centinel. Just——to witness his death.

Rolla. Soldier—I must speak with him.

Centinel. Back,—back.—It is impossible!—

Rolla. I do entreat you, but for one moment!

Centinel. You entreat in vain—my orders are most strict.

Rolla. Even now, I saw a messenger go hence.

Centinel. He brought a pass, which we are all accustomed to obey.

Rolla. Look on this wedge of massive gold—look on these precious gems.—In thy own land they will be wealth for thee and thine, beyond thy hope or wish. Take them—they are thine.— Let me pass one minute with Alonzo.

Centinel. Away!—wou'dst thou corrupt me?—Me!—an old Castilian!—I know my duty better.

Rolla. Soldier!—hast thou a wife?

Centinel. I have.

Rolla. Haſt thou children?

Centinel. Four—honeſt, lively boys.

Rolla. Where did'ſt thou leave them?

Centinel. In my native village—even in the cot where myself was born.

Rolla. Do'ſt thou love thy children and thy wife?

Centinel. Do I love them! God knows my heart,—I do.

Rolla. Soldier! imagine thou wer't doom'd to die a cruel death in this ſtrange land—What would be thy laſt requeſt?

Centinel. That some of my comrades should carry my dying blessing to my wife and children.

Rolla. Oh! but if that comrade was at thy prison gate—and should there be told——thy fellow soldier dies at sun-rise,—yet thou shalt not for a moment see him—nor shalt thou bear his dying blessing to his poor children or his wretched wife,—what would'ſt thou think of him, who thus cou'd drive thy comrade from the door?

Centinel. How!

Rolla. Alonzo has a wife and child—I am come but to receive for *her*, and for her *babe*, the laſt blessing of my friend.

Centinel. Go in.—[*Retires.*]

Rolla. Oh! holy Nature! thou do'ſt never plead in vain.—There is not, of our earth, a creature bearing form, and life, human or savage—native of the foreſt wild, or giddy air—around whose parent bosom, thou haſt not a cord entwined of power to tie them to their offspring's claims, and at thy will to draw them back to thee. On iron pennons borne—the blood-ſtain'd vulture, cleaves the ſtorm—yet, is the plumage closeſt to her heart, soft as the Cygnet's down, and o'er her unshell'd brood, the murmuring ring-dove sits not more gently!—Yes—now he is beyond the porch, barring the outer gate! Alonzo!—Alonzo!—my friend! Ha!—in gentle sleep!—Alonzo—rise!

Alonzo. How!—Is my hour elaps'd?—Well [*Returning from the recess.*] I am ready.

Rolla. Alonzo,—know me.

Alonzo. What voice is that?

Rolla. 'Tis Rolla's.

Alonzo. Rolla!—my friend!—[*Embraces him.*] Heavens! how could'ſt thou pass the guard? Did this habit————

Rolla. There is not a moment to be loſt in words;—this disguise I tore from the dead body of a Friar, as I pass'd our field of battle—it has gain'd me entrance to thy dungeon—now take it, thou, and fly.

Alonzo. And Rolla——

Rolla. Will remain here in thy place.

Alonzo. And die for me!—No!—Rather eternal tortures rack me.

Rolla. I shall not die, Alonzo.—It is thy life Pizarro seeks, not Rolla's—and from my prison soon will thy arm deliver me;—or, should it be otherwise—I am as a blighted Plantain ſtanding alone amid the sandy desart—Nothing seeks or lives beneath my shelter—Thou art a husband, and a father—The being of a lovely wife and helpless infant hang upon thy life—Go!—Go!— Alonzo!—Go—to save—not thyself—but Cora, and thy child!

Alonzo. Urge me not thus, my friend—I had prepar'd to die in peace.

Rolla. To die in peace!—devoting her you've sworn to live for,—to madness, misery, and death!—For, be assured—the ſtate I left her in forbids all hope, but from thy quick return.

Alonzo. Oh! God!

Rolla. If thou art yet irresolute, Alonzo—now heed me well. —I think thou haſt not known that Rolla ever pledg'd his word, and shrunk from its fulfilment.—And, by the heart of truth I swear, if thou art proudly obſtinate to deny thy friend the transport of preserving Cora's life, in thee,—no power that sways the will of man shall ſtir me hence;—and thou'lt but have the desperate triumph, of seeing Rolla perish by thy side,—with the assur'd conviction, that Cora, and thy child, are loſt for ever.

Alonzo. Oh! Rolla!—you diſtract me!

Rolla. A moment's further pause, and all is loſt—The dawn approaches—Fear not for me—I will treat with Pizarro as for surrender and submission;—I shall gain time, doubt not—while thou, with a chosen band, passing the secret way, may'st at night return—release thy friend, and bear him back in triumph.—Yes—hasten—dear Alonzo!—Even now I hear the frantic Cora call thee!—Haste!—Haste!—Haste!

Alonzo. Rolla, I fear your friendship drives me from honour, and from right.

Rolla. Did Rolla ever counsel dishonour to his friend?

Alonzo. Oh! my preserver!—[*Embracing him.*]

Rolla. I feel thy warm tears dropping on my cheek—Go! I am rewarded—[*Throws the Friar's garment over* ALONZO.]—There! —conceal thy face; and that they may not clank, hold fast thy chains—Now—God be with thee!

Alonzo. At night we meet again.—Then,—so aid me Heaven! I return to save—or—perish with thee!   [*Exit.*

Rolla [*alone*]. He has pass'd the outer porch—He is safe!—He will soon embrace his wife and child!—Now, Cora, did'st thou not wrong me? This is the first time throughout my life I ever deceived man—Forgive me, God of truth! if I am wrong—Alonzo flatters himself that we shall meet again—Yes—There! [*Lifting his hands to heaven.*] assuredly, we shall meet again:—there possess in peace, the joys of everlasting love, and friendship—on earth, imperfect, and embitter'd.—I will retire, lest the guard return before Alonzo may have pass'd their lines.

[*Retires into the Recess.*

Enter ELVIRA.

Elvira. No—not Pizarro's brutal taunts—not the glowing admiration which I feel for this noble youth, shall raise an interest in this harass'd bosom which honour would not sanction. If he reject the vengeance my heart has sworn against the tyrant, whose death alone can save this land—yet, shall the delight be mine to restore him to his Cora's arms, to his dear child, and to the unoffending people, whom his virtues guide, and valour guards.—Alonzo, come forth!

Enter ROLLA.

Ha!—who art thou?—Where is Alonzo?

Rolla. Alonzo's fled.

Elvira. Fled!

Rolla. Yes—and he muſt not be pursued—Pardonthisrough-ness. [*Seizing her hand.*]—but a moment's precious to Alonzo's flight.

Elvira. What if I call the guard?

Rolla. Do so—Alonzo ſtill gains time.

Elvira. What if thus I free myself? [*Shows a dagger.*]

Rolla. Strike it to my heart—Still, with the convulsive grasp of death, I'll hold thee faſt.

Elvira. Release me—I give my faith, I neither will alarm the guard, nor cause pursuit.

Rolla. At once, I truſt thy word—A feeling boldness in those eyes assures me that thy soul is noble.

Elvira. What is thy name? Speak freely—By my order the guard is remov'd beyond the outer porch.

Rolla. My name is Rolla.

Elvira. The Peruvian Leader?

Rolla. I was so yeſterday—To-day, the Spaniard's captive.

Elvira. And friendship for Alonzo, moved thee to this act?

Rolla. Alonzo is my friend—I am prepared to die for him. Yet is the cause a motive ſtronger far than friendship.

Elvira. One only passion else could urge such generous rash-ness.

Rolla. And that is—

Elvira. Love?

Rolla. True!

Elvira. Gallant!—ingenuous Rolla!—Know that my purpose here was thine; and were I to save thy friend——

Rolla. How!—a woman bless'd with gentleness and courage, and yet not Cora!

Elvira. Does Rolla think so meanly of all female hearts?

Rolla. Not so—you are worse and better than we are!——

Elvira. To save thee, Rolla, from the tyrant's vengeance—re-ſtore thee to thy native land—and thy native land to peace—would'ſt thou not rank Elvira with the good?

Rolla. To judge the action, I muſt know the means.

Elvira. Take this dagger.

Rolla. How to be used?

Elvira. I will conduct thee to the tent where fell Pizarro sleeps —The scourge of innocence—the terror of thy race—the fiend, that desolates thy afflicted country.

Rolla. Have you not been injur'd by Pizarro?

Elvira. Deeply as scorn and insult can infuse their deadly venom.

Rolla. And you ask that I shall murder him in his sleep!

Elvira. Would he not have murder'd Alonzo in his chains? He that sleeps, and he that's bound, are equally defenceless. Hear me, Rolla—so may I prosper in this perilous act as searching my full heart, I have put by all rancorous motive of private vengeance there, and feel that I advance to my dread purpose in the cause of human nature, and at the call of sacred justice.

Rolla. The God of Justice sanctifies no evil as a step towards good. Great actions cannot be achieved by wicked means.

Elvira. Then, Peruvian, since thou dost feel so coldly for thy country's wrong, this hand, tho' it revolt my soul, shall strike the blow.

Rolla. Then is thy destruction certain, and for Peru thou perishest!—Give me the dagger!

Elvira. Now follow me;—but first—and dreadful is the hard necessity—you must strike down the guard.

Rolla. The soldier who was on duty here?

Elvira. Yes, him—else, seeing thee, the alarm will be instant.

Rolla. And I must stab that soldier as I pass?—Take back thy dagger.

Elvira. Rolla!

Rolla. That soldier, mark me, is a man.—All are not men that bear the human form. He refus'd my prayers—refus'd my gold —denying to admit me—till his own feelings brib'd him.—For my nation's safety, I would not harm that man!

Elvira. Then he must with us—I will answer for his safety.

Rolla. Be that plainly understood between us:—for, whate'er betide our enterprise, I will not risk a hair of that man's head, to save my heartstrings from consuming fire.

[*Exeunt.*

SCENE III.

The inside of PIZARRO'*s Tent.*—PIZARRO *on a Couch, in disturbed sleep.*

Pizarro [*in his sleep*]. No mercy, traitor.—Now at his heart!—Stand off there, you—Let me see him bleed!—Ha! ha! ha!—Let me hear that groan again.

Enter ROLLA *and* ELVIRA.

Elvira. There!—Now, lose not a moment.

Rolla. You must leave me now.—This scene of blood is not for a woman's presence.

Elvira. But a moment's pause may——

Rolla. Go!—Retire to your own tent—and return not here—I will come to you—Be thou not known in this business, I implore you!

Elvira. I will withdraw the guard that waits. [*Exit* ELVIRA.

Rolla. Now have I in my power the accurs'd destroyer of my country's peace: yet tranquilly he rests.—God!—can this man sleep?

Pizarro [*in his sleep*]. Away! away!—Hideous fiends!—Tear not my bosom thus!

Rolla. No:—I was in error—the balm of sweet repose he never more can know.—Look here, ambition's fools!—Ye, by whose inhuman pride, the bleeding sacrifice of nations is held as nothing—behold the rest of the guilty!—He is at my mercy—and one blow!—No!—my heart and hand refuse the act: Rolla cannot be an assassin!—Yet Elvira must be saved! [*Approaches the Couch.*] Pizarro awake!—

Pizarro [*starts up.*] Who?—Guard!—

Rolla. Speak not—another word is thy death—Call not for aid!—this arm will be swifter than thy guard.

Pizarro. Who art thou? and what is thy will?

Rolla. I am thine enemy! Peruvian Rolla!—Thy death is not my will, or I could have slain thee sleeping.

Pizarro. Speak, what else?

Rolla. Now thou art at my mercy—answer me! Did a Peruvian ever yet wrong or injure thee, or any of thy nation? Didst thou, or any of thy nation, ever yet show mercy to a Peruvian in your power? Now shalt thou feel—and if thou hast a heart, thou'lt feel it keenly!—a Peruvian's vengeance! [*Drops the dagger at his feet*.] There!

Pizarro. Is it possible!   [*Walks aside confounded*.

Rolla. Can Pizarro be surprised at this! I thought Forgiveness of Injuries had been the Christians' precept—Thou seest, at least, it is the Peruvian's practice.

Pizarro. Rolla—thou hast indeed surpris'd—subdued me.

[*Walks again aside as in irresolute thought*.

Re-enter ELVIRA, [*not seeing* PIZARRO.]

Elvira. Is it done? Is he dead? [*Sees* PIZARRO.] How!—Still living! Then I am lost! And for you, wretched Peruvian! mercy is no more!—Oh! Rolla! treacherous, or cowardly?—

Pizarro. How can it be, that—

Rolla. Away! Elvira speaks she knows not what! Leave me [*to* ELVIRA] I conjure you, with Pizarro.

Elvira. How!—Rolla, do'st thou think I shall retract—or that I meanly will deny, that in thy hand *I* plac'd a poignard to be plung'd into that tyrant's heart? No:—my sole regret is, that I trusted to thy weakness, and did not strike the blow myself.— Too soon thou'lt learn that mercy to that man is direct cruelty to all thy race!

Pizarro. Guard! quick! a guard, to seize this frantic woman.

Elvira. Yes, a guard! I call them too! And soon I know they'll lead me to my death. But think not, Pizarro, the fury of thy flashing eyes shall awe me for a moment!—Nor think that woman's anger, or the feelings of an injur'd heart, prompted me to this design—No! Had I been only influenced so;—thus failing— shame and remorse would weigh me down. But tho' defeated and destroyed, as now I am, such is the greatness of the cause that urged me, I shall perish, glorying in the attempt, and my last breath of life shall speak the proud avowal of my purpose—to have rescued millions of innocents from the bloodthirsty tyranny of ONE—by ridding the insulted world of THEE.

Rolla. Had the act been noble as the motive—Rolla would not have shrunk from its performance.

Enter Guards.

Pizarro. Seize this discover'd fiend, who sought to kill your Leader.

Elvira. Touch me not, at the peril of your souls;—I am your prisoner, and will follow you.—But thou, their triumphant Leader, shalt hear me. Yet, first—for thee, Rolla, accept my forgiveness: even had I been the victim of thy nobleness of heart, I should have admir'd thee for it—But 'twas myself provok'd my doom—Thou would'st have shielded me.—Let not thy contempt follow me to the grave. Didst thou but know the spell-like arts, by which this hypocrite first undermin'd the virtue of a guileless heart! how, even in the pious sanctuary wherein I dwelt, by corruption and by fraud, he practis'd upon those in whom I most confided—'till my distemper'd fancy led me, step by step, into the abyss of—guilt——

Pizarro. Why am I not obey'd?—Tear her hence!

Elvira. 'Tis past—but didst thou know my story, Rolla, thou would'st pity me.

Rolla. From my soul I do pity thee!

Pizarro. Villains! drag her to the dungeon!—prepare the torture instantly.

Elvira. Soldiers—but a moment more—'Tis to applaud your General—It is to tell the astonished world, that, for once, Pizarro's sentence is an act of justice: Yes, rack me with the sharpest tortures that ever agoniz'd the human frame; it will be justice. Yes—bid the minions of thy fury—wrench forth the sinews of those arms that have caress'd, and—even have defended thee! Bid them pour burning metal into the bleeding cases of these eyes, that so oft—oh, God!—have hung with love and homage on thy looks—then approach me bound on the abhorred wheel —there glut thy savage eyes with the convulsive spasms of that dishonour'd bosom, which was once thy pillow!—Yet, will I bear it all; for it will be justice, all! And when thou shalt bid them tear me to my death, hoping that thy unshrinking ears may at last be feasted with the music of my cries, I will not utter one shriek or groan—but to the last gasp, my body's patience shall deride thy vengeance, as my soul defies thy power.

Pizarro [*endeavouring to conceal his agitation*]. Hear'st thou the wretch whose hands were even now prepared for murder?

Rolla. Yes! And if her accusation's false, thou wilt not shrink from hearing her: if true, thy barbarity cannot make *her* suffer the pangs thy conscience will inflict on *thee.*

Elvira. And now, farewell, world!—Rolla, farewell!—Farewell, thou condemn'd of Heaven! [*To* PIZARRO.] For repentance and remorse, I know will never touch thy heart.—We shall meet again.—Ha! be it thy horror here, to know that we shall meet hereafter! And when thy parting hour approaches—hark! to the knell, whose dreadful beat will strike to thy despairing soul. Then, will vibrate on thy ear the curses of the cloister'd saint from whom you stole me. Then, the last shrieks which burst from my mother's breaking heart, as she died, appealing to her God against the seducer of her child! Then the blood-stifled groan of my murder'd brother—murdered by thee, fell monster!—seeking atonement for his sister's ruin'd honour.—I hear them now! To me, the recollection's madness!—At such an hour,—what will it be to thee?

Pizarro. A moment's more delay, and at the peril of your lives

---

Elvira. I have spoken—and the last mortal frailty of my heart is past.—And now, with an undaunted spirit, and unshaken firmness, I go to meet my destiny. That I could not *live* nobly, has been PIZARRO's ACT. That I will *die* nobly, shall be my own.

[*Exit, guarded.*

Pizarro. Rolla, I would not thou, a warrior, valiant and renown'd, should'st credit the vile tales of this frantic woman. The cause of all this fury—O—a wanton passion for the rebel youth Alonzo, now my prisoner.

Rolla. Alonzo is not now thy prisoner.

Pizarro. How!

Rolla. I came to rescue him—to deceive his guard—I have succeeded;—I remain thy prisoner.

Pizarro. Alonzo fled!—Is then the vengeance dearest to my heart never to be gratified?

Rolla. Dismiss such passions from thy heart; then thou'lt consult its peace.

Pizarro. I can face all enemies that dare confront me—I cannot war against my nature.

Rolla. Then, Pizarro, ask not to be deem'd a hero—To triumph o'er ourselves, is the only conquest, where fortune makes no claim. In battle, chance may snatch the laurel from thee, or chance may place it on thy brow—but in a contest with yourself, be resolute, and the virtuous impulse must be the victor.

Pizarro. Peruvian! thou shalt not find me to thee ungrateful, or ungenerous—Return to your countrymen—You are at liberty.

Rolla. Thou do'st act in this, as honour, and as duty, bid thee.

Pizarro. I cannot but admire thee, Rolla; I wou'd we might be friends.

Rolla. Farewell.—Pity Elvira!—Become the friend of virtue —and thou wilt be mine. [*Exit.*

Pizarro. Ambition! tell me what is the phantom I have follow'd, where is the one delight which it has made my own? My fame is the mark of envy—my love the dupe of treachery—my glory eclips'd by the boy I taught—my revenge defeated and rebuked by the rude honour of a savage foe—before whose native dignity of soul I have sunk confounded and subdued! I would I cou'd retrace my steps—I cannot—Would I could evade my own reflections!—no living!—thought and memory are my Hell.

[*Exit.*

END OF THE FOURTH ACT.

Act the Fifth

SCENE I

A thick Forest—In the back ground, a Hut almost covered by Boughs of Trees—A dreadful Storm, with Thunder and Lightning.— CORA has covered her Child on a Bed of Leaves and Moss—Her whole appearance is wild and distracted.

Cora. O NATURE! thou hast not the strength of love. My anxious spirit is untired in its march; my wearied, shivering frame, sinks under it. And, for thee, my boy—when faint beneath thy lovely burthen, could I refuse to give thy slumbers that poor bed of rest! O my child! were I assured thy father breathes no more, how quickly would I lay me down by thy dear side—but down—down for ever. [*Thunder and lightning.*] I ask thee not, unpitying storm! to abate thy rage, in mercy to poor Cora's misery; nor while thy thunders spare his slumbers will I disturb my sleeping cherub. Though Heaven knows I wish to hear the voice of life, and feel that life is near me. But I will endure all while what I have of reason holds.

SONG.[1]

Yes, yes, be merciless, thou Tempest dire;
Unaw'd, unshelter'd, I thy fury brave,
I'll bare my bosom to thy forked fire,
Let it but guide me to ALONZO's grave!

O'er his pale corse then while thy lightnings glare,
I'll press his clay-cold lips, and perish there.

[1] This song appeared in the 1st Edition and all others by Ridgway. It is the only song whose words were by Sheridan. (See Introduction.)

But thou wilt wake again, my boy,
Again thou'lt rise to life and joy,
   Thy father never!——
Thy laughing eyes will meet the light,
Unconscious that eternal night
   Veils his for ever.

On yon green bed of moss there lies my child,
   Oh! safer lies from these chill'd arms apart;
He sleeps, sweet lamb! nor heeds the tempest wild,
   Oh! sweeter sleeps, than near this breaking heart.

Alas! my babe, if thou would'st peaceful rest,
Thy cradle must not be thy mother's breast.

Yet, thou wilt wake again, my boy,
Again thou'lt rise to life and joy,
   Thy father never!——
Thy laughing eyes will meet the light,
Unconscious that eternal night
   Veils his for ever.
                [*Thunder and lightning.*

Cora. Still, still, implacable! unfeeling elements! yet still dost thou sleep, my smiling innocent! O, death! when wilt thou grant to this babe's mother such repose? Sure I may shield thee better from the storm; my veil may——

    [*While she is wrapping her mantle and her veil over him,* ALONZO's *voice is heard at a great distance.*

Alonzo. Cora!

Cora. Hah!!! [*Rises.*]

Alonzo [*again*]. Cora!

Cora. O, my heart! Sweet Heaven deceive me not!—Is it not Alonzo's voice?

Alonzo [*nearer*]. Cora!

Cora. It is—it is Alonzo!

Alonzo [*nearer still*]. Cora! my beloved!——

Cora. Alonzo!—Here!—here!—Alonzo!   [*Runs out.*

Enter two Spanish Soldiers.

1st Soldier. I tell you we are near our out-posts, and the word we heard just now was the countersign.

2nd Soldier. Well, in our escape from the enemy, to have discover'd their secret passage thro' the rocks, will prove a lucky chance to us—Pizarro will reward us.

1st Soldier. This way—The sun, though clouded, is on our left. [*Perceives the child.*] What have we here?—A child!—as I'm a soldier.

2nd Soldier. 'Tis a sweet little babe. Now would it be a great charity to take this infant from its pagan mother's power.

1st Soldier. It would so—I have one at home shall play with it. —Come along.   [*Takes the child.   Exeunt.*

Re-enter CORA *with* ALONZO.

Cora [*speaking without*]. This way, dear Alonzo. Now am I right—there—there—under that tree. Was it possible the instinct of a mother's heart could mistake the spot! Now will you look at him as he sleeps, or shall I bring him waking with his full blue laughing eyes to welcome you at once—Yes—yes.—Stand thou there—I'll snatch him from his rosy slumber, blushing like the perfum'd morn.

> [*She runs up to the spot, and, finding only the mantle and veil, which she tears from the ground, and the child gone, (shrieks) and stands in speechless agony.*

Alonzo [*running to her*]. Cora!—my heart's beloved!

Cora. He is gone!

Alonzo. Eternal God!

Cora. He is gone!—my child! my child!

Alonzo. Where did you leave him?

Cora [*dashing herself on the spot*]. Here!

Alonzo. Be calm, beloved Cora—he has wak'd, and crept to a little distance—we shall find him—Are you assured this was the spot you left him in?

Cora. Did not these hands make that bed, and shelter for him? —and is not this the veil that covered him?

Alonzo. Here is a hut yet unobserved.

Cora. Ha!yes, yes! there lives the savage that has robb'd me of my child—[*Beats at the door, exclaiming*] Give me back my child! restore to me my boy!

Enter LAS-CASAS *from the Hut.*

Las-Casas. Who calls me from my wretched solitude?

Cora. Give me back my child! [*Goes into the hut, and calls.*] Fernando!

Alonzo. Almighty powers! do my eyes deceive me! Las-Casas!

Las-Casas. Alonzo,—my belov'd young friend!

Alonzo. My rever'd instructor. [*Embracing.*]

Cora [*return'd*]. Will you embrace this man before he restores my boy?

Alonzo. Alas, my friend—in what a moment of misery do we meet!

Cora. Yet his look is goodness and humanity.—Good old man have compassion on a wretched mother—and I will be your servant while I live.—But do not, for pity's sake—do not say, you have him not—do not say, you have not seen him.

[*Runs into the Wood.*

Las-Casas. What can this mean?

Alonzo. She is my wife, just rescued from the Spaniards' prison. —I learn'd she had fled to this wild forest—Hearing my voice, she left the child, and flew to meet me—he was left sleeping under yonder tree.

Las Casas. How! did you *leave* him?—   [CORA *returns.*

Cora. O, you are right!—right!—unnatural mother, that I was—I left my child—I forsook my innocent—but I will fly to the earth's brink, but I will find him.   [*Runs out.*

Alonzo. Forgive me, Las-Casas, I must follow her: for at night, I must attempt brave Rolla's rescue.

Las-Casas. I will not leave thee, Alonzo—you must try to lead her to the right—that way lies your camp—Wait not my infirm steps,—I follow thee, my friend.

[*Exeunt.*

SCENE II.

The Out-Post of the Spanish Camp.—The back ground wild and rocky, with a Torrent falling down the Precipice, over which a Bridge is formed. A fell'd Tree.   [Trumpets sound without.

Almagro [without]. Bear him along—his story must be false
[*Entering.*

Enter ROLLA [*in Chains*] *brought in by Soldiers.*

Rolla. False!—Rolla, utter falsehood!—I would I had thee in a desert with thy troop around thee;—and I, but with my sword in this unshackled hand!—[*Trumpets without.*]

Almagro. Is it to be credited that Rolla, the renown'd Peruvian hero—shou'd be detected like a spy, skulking thro' our camp?

Rolla. Skulking!

Almagro. But answer to the General—he is here.

Enter PIZARRO.

Pizarro. What do I see! Rolla!

Rolla. O! to thy surprise, no doubt.

Pizarro. And bound too!

Rolla. So fast, thou need'st not fear approaching me.

Almagro. The guards surpris'd him, passing our out-post.

Pizarro. Release him instantly.—Believe me, I regret this insult.

Rolla. You feel then as you ought.

Pizarro. Nor can I brook to see a warrior of Rolla's fame disarm'd—Accept this, tho' it has been thy enemy's. [*Gives a sword.*] The Spaniards know the courtesy that's due to valour.

Rolla. And the Peruvian, how to forget offence.

Pizarro. May not Rolla and Pizarro cease to be foes?

Rolla. When the sea divides us; yes!—May I now depart?

Pizarro. Freely.

Rolla. And shall I not again be intercepted?

Pizarro. No!—let the word be given that Rolla passes freely.

Enter DAVILLA *and Soldiers, with the Child.*

Davilla. Here are two soldiers, captived yesterday, who have escap'd from the Peruvian hold,—and by the secret way we have so long endeavoured to discover.

Pizarro. Silence,—imprudent!—Seest thou not—? [*Pointing to* ROLLA.]

Davilla. In their way, they found a Peruvian child, who seems——

Pizarro. What is the imp to me?—Bid them toss it into the sea.

Rolla. Gracious heaven! it is Alonzo's child!—give it to me.

Pizarro. Ha! Alonzo's child!—Welcome, thou pretty hostage.—Now Alonzo is again my prisoner!

Rolla. Thou wilt not keep the infant from its mother?

Pizarro. Will I not!—What, when I shall meet Alonzo in the heat of the victorious fight—think'st thou I shall not have a check upon the valour of his heart, when he is reminded that a word of mine is this child's death?

Rolla. I do not understand you.

Pizarro. My vengeance has a long arrear of hate to settle with Alonzo!—and this pledge my help to settle the account.

Rolla. Man! Man!—Art thou a man?—Could'st thou hurt that innocent?—By Heaven! it's smiling in thy face.

Pizarro. Tell me, does it resemble Cora?

Rolla. Pizarro! thou hast set my heart on fire—If thou do'st harm that child—think not his blood will sink into the barren sand—No!—faithful to the eager hope that now trembles in this indignant heart—'twill rise to the common God of nature and humanity, and cry aloud for vengeance on it's accurs'd destroyer's *head.*

Pizarro. Be that peril mine.

Rolla [*throwing himself at his feet*]. Behold me at thy feet—Me, Rolla!—Me, the preserver of thy life!—Me, that have never yet bent or bow'd before created man!—In humble agony I sue to you—prostrate I implore you—but spare that child, and I will be your slave.

Pizarro. Rolla! still art thou free to go—this boy remains with me.

Rolla. Then was this sword Heaven's gift, not thine! [*Seizes the Child.*]—Who moves one step to follow me, dies upon the spot.   [*Exit, with the Child.*

Pizarro. Pursue him instantly—but spare his life. [*Exeunt* ALMAGRO *and soldiers.*] With what fury he defends himself!—Ha!—he falls them to the ground—and now——

Enter ALMAGRO.

Almagro. Three of your brave soldiers are already victims to your command to spare this madman's life; and if he once gains the thicket——

Pizarro. Spare him no longer. [*Exit* ALMAGRO.] Their guns must reach him—he'll yet escape—hollow to those horse—the Peruvian sees them—and now he turns among the rocks—then is his retreat cut off.

[ROLLA *crosses a wooden bridge over the cataract, pursued by the soldiers—they fire at him—a shot strikes him—* PIZARRO *exclaims.*——

Pizarro. Now! quick! quick! seize the child!—

[ROLLA *tears from the rock the tree which supports the bridge, and retreats by the back ground, bearing off the child.*

Re-enter ALMAGRO.

Almagro. By Hell! he has escaped!—and with the child unhurt.

Davilla. No—he bears his death with him—Believe me, I saw him struck upon the side.

Pizarro. But the child is sav'd—Alonzo's child! Oh! the furies of disappointed vengeance!

Almagro. Away with the revenge of words—let us to deeds—Forget not we have acquired the knowledge of the secret pass, which thro' the rocky cavern's gloom brings you at once to the stronghold, where are lodg'd their women, and their treasures.

Pizarro. Right, Almagro! Swift as thy thought draw forth a daring and a chosen band—I will not wait for numbers.—Stay, Almagro! Valverde is informed Elvira dies to-day?

Valverde. He is—and one request alone she——

Pizarro. I'll hear of none.

Valverde. The boon is small—'tis but for the novitiate habit which you firſt beheld her in—she wishes not to suffer in the gaudy trappings, which remind her of her shame.

Pizarro. Well, do as thou wilt—but tell Valverde, that at our return, as his life shall answer it, to let me hear that she is dead.

[*Exeunt, severally.*

SCENE III

ATALIBA's *Tent.*

Enter ATALIBA, *follow'd by* CORA *and* ALONZO.

Cora. Oh! Avoid me not, Ataliba! To whom, but to her King, is the wretched mother to address her griefs?—The Gods refuse to hear my prayers! Did not my Alonzo fight for *you?*—and will not my sweet boy, if thou'lt but reſtore him to me, one day fight thy battles too?

Ataliba. Oh! my suffering love—my poor heart-broken Cora! —you but wound our Sovereign's feeling soul, and not relieve thy own.

Cora. Is he our Sovereign, and has he not the power to give me back my child?

Ataliba. When I reward desert, or can relieve my people, I feel what is the real glory of a King—when I hear them suffer, and cannot aid them, I mourn the impotence of all mortal power.

[*Voices behind*]. Rolla! Rolla! Rolla!

Enter ROLLA, *bleeding, with the child, follow'd by Peruvian soldiers.*

Rolla. Thy child! [*Gives the child into* CORA's *arms, and falls.*]

Cora. Oh God!—there's blood upon him!

Rolla. 'Tis my blood, Cora!

Alonzo. Rolla, thou dieſt!

Rolla. For thee, and Cora.—[*Dies.*]

Enter ORANO.

Orano. Treachery has revealed our asylum in the rocks. Even now the foe assails the peaceful band retired for proteƈtion there.

Alonzo. Lose not a moment!—Swords be quick!—Your wives and children cry to you—Bear our lov'd hero's body in the van— 'Twill raise the fury of our men to madness.—Now, fell Pizarro! the death of one of us is near!—Away! be the word of assault, Revenge and Rolla!——   [*Exeunt.* Charge.

SCENE IV

A romantic part of the Recess among the Rocks—[*Alarms*] *Women are seen flying, pursued by the Spanish Soldiers.*—*The Peruvian Soldiers drive the Spaniards back from the Field.*—*The Fight is continued on the Heights.*

Enter PIZARRO, ALMAGRO, VALVERDE, *and Spanish soldiers.*
Pizarro. Well!—if surrounded, we must perish in the centre of them—Where do Rolla and Alonzo hide their heads?

Enter ALONZO, ORANO, *and Peruvians.*
Alonzo. Alonzo answers thee, and Alonzo's sword shall speak for Rolla.
Pizarro. Thou know'st the advantage of thy numbers.—Thou dar'st not singly face Pizarro.
Alonzo. Peruvians, stir not a man!—Be this contest only ours.
Pizarro. Spaniards!—observe ye the same.   [*Charge.*
They fight. ALONZO'S *shield is broken, and he is beat down.*
Pizarro. Now, traitor, to thy heart!
At this moment ELVIRA *enters, habited as when* PIZARRO *first beheld her.*—PIZARRO, *appalled, staggers back* —ALONZO *renews the Fight, and slays him.*
          [*Loud shouts from the Peruvians.*

ATALIBA *enters, and embraces* ALONZO.
Ataliba. My brave Alonzo!
Almagro. Alonzo, we submit.—Spare us! we will embark, and leave the coast.
Valverde. Elvira will confess I sav'd her life; she has sav'd thine.

Alonzo. Fear not. You are safe. [*Spaniards lay down their arms.*

Elvira. Valverde speaks the truth;—nor could he think to meet me here.—An awful impulse which my soul could not resist, impell'd me hither.

Alonzo. Noble Elvira! my preserver! How can I speak what I, Ataliba, and his rescued country, owe to thee? If amid these grateful innocents thou would'st remain——

Elvira. Alonzo, no!—the destination of my future life is fix'd. Humbled in penitence, I will endeavour to atone the guilty errors, which, however mask'd by shallow cheerfulness, have long consum'd my secret heart.—When, by my sufferings purified, and penitence sincere, my soul shall dare address the Throne of Mercy in behalf of others,—for thee, Alonzo—for thee, Cora, and thy child—for thee, thou virtuous Monarch, and the innocent race you reign over, shall Elvira's prayers address the God of Nature.—Valverde, you have preserved my life. Cherish humanity—avoid the foul examples thou hast view'd.—Spaniards returning to your native home, assure your rulers, they mistake the road to glory, or to power.—Tell them, that the pursuits of avarice, conquest, and ambition, never yet made a people happy, or a nation great.—[*Casts a look of agony on the dead body of Pizarro as she passes, and exit.*]

[*Flourish of Trumpets.*

[VALVERDE, ALMAGRO, *and Spanish Soldiers, exeunt, bearing off* PIZARRO'*s Body.*—*On a signal from* ALONZO, *flourish of Music.*

Alonzo. Ataliba! think not I wish to check the voice of triumph —when I entreat we first may pay the tribute due to our lov'd Rolla's memory.

A solemn March—*Procession of Peruvian Soldiers, bearing* ROLLA'*s Body on a Bier, surrounded by Military Trophies. The Priests and Priestesses attending chaunt a Dirge over the Bier.*—ALONZO *and* CORA *kneel on either side of it, and kiss* ROLLA'*s hands in silent agony* —*In the looks of the King, and of all present, the Triumph of the Day is lost, in mourning for their Hero.*

LAMENTATION FOR THE DEATH OF ROLLA.

Priests and Priestesses.   Let tears of gratitude and woe
                 For the brave Rolla ever flow!][1]
                 [*The Curtain slowly descends.*]

END OF THE FIFTH ACT

[1]From Kelly's edition of the music.

Epilogue

Written by the HON. WILLIAM LAMB.

Spoken by MRS. JORDAN.

ERE yet Suspense has ſtill'd its throbbing fear,
Or Melancholy wip'd the grateful tear,
While e'en the miseries of a sinking State,
A Monarch's danger, and a Nation's fate,
Command not now your eyes with grief to flow,
Loſt in a trembling Mother's nearer woe;
What moral lay shall Poetry rehearse,
Or how shall Elocution pour the verse
So sweetly, that its music shall repay
The lov'd illusion, which it drives away?
Mine is the task, to rigid cuſtom due,
To me ungrateful, as 'tis harsh to you,
To mar the work the tragic scene has wrought,
To rouse the mind that broods in pensive thought,
To scare Reflection, which, in absent dreams,
Still lingers musing on the recent themes;
Attention, ere with contemplation tir'd,
To turn from all that pleas'd, from all that fir'd;
To weaken lessons ſtrongly now impreſt,
And chill the intereſt glowing in the breaſt—
Mine is the task; and be it mine to spare
The souls that pant, the griefs they see, to share;
Let me with no unhallow'd jeſt deride
The sigh, that sweet Compassion owns with pride—
The sigh of Comfort, to Affliction dear,
That Kindness heaves, and Virtue loves to hear.
E'en gay THALIA will not now refuse
This gentle homage to her Siſter-Muse.
  O ye, who liſten to the plantive ſtrain,
With ſtrange enjoyment, and with rapturous pain,

Who erst have felt the *Stranger*'s lone despair,
And *Haller*'s settled, sad, remorseful care,
Does *Rolla*'s pure affection less excite
The inexpressive anguish of delight?
Do *Cora*'s fears, which beat without control,
With less solicitude engross the soul?
Ah, no! your minds with kindred zeal approve
Maternal feeling, and heroic love.
You must approve; where Man exists below,
In temperate climes, or 'midst drear wastes of snow,
Or where the solar fires incessant flame,
Thy laws, all-powerful Nature, are the same:
Vainly the Sophist boasts, he can explain
The causes of thy universal reign—
More vainly would his cold presumptuous art
Disprove thy general empire o'er the heart:
A voice proclaims thee, that we must believe,
A voice, that surely speaks not to deceive;
That voice poor *Cora* heard, and closely prest
Her darling infant to her fearful breast;
Distracted dar'd the bloody field to tread,
And sought *Alonzo* through the heaps of dead,
Eager to catch the music of his breath,
Though faltering in the agonies of death,
To touch his lips, though pale and cold, once more,
And clasp his bosom, though it stream'd with gore;
That voice too *Rolla* heard, and, greatly brave,
His *Cora*'s dearest treasure died to save,
Gave to the hopeless Parent's arms her child,
Beheld her transports, and expiring smil'd.
That voice ye hear—Oh! be its will obey'd!
'Tis Valour's impulse and 'tis Virtue's aid—
It prompts to all Benevolence admires,
To all that heav'nly Piety inspires,
To all that Praise repeats through lengthen'd years,
That Honour sanctifies, and Time reveres.

THE END

Bibliography of *Pizarro*[1]

I. RIDGWAY'S EDITIONS

Pizarro; a Tragedy, In Five Acts; As performed at the Theatre-Royal in Drury-Lane: Taken from the German Drama of
Kotzebue; and Adapted to the English Stage by Richard Brinsley Sheridan. London: Printed for James Ridgway, York Street,
St. James's Square, 1799. Price 2s 6d. A superior Edition on
fine wove Paper, hot-pressed. Price 5s.

8vo.

Pagination [i] title-page [ii] blank [iii] *Advertisement* [iv]
blank; [v] *Dedication*; [vi] blank; [vii] *Prologue*; [viii] *Dramatis
Personæ*. Pp. [1] and 2-76, text. [77-79] *Epilogue*; [80] blank.

[James Ridgway issued a large number of Editions, at least
twenty in 1799. The Thirtieth Edition is dated 1814. Those I
have examined have no peculiarities beyond the trivial points
here recorded. There is therefore no reason for detailed bibio-
graphies. The Editions are all 8vo.]

*Pizarro. The Second Edition. 1799.

*Pizarro. The Third Edition. 1799.

*Pizarro. The Fourth Edition. 1799.

*Pizarro. The Fifth Edition. 1799.

*Pizarro. The Seventh Edition. 1799. With a Portrait.

*Pizarro. The Eighth Edition. 1799.

*Pizarro. The Tenth Edition. 1799.

*Pizarro. The Eleventh Edition. 1799.

*Pizarro. The Thirteenth Edition. 1799.

*Pizarro. The Fourteenth Edition. 1799.

[1]The Editions marked with an asterisk are not recorded by Sichel.

*Pizarro. The Fifteenth Edition. 1799.

[This Edition contains an advertisement.

SCHOOL FOR SCANDAL
A genuine Edition, from the Original Copy,
By R. B. SHERIDAN, Esq.
Is in the Press, and will be published on *Monday*,
30*th Sept. instant*, 1799.

JAMES RIDGWAY having purchased the Copyright of the above celebrated Comedy, gives Notice, that the Venders of the *Spurious Copies* which have been attempted to be imposed on the Public, will be prosecuted as the Law directs.]

Pizarro. The Twentieth Edition. 1799.

*Pizarro. The Twenty-Third Edition. 1800.

Pizarro. The Twenty-Fourth Edition. 1800.

Pizarro. The Twenty-Sixth Edition. 1800. With a Portrait.

*Pizarro. The Twenty-Seventh Edition. 1804.

*Pizarro. The Twenty-Eighth Edition. 1811.

*Pizarro. The Twenty-Ninth Edition. 1811.

Pizarro. The Thirtieth Edition. 1814.

[It will be noted that there are ten Editions still to be accounted for. Sichel records "An Edition printed on fine paper. London: 1799. 8vo." This appears to be unnumbered, and must be the "superior Edition. Price 5s." announced in the First Edition.]

2. POSTHUMOUS LONDON EDITIONS

[Between 1814 and 1823 there appears to have been no London Edition of *Pizarro*, though, of course, such may be discovered. In the next two years, however, it was issued, originally, in wrappers, in at least four serial collections of "Acting-Editions."]

*Pizarro ... As performed at Drury Lane and Covent Garden. London. T. Hughes, 35 Ludgate-Street, 1823.

12mo. pp. 48.

[This Edition (with a frontispiece by Cruikshank of Young as Rolla) appears to be the first to contain the four songs omitted from the Ridgway editions. It has some trivial textual differences, the first word reading "Insolent!" for "Audacious!" The frontispiece is dated August, 1821.

*Pizarro . . . . Printed from the Prompt-Book. London. T. Dolby. Britannia Press. 299 Strand. 1823.

12mo.

Pizarro. . . . Faithfully marked with the stage-business by W. Oxberry. Comedian. London. W. Simpkin and H. Marshall, Stationers' Court, Ludgate Street; and C. Chapple, 59, Pall Mall. 1824.

12mo. (large) pp. xvi— 64.

[Frontispiece of Kemble as Rolla. *Remarks* by P. P. Issued in buff wrappers as No. CIX of *Oxberry's New English Drama* "Price 1s." The wrapper states "A superior Edition may be had. Price 2s."]

*Pizarro. Printed from the Acting Copy. London. John Cumberland. 19 Ludgate Hill. [1826.]

12mo. pp. 60.

[Frontispiece by R. Cruikshank. Remarks by D—G [George Daniel]. The earlier issues are really Dolby's Edition; with a new title-page and prefatory matter. The later issues are "printed from stereotype" by Davidson [1829?]. No dated issues.]

3. EDITIONS OTHER THAN LONDON, 1799—1804.

*Pizarro. Adapted to the English Stage by Richard Brinsley Sheridan. Dublin: Printed for J. Moore, 45, College Green, 1799.

12mo. pp. vi— 76. [Sig. B on p. 1.]

[The Advertisement mentions only Miss Plumptre's translation. Copies in the National Library and Municipal Library, Dublin.—E. R. Mc.C. D.]

Pizarro, A Tragedy in Five Acts. . . The Genuine Edition. Dublin: Printed for Burnet [and others] 1799.

12mo. pp. vi—76. [Sigs. A.-G 6.]

[Copy in National Library, Dublin.—E. R. McC. D.]

*Pizarro . . . Genuine Edition. Cork. Printed by A. Edwards. 1799.

12mo. pp. iv—66.

[Copy in National Library, Dublin.—E. R. McC. D.]

Pizarro . . . Genuine Edition. Philadelphia. Printed for H. &
P. Rice. 16, South Second Street. 1799.

12mo.

[From Sichel, *Sheridan,* vol. II, p. 278.]

*Pizarro . . . A New Edition. Paris. Printed for Theophilus
Barrois junior. Bookseller, quay Voltaire, No. 3. 1804.

12mo. pp. 80.

[Apparently the first Paris Edition. Announced as *sous presse* in *The School for Scandal*
1804.]

4. MISCELLANEOUS.

The Music of Pizarro. A Play. As now performing at the
Theatre Royal, Drury Lane. With unbounded Applause. The
Music composed and selected by Michael Kelly. Ent. at Stationers' Hall. Pr. 6s. Published for Mr. Kelly, New Lisle Street,
and to be had at the Music Shops.

Folio. pp. 32.

Pagination. P. [i] title-page; p. [ii] blank; Pp. 1-30 Music
and Words from engraved plates.

[Pp. 25-28 contains, "Yes, yes, be merciless thou tempest dire. Sung by Mrs. Jordan.
Written by R. B. Sheridan, Esqr." This was also sold separately at 1s. The music is very
rare.]

Pizarro. Translated into German by Constantine Geisweiler.
(With the English Text). 1800. 8vo.

[From Allardyce Nicoll, *XVIII Century Drama,* 1750-1800. Boaden ascribes the
translation to Maria Geisweiler.]

Sheridan and Kotzebue. The Adventures of Pizarro. With
criticisms on the Play. London: Fairburn. 1799. 8vo.

[From Sichel, *Sheridan,* vol. II, p. 454. By J. Britton; according to Anderson,
Sheridan Bibliography, p. vii.]

A Critique on the Tragedy of Pizarro, As represented at
Drury Lane Theatre With such uncommon Applause. To which
is added a new Prologue. London. 1799. 8vo.

[From Anderson, *Sheridan Bibliography,* p. ix.]

*Memoir of R. B. Sheridan, with a concise critique upon the New Tragedy of Pizarro. London. 1799. 8vo.

[From Anderson, *Sheridan Bibliography*, p. ix.]

*More Kotzebue. By Bamley Satyricon. The origin of My Own Pizarro. A farce. London. 1799. 8vo.

[From Anderson, *Sheridan Bibliography*, p. viii. It is a satire on *Pizarro*.]

*Critical Remarks on Pizarro, a tragedy, taken from the German drama of Kotzebue, and adapted to the English Stage by R. B. Sheridan. By Samuel A. Bardsley. London. 1800. 8vo.

[From Anderson, *Sheridan Bibliography*, p. vii.]

[*Pizarro* was, of course, printed in all the Collected Editions after John Murray's of 1821, and in numerous collections. The only late Edition of interest is one "With Historical Notes by Charles Kean." London. 1856. 8vo.]

Four other translations of *Die Spanier in Peru* appeared in 1799:

Matthew Gregory Lewis. *Rolla; or, The Peruvian Hero*. 8vo. 1799.

[Four Editions. A remark of Moore's implies that this preceded the production of the Sheridan version.]

Anna Plumptre. *The Spaniards in Peru; or, The Death of Rolla.* The Original of the Play Performed under the title of *Pizarro*. 8vo. 1799.

[Six Editions. Reprinted in Dublin, and elsewhere also.]

*Thomas Dutton. *Pizarro in Peru, or the Death of Rolla*. With Notes. 8vo. 1799.

*Robert Heron. *Pizarro or The Death of Rolla*. 8vo. 1799.

Clio's Protest, with other Poems

Note

"CLIO'S PROTEST . . . With Other Poems by the late Right Honourable R. B. Sheridan" was printed in 1819. It contains four poems by Sheridan, the "Verses to Laura" being printed from MS. The last of these, the Epilogue to *Semiramis*, is omitted, being reprinted in another section of the present edition. The Introduction and annotations to the edition of 1819 are here included, as also is *The Bath Picture*, to which Sheridan's *Clio's Protest* was a reply.

R . C . R.

CONTENTS

Introduction

SHERIDAN got himself into print for the first time as an original author in *The Bath Chronicle* on October 10th, 1771. In this newspaper appeared *The Ridotto of Bath*, "a Panegyrick, Being an Epistle from Timothy Screw, Under Server to Messrs. Kuhf and Fitzwater, to his brother Henry, Waiter at Almack's." It was, in the strictest sense, occasional verse, for it satirised the opening ball at the New Assembly Rooms at Bath on September 30th of that year; the piece, therefore, must have been written in a week, perhaps, indeed, in two or three days. It is a swift and spirited essay in the manner of the New Bath Guide, a neat and clever imitation of Anstey, by a young man of nineteen. The first lines of *The Ridotto of Bath* are:

> At many grand Routs in my time I have been,
> And many fine Rooms to be sure I have seen,
> Al Fresco's, rich Gala's, Ridotto's and Balls,
> From Carlisle's sweet palace to black city Halls,
> From Almack's Long-Room to the Inn at Devizes,
> From *birth-night* eclat to the dance at Assizes;
> All these have I serv'd at these twelve years or more,
> Yet, 'faith, I've seen *here* what I ne'er saw before.

Sheridan had certainly caught the manner of Anstey, who began his letter from Mr. Simkin Barnard to his lady mother, "A Panegyric on Bath," in the same style:

> Of all the gay places the world can afford,
> By gentle and simple for pastime ador'd,
> Fine balls, and fine concerts, fine buildings, and springs,
> Fine walks, and fine views, and a thousand fine things,

Not to mention the sweet situation and air,
What place, my dear mother, with Bath can compare?

Some of Sheridan's echoes were deliberate.   In another
epistle concerning "A Public Breakfast at Spring Gardens"
Anstey wrote:—

The company made a most brilliant appearance,
And eat bread and butter with great perseverance,
All the chocolate, too, that my Lord set before 'em
The ladies despatched with the utmost decorum.

Timothy Screw's "good prudent Lords" ("Messrs. Kuhf
and Fitzwater") were less fortunate: the people at their Ridotto
laid hands on all they could:

So you see, my dear Hal, they bore all things before 'em
And trampled on *sweetmeats* as well as *decorum*.

Of course, Sheridan was no match for Anstey at his best,
though Mr. Sichel's condemnation of *The Ridotto of Bath* as
"commonplace and colloquial" is rather too strong. Still, there
is much truth in Moore's assertion that the allusions in this
trifle have lost their zest by time, although (it may be noted)
when the poem was reprinted as a broadsheet it was already
necessary—a few days after the event—to add the footnotes
which are now reprinted, as they were in the Bath edition of *The
Rival Beauties* (1773) and in *Clio's Protest: With Other Poems*
(1819). The poem might, of course, be annotated further—to
explain that "Carlisle's sweet palace" meant Carlisle House in
London, where Teresa Cornelys held her masquerades; that
"birth-night éclat" meant the Court Balls on the King's Birth-
day—that the "dance at Assizes" were the great County Balls
of the period. Or again, it might be added that when Wade, the
Master of Ceremonies, prohibited the wearing of black, it was
because such was the custom of London at Ridottos, which were
held during Lent, when some concession to decorum was considered necessary. But annotations of that type would indeed be
endless.

CLIO'S PROTEST

A few weeks after *The Ridotto of Bath* Sheridan wrote, with the same haste but with greater accomplishment, another piece with the title of *Clio's Protest, or the Picture Varnish'd*. This has a curious history, even more curious, it seems, than has hitherto been suspected. It is a reply to some verses—"doggerel," says Mr. Sichel, "balderdash," says Mr. Iolo Williams—with the title of *The Bath Picture*; "or a Slight Sketch of its Beauties in 1771." The author of this poem exerted himself to compliment the ladies who had assembled for the Bath Season in the autumn of that year. It was, no doubt, a hasty and headlong piece of versification, in which was achieved the distinction of some of the world's worst verses. For the moment two stanzas will suffice. The one celebrated the graces of two sisters, Lady Margaret Fordyce and Lady Ann Lindsay:

> Remark, too, the dimpling sweet smile,
>   Lady *Marg'ret's* fair countenance wears;
> And Lady *Ann*, whom so beauteous we stile,
>   As quite free of affected fine airs.

The other, following a compliment to Miss Waller, a singer, was intended as a tribute to Elizabeth Linley:

> We can boast of one other beside
>   Who's a mistress of harmony too;
> She's well-tempered and void of all pride,
>   The whole family's equally so.

Despite Mr. Sichel, neither this *Picture* nor Sheridan's answer, are to be found in "Crutwell's newspaper" *The Bath Chronicle*—at least by my seeking. But in its columns there appeared these notices:

November 21st, 1771.—"*The Picture* was received too late for this day's paper."

December 5th, 1771.—"*The Bath Picture*, or a Slight

Sketch of its Beauties in 1771, a Ballad, may be had at Crutwell's Printing-Office. Price 2d.

Where may be had

Clio's Protest; or, the Picture Varnished. Addressed to the Lady M—rg—r—t F—d—ce. Price 6d. . . .

And the Poetical Panegyrick of the *Ridotto of Bath.* Price 1d.

It would seem that Crutwell had handed *The Picture* to the young author of *The Ridotto of Bath*, who in ten days at the most, improvised his reply, which was published simultaneously with the Ballad. Collusion between the authors seems to have been impossible, for Sheridan misunderstood the allusion to Elizabeth Linley, which he thought was intended for the other singer, writing:

> Waller, could I say more of thee—
> But soft—here's all your family:
> A compliment—that none may grumble,
> They're all, it seems, extremely humble.

"With more of the tact of the man of the world than the ardour of a poet," says Moore, Sheridan "dismissed the object of his heart with the mere passing gallantry of a compliment":

> O! should your genius ever rise,
> And make you *Laureate* in the skies,
> I'd hold my life, in twenty years,
> You'd spoil the *music* of the *spheres.*
> —Nay, should the rapture-breathing Nine
> In one celestial concert join,
> Their sovereign's power to rehearse,
> —Were you to furnish them with verse,
> By Jove, I'd fly the heavenly throng,
> Tho' *Phœbus* play'd and *Linley* sung.

But the finest lines in *Clio's Protest* are those which embody the graceful anacreontic that was to become a favourite song, "Mark'd you her eye?":

But hark—Did not our Bard repeat
The love-borne name of Margaret?

. . . . .

And could you really discover,
In gazing those sweet beauties over,
No other charm, no winning grace,
Adorning either mind or face,
But one poor *dimple* to express
The *quintessence* of Loveliness?
—Marked you her cheek, of rosy hue?
Marked you her eye of sparkling blue
That eye in liquid circles moving!
That cheek, abashed at man's approving!
The *one* . . . Love's arrows darting round;
The *other* . . . blushing for the wound:
Did she not speak . . . did she not move . . . .
Now Pallas . . . now the Queen of Love!
O that the Muse . . . I mean, that you,
With such a model in your view,
Should prove so weak, so very simple,
To mock us with an idle *dimple*!
Nor ought you, *Pindar*, to accuse
The absence of your favourite *Muse*;
Her flight is here no palliation:
The *Theme* itself was inspiration.

Apparently *The Bath Picture* had been signed "Pindar," and
not as Mr. Sichel says "Clio"—a mistake which seems due to
the presence of the catchword " Clio" at the foot of an edition.
Sheridan used the pseudonym of "Asmodeo," derived from
Cumberland's epilogue to *The Maid of Bath*, Foote's play about
Elizabeth Linley. The author of *The Bath Picture* is described
in the edition of 1819 as " a wretched scribbler named Fitzpatrick" by which, despite the Editors, can scarcely have been
supposed to mean so distinguished a person as General Richard
Fitzpatrick, the author of the prologue to *The Critic*. Moore

identified the author as Miles Peter Andrews. It would be kinder to leave the "Bath Pindar" to languish undetected in his chosen pseudonym.

Clio's Protest is essentially occasional verse, but it is well-turned, witty, and melodious, and memorable (at all events) for its well-known epigram:—

> You write with *ease*, to show your breeding;
> But *easy writing*'s vile *hard reading*,

which is not less effective because of its echo of Pope's contemptuous phrase, "the mob of gentlemen who writ with ease."

Introduction

*T*HE *last four of the following Poems are submitted to the Public
in the fullest confidence of their authenticity.*

Clio's Protest, *and the* Ridotto *were delivered by Mr. Sheridan
himself, when a resident at Bath, to the late Mr. Crutwell, the pro-
prietor of the* Bath Chronicle, *for the purpose of publication in that
Journal, so far back as the year* 1771.

*The former was written in answer to a wretched scribler, of the
name of Fitzpatrick, who had published a Ballad, called* The Bath
Picture, *in celebration of the principal local beauties of that period.
This farrago is now prefixed, simply from its rendering the public more
competent judges of the admirable wit and humour of Mr. Sheridan's
satirical reply. Fitzpatrick (to whom although worsted, such an an-
tagonist was preferment), wrote a very angry rejoinder; but as it is
not clear that its republication would produce any other effect, beyond
that of increasing the number of pages, it is omitted.*

The easy style of The Ridotto of Bath, *hastily composed about the
same time, in consequence of an entertainment of that kind given in the
City, will not suffer by a comparison with the amusing vivacity of*
The Bath Guide.

*It is only necessary to add, that at that day there existed on the
spot no dispute as to these Poems being Mr. Sheridan's,—no secrecy
being observed with regard to the Author, who, in a confined circle
was more easily ascertained; and who, besides, had not then attained
his subsequent and well-earned celebrity; and that they were con-
stantly repeated and quoted by his contemporaries as his undoubted
productions.* [1]*This question is, however, willingly left to the judgment
and discrimination of the Reader; who, in these irregular and early*

---

[1]*There are a few still living who recollect him, when a very young man, walking about
Bath in a cocked hat and scarlet waistcoat, the then fashionable costume; much in the situation, with respect to finances, of his own Sir Lucius O' Trigger.*

efforts, will readily discern much of the brilliancy, that afterwards illuminated the Author's later and more mature compositions.

The Verses to Laura *were addressed to Miss* Ogle *(laterly Mrs. Sheridan), on the death of her former admirer, Col. M. who was killed in the battle at the Helder, during the British expedition to Holland, under his R. H. the Duke of York. They will be found pointedly to express the well-known sentiments of the writer on the justice and policy of the war consequent upon the French Revolution; and though manuscript copies were then in circulation, it is believed they were never before printed.*

The Epilogue to Capt. Ayscough's tragedy of Semiramis *is differently circumstanced, having been printed in* 1776; *but as that play was only performed seven or eight nights, and has never been heard of since, the Epilogue is now included, both on account of its own intrinsic merit, and of its hitherto very limited and imperfect circulation.*

The Editor is well aware that the Public require no apology for being presented with any works really proceeding from Mr. Sheridan's pen; and it is solely the anxiety to state the grounds of a firm belief in the legitimacy of his early but unknown offspring, that has occasioned their being troubled with the foregoing observations.[1]

[1]*As, on the recent publication of two poetical trifles of Mr. Sheridan's, the* Morning Herald *boldly declared them to be juvenile sallies of Mr.* Tierney's; *it is expected that on this occasion it will ascribe these to Mr.* Vansittart!

[For The Epilogue to *Semiramis* see the Prologues & Epilogues.]

The Bath Picture

COME exert yourself, *Clio*, I pray;
   Such a theme sure was never before;
  But acquit yourself well of the lay,
   And I never will pester you more.

Tho' no verse can with justice describe
   The sweet Beauties which *Bath* now may boast,
Yet I wish—must I speak it aside—
   You'd descant on each favourite toast.

I'd not have you to beauty of face,
   To manners or form be confin'd;
But display ev'ry charm, ev'ry grace,
   And each excellence too of the mind.

Tho' the beauty that's maiden, 'tis true,
   Stands most commonly foremost in fame;
Yet give that to each wife which is due,
   —Wou'd their husbands but practise the same!

Now my fair ones, you've nothing to fear,
   No ill-natur'd satirical style;
When the Graces with beauty appear,
   Envy can't but look pleasant the while.

When the elegant *Jennings* appears,
   What a buz through the room do they raise,
Tho' her beauty's the subject she hears,
   Not one scrap of conceit she betrays.

What eyes! and what lips! and what hair!
  Such a mouth too! what pleasure to kiss!
When I look, I can scarcely forbear
  Rushing on to such heavenly bliss.

I'd pronounce him a snarling poor wight,
  Void of taste too in ev'ry degree,
Who would dare, my sweet girl, for to write
  Or e'en speak with detraction of thee.

Mark the graceful fine figure of *Moore*,
  Who with ease and gentility moves;
Her eyes are delightful, that's sure—
  They must rapture whomever she loves.

When *Calder* too trips down the dance,
  All croud the sweet maid to observe;
She's distinguish'd by great complaisance,
  Good sense, and a prudent reserve.

For your life don't the *Seymours* forget,
  Who so rival each other all day,
That you'd not decide, should you bet,
  The most lively, good-humour'd, and gay.

Remark too the dimpling sweet smile,
  Lady *Marg'ret's* fair countenance wears;
And Lady *Ann*, whom so beauteous we style,
  As quite free of affected fine airs.

Gentle *Nappier* deserves to be nam'd:
  She's cautious—yet pleasing withal:
And *Drax* too must ever be fam'd—
  As a wife she's a pattern to all.

Pretty *Cheshire* you muſt not pass o'er,
    Who's so joyous and arch in her look:
You might mention at leaſt fifty more,
    But your ballad would swell to a book.

How my *Clio* you now will rejoice!
    For I'm come to your favourite name;
And our *Waller*'s as sweet in her voice,
    As your bard of poetical fame.

We can boaſt of one other beside,
    Who's a miſtress of harmony too;
She's well-temper'd, and void of all pride;
    The whole family's equally so.

'Twould be wrong, and one could not excuse,
    If your song was not happily grac'd
With *Matthews*'s name; whom my Muse
    Deserves with the firſt to be plac'd:

She's agreeable, courteous, and kind;
    Loves good-humour I'm sure to her heart;
And so bleſt with an amiable mind,
    She can't fail every bliss to impart.

Both the siſters for sense too we prize;
    With the *Sharps*, their conversable friends;
Milly, faith, has moſt excellent eyes,
    Which speaks more than, perhaps, she intends.

Give smart-looking fair *Hankle* a verse;
    She's always neat dress'd, and well bred;
And remember soft-speaking Miss *Nourse*,
    Who muſt look quite delicious in bed.

The laſt I shall name to you now,
  Is a beauty that all muſt admire;
She's juſt to a tittle, I vow,
  The thing one would wish and desire.

Her comedy-looking sweet face
  Spreads a joy round wherever she goes;
And vivacity chose it her place
  For to dwell with good-natur'd repose:

Affability marks her address,
  She with cheerfulness ever appears;
And *Pauncefort*—we all muſt confess,
  Wou'd rouse passion, tho' bury'd in years.

Clio's Protest

WHEREAS a certain Poetaster,
Pretending *Phœbus* was his Master,
Has modestly made up the Trio,
By lugging in the name of *Clio*,
To grace a fine descriptive stricture,
Which he is pleased to call *the Picture*—
I, in behalf of Muse aforesaid,
(By *Phœbus*, secund. leg. indorsed)
Present to all who chuse to have it,
Enclos'd, the *Muse's* affidavit:
By which it plainly will appear,
(As sworn 'fore Justice *Jupiter*)
That *Clio* never did assist
That daubing Panegyrist's fist;
Who lays his praise so thickly on,
That ev'ry *Goose* with him's a *Swan*:
Nor did she ever see the Piece
Which so *be-swans* these motley *Geese*.
And I too, for the *Muse's* sake,
Though *uninspir'd*, will undertake
To prove that, 'stead of aid divine,
True *Dullness* breathes in ev'ry line.

First then—(your Ancients will aver it)
This *Clio* was a girl of *spirit*;
Could point her periods to a tittle,
And was allow'd to *spell* a little:
Then being sister to *Apollo*,
I think it probably will follow,
That she could rhyme at least at pleasure;
And had some little skill in measure.

But our great Bard, whose genius tow'rs
Above such *low mechanic* powers;
Whose *Pegasus*, as bold as thunder,
All bonds of metre breaks asunder;
Kicks simple adverbs into fractions,
Snorting out furious *interjections!*
On concords and agreements tramples—
(Vide each stanza for examples)
This bard forsooth 'twas *Clio* fir'd!
O wonderful! how he's *inspir'd!*—
But as I would not seem to write
From idle prejudice or spite,
If there be faults, 'tis fit I shew 'em,
So let us just review the Poem.

He first begins, as Poets use,
To pay his devoirs to the *Muse;*
Then vows, if now she'll mend his pen,
He'll never *pester* her again.
(And no bad argument it was
To bribe her to befriend his cause.)
Ladies, it seems you've *nought* to *fear;*
The Poet will not be *severe:*
Alas! poor Bard, you little knew
The *fear* was—being *prais'd* by you.
If e'er by wine or fancy fir'd,
A witling thinks that he's inspir'd;
Mistaking, for a Poet's vein,
The itching of a rhyme-fed brain,
His pen he grasps, his subject chuses,
Then whips me down a brace of *Muses;*
Scales all *Parnassus* with his rhymes,
And wonders with what ease he climbs!
—But O! defend me from the *praise*
Of such! and let them wear the bays:
Their coarse good-will proves right ill-nature;
For ill- judg'd praise is worse than satire.

But tell me, lofty Bard, I pray,
What's this *acquitting of a lay?*
Or who, I beg, from prince to peasant,
E'er heard of *Envy looking pleasant?*

But Panegyrick's now the plan—
So enter *Jennings* in the van:
Behold she comes in beauty's ſtate;
(The hobbling verse proclaims her gait)
Hark, what a general *buz* is spread!
(Tho' only with a single *z*)
The nymph, unconscious that we raise
This *buzzing buzz* to *buzz* her praise;
Or, skill'd that consciousness to hide,
Ne'er shews the smalleſt scrap of pride.
But we ſtill *buzz* her noble size,
Her *pretty hair*, and *pretty eyes*,
And *pretty* brows those eyes to suit,
And *pretty*—God knows what to boot;
'Till echo, charm'd at beauty's reign,
With double *buzz* repeats the ſtrain.
—But here, to drop all quaint allusion,
How grand and new is the conclusion!
When all her other charms are paſt,
The Poet's *bonne Bouche* comes at laſt:—
This, literatim, would be truth:—
What think ye of her *kissing mouth?*
Nor does he here with flatt'ry treat her;
(I only wish it had been metre.)
Well, next in rank, you may be *sure*,
Comes in so pat the name of *Moore*;[1]
Or had the surname been *Moresco*,
'Tis ten to one he'd lugg'd in *fresco:*
For when a *proper name* will chime,
It has a fine effect in rhyme.
Here now, to judge by *vulgar* law,

[1] The daughter of Admiral Moore, and afterwards Lady Bamfylde.

A *scrup'lous* drudge might find a flaw;
Might doubt if 'twere a lawful capture,
Boldly to make a *verb* of *rapture*.
But shall the ſtanza-teeming mind,
By paltry *syntax* be confin'd?
Shall *Inspiration*, wild and free,
Be cramp'd by laws of *prosody*?
Shall *He*, whose soul perspires with *feeling*,
Be interrupted by the *spelling*?
Or when *enraptur'd*, ſtop to hammer
Those *raptures* into dirty *grammar*?
Never!—Let others dully beat
The *common* track with shackled feet,
Our *Pindar* ſtill disdains the road,
By prejudice ignobly trod:
There's not a hackney'd scribbling sot,
But *coins* you *beauties* where they're not:
—But our great bard extends his reach,
And nobly coins us *parts* of *speech*!

But soft—brisk *Calder's* next in ſtation,
Jigging it down to admiration:
But jigging how—perhaps you'll say—
O fear not, in the common way!
No—she's *diſtinguiſh'd* in the *Dance*
By her *prodigious complaisance*!
Reserv'd and *prudent* as she goes,
With *good sense* waiting on her toes.
—A pretty mode of dancing this!—
And yet for my part, gentle Miss,
I hope thy *real* feet are fleeter
Than those you halt upon in metre;
And pay too more regard to *time*
Than He, who made you dance in rhyme.

The *Rival Siſters* next appear!—
(At leaſt we find them rivals here);

But wherefore?—Didst thou never see
Beauty's twin-sisters yet agree?
Pause *here*, then, Trifler, and you'll find
Less parity of charms than mind:
For when true sense and mild good-nature,
Scarce ask the aid of youth and feature;
When the *fair mind*, and inborn grace,
Are but denoted by the face;
What need great Nature's band to move
The twin possessors hearts to love?
—Form'd in the self-same mould of heav'n,
To each the same attractions given;
Like polish'd mirrors they unite,
And lend each other mutual light—
What *Nature's* tie can *farther* do,
Sweet *Seymours*,[1] we behold in *you*.

But hark—did not our Bard repeat
The love-borne name of *Margaret*?
Attention seizes ev'ry ear;
We pant for the description *here*:—
"If ever Dullness left thy brow,
"*Pindar*, we say, 'twill leave thee now."
—But O! old Dullness' son anointed
His mother never disappointed!
And here we all were left to seek
A dimple in *Fordyce's* cheek!

And could you really then discover,
In gazing those sweet beauties over,
No other charm, no winning grace,
Adorning either mind or face,
But one poor *dimple*, to express
The *quintessence* of *Loveliness*?
—Mark'd you her cheek of rosy hue?

[1] The daughters of Lord Francis Seymour and one of them afterwards married to Mr. Newton.

Mark'd you her eye of sparkling blue?
That eye, in liquid circles moving;
That cheek, abash'd at man's approving;
The *one*—Love's arrows darting round
The *other*—blushing for the wound:
Did she not speak—did she not move—
Now *Pallas*—now the Queen of Love

O that the Muse—I mean that you,
With such a model in your view,
Should prove so weak, so very simple,
To mock us with an idle *dimple*!
Nor ought you, *Pindar*, to accuse
The absence of your favourite *Muse*;
Her flight is here no palliation:
The *Theme* itself was *inspiration*.

But surely here I ought to name
The *Sister* of this heav'nly dame—
Thee, gentle *Anne*,[1] I'll not pass o'er,
Tho' *Pindar*'s praise has gone before:
I'll paint—yet wherefore should I dwell
On what all feel and know too well?
Come forth, ye beauteous Idols then,
Who love the panegyrist's pen;
Her conscious heart, to whom I'd raise
My notes, disdains the pomp of praise.

But now, my trusty pen and paper!
(For I've no *Muse* to shew her shape here)
Return we to our humble strain,
And touch this Picture once again;
Or yawning wits will swear 'tis time
To let them sleep, and close our rhyme.

[1]Lady Anne Lindsay, afterwards Lady Anne Barnard. These two ladies were the daughters of the Earl of Balcarras.

For modern beaus, who scarcely spare
More time to reading than to pray'r,
If chance, when under hands of *Frizeur*,
On some quaint piece they make a seizure,
Or ſtroll from LEAKE's[1] with verses homewards,
(Allowing time for spelling some words)
If *minutes ten* don't get them through it,
They tear the sheet, and d—n the Poet.
But me such drones shall never hinder—
Have at you then, my noble *Pindar*.

Well now—(I hope he fits the cap here)
He introduces gentle *Napier*.
And here I mark *Minerva*'s frown,
To miss her fav'rite *Ogleton*.

Anon facetiously he cracks
His jokes upon *good Mrs. Drax*:
For where's the dame of common spirit
Will hear of *matrimonial* merit?
Or thank a poet who shall make her
A *poor domeſtic Bible-raker*?
It brings such notions in one's head
Of ſturdy females *country-bred*!
—We see the dame in ruſtic pride,
A bunch of keys to grace her side,
Stalking across the well-swept entry,
To hold her council in the pantry;
Or, with prophetic soul, foretelling
The peas will boil well by the shelling;
Or buſtling in her private closet,
Prepare her lord his morning posset;
And while the hallow'd mixture thickens,
Signing death-warrants for the chickens:
Else, greatly pensive, poring o'er
Accounts her cook had thumb'd before;

[1] Leake's Library, afterwards Bull's, and now Upham's.

III. I

One eye cast upon that *great Book*,
Yclep'd the *Family Receipt-Book*;
By which she's ruled in all her courses,
From stewing figs, to drenching horses.
—Then pans and pickling skillets rise
In dreadful lustre to our eyes,
With store of sweetmeats rang'd in order,
And *potted nothings* on the border;
While salves and caudle-cups between,
With squalling children, close the scene.

Here sure you fairly had a title,
My *Pindar*, to digress a little:
Nor would the lowly subject stain,
Sweet Bard, thy fine descriptive vein.
When next then you would shew a *pattern*
To each untidy married slattern,
Be sure you make a country life
The scene of action for your wife;
Chuse out a fine old mould'ring hall,
With moral tap'stry on the wall;
A farm-house too,—be sure you thatch it,
With barns on t'other side to match it;
A pig-stye, and a poultry-yard,
And *Shock*, you know, the faithful guard:
Describe the nurses, girls, and boys,
With all "the dear domestic joys";
And then, with hogs, babes, chicks, and all,
Bring *Goody Drax* to grace the ball.

But now behold, in stately march,
Miss *Cheshire*, with her looks so *arch*!
—(Tho' that is better, by the bye,
Then if he'd said her looks so *sly*.)—
But why not introduce her sister,
I see no reason why you've miss'd her:

For sure, my dear poetic brother,
The one looks full as *arch* as t'other.

Sudden our Bard begins to vapour,
And calls on *Clio* for a caper;
And she, poor girl! must now turn squaller,
To join in concert with his *Waller*!
There's music in the name, 'tis true;
But when that name is sung by you,
The *verse* and *theme* so disagree,
I cannot think of harmony.
O! should your genius ever rise,
And make you *Laureate* in the Skies,
I'd hold my life, in twenty years,
You'd spoil the *music* of the *spheres*.
—Nay, should the rapture-breathing Nine,
In one celestial concert join,
Their Sov'reign's power to rehearse,
—Were thou to furnish them with verse,
By *Jove*, I'd fly the heav'nly throng,
Tho' *Phœbus* play'd, and *Linley*[1] sung.

Waller, could I say more of thee—
But soft—here's all your family—
A compliment—that none may grumble;
They're all, it seems, *extremely humble*.

Here *Matthews* comes too, and a few more
Remarkable for their *good-humour*.
Pindar, 'tis thought (though not by me)
That here you aim'd at *Irony*:
For my part, I could wish you had;
For though th' attempt were wretched bad,
Yet one, whose merit mocks thy lays,
Might boast she had escap'd your praise.

[1] Subsequently, the first Mrs. Sheridan.

—*Conversable!*—can this be true?
And, *Pindar*, can this come from you?
What! shall the *Sharps*, for learning fam'd,
As mere Chitchatterers be nam'd?
Shall they, who've roam'd thro' *Rome* and *Greece*,
Sleep in a *conversation-piece?*
Shall they—yet hold, they must despise you,
Else, know, they could themselves chastise you.
—Ah! sure here was a subject fit,
For fancy to display its wit!
What, *sisters three*, with such sweet faces,
And no allusion to the Graces!
Or Goddesses on lofty Ide;
And you the *Trojan* by their side!
—There's *Anne*, whose wit and lively sallies
Would make a very decent *Pallas:*
And *Fan*, tho' short, as scholar you know,
Would be no bad *Bo-opis Juno:*
And then, (hang empty face or mein)
The *third*, of course, is beauty's queen.
—If any prude find fault with these
My new-created deities,
Out with the hag from *Bath*, and let her
At *Hyde-Park Corner* look for better.

Alas! unfortunate Miss *Nourse*,
That e'er your name should rhyme to verse!
(Tho' faith there's few could do it *worse*)
Else, sure our Bard, with fancy vicious,
Had never told us how *delicious*,
With powder'd night-cap on your head,
Your beauties would appear in bed!
Here follow lines of good dimension;
But as they're past my comprehension,
I will not grope thro' the confusion
In search of sense:—so come conclusion.

If in my strictures I've been free,
—You know the Muse's liberty.
Howe'er, I'll make all matters equal
By wholesome council, in the sequel:
And first—leave *Panegyrick*, pray;
Your genius does not lead that way:
You write with *ease*, to shew your breeding;
But *easy writing*'s vile *hard reading*,
—Henceforward Satire guide your pen;
But spare the women—lash the men.
Tho' possibly your Muse may stare,
To find such little diff'rence there;
So oft her verse would strike, in common,
The *flirting Man*, and *rakish Woman*.

Would not mild *Puffo* grace thy song,
And *Raucus*, with his fluent tongue?
—So rough, and yet so glib a tool;
'Twould silence a whole *boarding-school*.
With skipping *Wagtail*, pretty puppet,
(Inhuman aunt, so soon to drop it!)
And *Lizard*, with his supple bones,
The lively Prince of Cotillions?
Then grinning *Witwould*—tho' no Teague—
Who more successful at intrigue?
So bold and curling in his trade, he's
Like *Wantley*'s dragon to the ladies.
Nor spare the *flirting Cassock'd Rogue*,
Nor ancient *Cullin*'s polished brogue;
Nor gay *Lothario*'s[1] nobler name,
That *Nimrod* to all female fame:—
Nor sullen *Philo*'s stiff grimace,
Great SELF all gathering in his face:
And then, to scare the jovial crew,
Raise wretched *Chillchit* to their view;

[1] The late Lord Lyttelton.

With body meagre, wan, and thin,
And heart as narrow as his chin.

—Let me, my PINDAR, be your tutor,
Be such your subjects for the future.
Hence with your *Muse*, your *Clio* hence,
And court instead—*Dame* COMMON-SENSE.

If any think that unprovok'd
I here have satiriz'd and jok'd,
I answer them, whoe'er they be,
Begin and deal the same by me.

We petty Sciolists in verse,
For ever make each other worse;
By turns this licence take and give,
—The Muses' known prerogative.—
This once allow'd—'tween you and me,
Great *Pindar*, there's no enmity.
But if my satire seems uncouth,
As back'd by that foul monster, TRUTH,
And you (true Bard!) are therefore vex'd;
—Be quit—and *praise* me in your next.

The Ridotto of Bath

AT many grand Routs in my time I have been,
And many fine Rooms to be sure I have seen;
Al Fresco's, rich *Gala's*, *Ridotto's*, and *Balls*,
From *Carlisle's* sweet palace to black City halls;
From *Almack's* Long-Room to the Inn at *Devizes*,
From *birth-night* eclat to the dance at *Assizes:*
All these have I serv'd at these twelve years or more,
Yet faith I've seen *here*—what I ne'er saw before.

You'd like a description, I'm sure, my dear brother,
For fifty to one we may n't have such another.
I told in my laſt of the new alterations,
Of all our confusion and grand preparations;
I think too I mention'd a secret affair,
How all had been nearly knock'd up by the May'r:
It seems tho' that all their parading and bouncing
Was caus'd by a little miſtake in pronouncing;
The Aldermen heard that ſtrange whims we had got here,
And meant to exhibit a flaming *Red Otter;*
This well they conceiv'd was a shameful abuse,
And hinted their fears should it ever break loose;
Or chain'd e'er so faſt, we had little to brag on,
In building a palace to hold a great dragon:
However, at laſt they were eas'd of their fright,
And Monday was fix'd for the wonderful night.

At seven we open'd, and not very long
Before all the passages smoak'd with the throng;
All dress'd in their beſt—for great Marshall WADE,
For Fear the *Coup de' Oïel* should be darken'd by shade,
Had issued his orders to dizen the back,

With singular caution 'gainst wearing of black;[1]
In gaudes all must shine, he had given them warning,
Tho' the ghosts of their kindred should bellow for mourning;
Nay more, this grand festival night to denote,
No creature must come with a cape to his coat;
Full trimm'd they should be, tho' a French frock would do,
But Officers must be in livery queüe:
And yet for all this, there were some so uncivil,
They came in their dolefuls as black as the devil;
Nay Cornets clapp'd bags to their soldiery locks,
And many performed in common fly frocks.
Two rooms were first open'd—the *long* and the *round* one—
(These *Hogstyegon*[2] names only serve to confound one)
Both splendidly lit with the new chandeliers,[3]
With drops hanging down like the bobs at *Peg*'s ears,
While jewels of *paste* reflected the rays,
And *Bristol-stone* di'monds gave strength to the blaze:
So that it was doubtful, to view the bright clusters,
Which sent the most light out, the ear-rings or lustres.

But here I must mention the best thing of all,
And what I'm inform'd ever marks a *Bath* ball;
The VARIETY 'tis which so reign'd in the crew,
That turn where one would the classes were new;
For here no dull level of rank and degrees,
No uniform mode, that shews all are at ease;
But like a chess table, part black and part white,
'Twas a delicate checquer of *low* and *polite*;
The motley assemblage so blended together,
'Twas Mob, or Ridotto—'twas both, or 'twas neither.
Here Taylors, in bags, might contemplate at leisure
Fine dress coats, for which they'd last week taken measure;
Or if a stich broke in a gentleman's pump,

---

[1] The master of the Ceremonies publickly requested the Company to appear full-dressed, and not in mourning. Gentlemen full-dressed, or in French frocks. Officers in their uniforms, and their hair *en queüe*.
[2] The Concert Room, where the sideboards were served, is an Octagon.
[3] The five Chandeliers of the large Ball Room cost upwards of £500, and the three in the Tea Room near £300.

Some *Crispin* be sure had an awl at his rump;
Or should Lady's coïef be derang'd in the fright,
Three to one her next neighbour could set it to right;
To blame such a mixture were surely *abuseful*,
When one out of three might be *really* useful.—
Nor less among you was the medley, ye fair!
I believe there *were* some beside Quality there:
Miss *Spiggot*, Miss *Brussels*, Miss *Tape*, and Miss *Socket*,
Miss *Trinket*, and aunt, with her leathern pocket;
With good Mrs *Soaker*, who made her old chin go,
For hours, hob-nobbing with Mrs. *Syringo;*
Had *Tib* staid at home, I b'lieve none would have miss'd her,
Or pretty *Peg Runt*, with her tight little sister:
But blame not *Pinkinny* herself for adorning;—
Her gown—was the gown which she made in the morning;
Miss *Chain-stich* had ruffles she tore without sorrow,
'Twas *mending-lace day* behind counter to-morrow.
From *Bristol* too come many dames of high breeding;—
Seven Shillings was *money*—but then there was feeding:
Nay more—there were some this grand ball to adorn,
Whose husbands were puffing above at the horn:[1]
O, spare not your Cornu's! secure you may blow—
Your spouses are planning you fresh ones below:
But sure I was charm'd to behold little *Rona*
Jig it down all in time to her husband's cremona;
While he, happy mortal, at sight of his love,
In sympathy beat the balcony above.—

But—silence, ye hautboys! ye fiddles, be dumb!
Ye dancers, stop instant—THE HOUR is come;[2]
The great—the all-wonderful hour—of EATING!
That hour—for which ye all know you've been waiting,
Well, the doors were unbolted, and in they all rush'd;
They crouded, they jostled, they jockey'd, and push'd:
Thus at a Mayor's feast, a disorderly mob
Breaks in after dinner to plunder and rob.—

[1] Some of the musician's wives were of the company.
[2] Precisely at nine o'clock the sideboards in the Octagon Room were opened.

I mean not by this to reflect on the gentry,
I'd only illustrate the *mode* of their *entry;*
For certain I am they meant no such foul play,
But only were wishing to help us away:
I believe too their hurry in clearing the platters
Was all in compassion to us the poor waiters;
In *London* I'm sure I've been kept many hours
In dangling attendance with sweetmeats and flow'rs;
But *here*, as if studious to ease us of trouble,
Each guest play'd his part, as if he'd paid double;
In files they march'd up to the sideboards, while each
Laid hands upon all the good things in his reach;
There stuck to his part, cramm'd while he was able,
And then carried off all he could from the table:
Our outworks they storm'd with prowess most manful,
And jellies and cakes carried off by the handful;[1]
While some our lines enter'd, with courage undaunted,
Nor quitted the trench till they'd got what they wanted.
There was Mrs. *M'Ribband*, and Mrs. *Vancasket*,
I believe from my soul they went halves in a basket;
While lank Madam *Crib'em* so work'd her old jaw,
Tom Handleflask swore she'd a pouch in her maw:
But let not the smirking Dame *Patch* be forgot here,
Who ate like her lap-dog, and drank like an Otter;
Nor pious Miss *Churchface*, whatever 'twas brought her,
Unless to crib cakes for her landlady's daughter;
However, the viands went off at such rate,
A lady's toupee often knock'd down a plate,
And many confess'd a fat citizen's belly
A terrible stop to the progress of jelly;
While salvers of biscuits around their ears flew,
O'erturn'd by the whisk of an officer's queüe;
And thus in ten minutes one half of the treat
Made a pretty check carpet squash'd under their feet.
O 'twas pleasing to see a collection of beaux

[1]The Author might have said pocket instead of hand, as many were really seen filling their pockets with sweetmeats, &c.

Parading with large macarons at their toes;
Or a delicate nymph give a languishing reel
On a marmalade kissing her little French heel.
So you see, my dear *Hal*, they bore all things before 'em,
And trampled on *sweetmeats* as well as *decorum*.
Our good prudent Lords had indeed given word
Not to truſt any vessels away from the board;[1]
For my part, I thought them so much in the right,
I fretted to see but a spoon out of sight;
Tho' 'twere beſt to have had 'em sure, had we been able,
As 'tis at St. Giles's, all chain'd to the table:
I muſt tho' in juſtice declare, that as yet
I hear of nought missing—but what could be eat—
If *dispatch* is a virtue, I here muſt aver it,
The whole congregation had infinite merit;
For sure, my dear *Hal*, you'll be charmed to hear
That within half an hour all the tables were clear.

The reſt, *Hal*, you know, is for ever the same,
With chatt'ring, and dancing, and all the old game;
Cotillons in one room, country-dance in another,
In ev'ry room—*folly, confusion*, and *pother*!
With unmeaning queſtions, of "which room's the hotter?"
And, "Madam, pray how do you like the *Rudotter?*
"To see Capt. *Plume* dance—sure none can dislike him—
"Wade's piƈture,[2] I think, is *purdigiously* like him—
"Do you dance, Sir, to-night?"—'No, Ma'am, I do not:"
"I don't wonder at it, 'tis *suffoking* hot."
But you, *Hal*, have heard out firſt quality praters,
Who English ne'er talk—but when d-mn-ng the waiters:
So I need only say, that at one all withdrew,
Which gives me the hint now to bid you adieu;
So believe me sincerely,

Your's,

Timothy Screw.

[1]It was publickly ordered by the managers, that no bottles or glasses should be taken from the sideboards.
[2]In the Octagon Room is a fine Portrait of Mr. Wade, painted by Mr. Gainsborough.

Verses Addressed to Laura

SCARCE hush'd the sigh, scarce dried the tear
Affliction pour'd upon a Brother's bier,
Another loss bids *Laura*'s sorrows flow:
As keen in anguish as a sister's woe.
Unknown to me the object of her grief,
I dare not counsel, did she ask relief;
Yet may the wish no vain intrusion prove,
To share her grief, for all who share her love.
Yes, gallant victim in this hateful strife,
Which pride maintains 'gainst man's and freedom's life
If quick and sensible to *Laura*'s worth,
Thy heart's first comment was affections birth,
If thy soul's day rose only in her sight,
And absence was thy clouded spirit's night;
If 'mid whatever busy tumults thrown,
Thy silent thought still turn'd to her alone.
If while ambition seem'd each act to move,
Thy secret hope was *Laura*, peace, and love;
If such thy feelings, and thy dying prayer
To wish that happiness thou couldst not share.
Let me with kindest claim thy name revere,
And give thy memory a brother's tear.—
But ah! not tears alone fill *Laura*'s eyes,
Resentment kindles with affliction's sighs;
Insulted patience borrows passion's breath,
To curse the plotters of these scenes of death;
Yet sooth'd to tranquil peace sweet Mourner be,
And every harsh emotion leave to me.
Remembrance sad, and soft regret be thine,
The wrath of hate and blow of vengeance mine;

And oh! by Heaven that hour shall surely come,
When fell Deſtroyers! ye shall meet your doom.
Yes, miscreant Statesmen! by the proud disdain
Which honour feels at base corruption's reign.
By the loud clamour of a nation's woes,
By the ſtill pang domeſtic sorrow knows,
By all that hope has loſt, or terror fears,
By England's injuries, and by *Laura*'s tears,
The hour shall come when fraud's short triumph paſt,
A people's vengeance shall ſtrike home at laſt:
Then, then shall foul remorse, the daſtard fiend,
That ne'er pollutes the noble Soldier's end;
And dark despair around the scaffold wait,
And not one look deplore the Traitor's fate;
But while remembrance shakes his coward frame,
And ſtarts of pride contend with inward shame.
The mute reproach, or execrations loud,
Of sober Juſtice, or the scoffing crowd,
Alike shall hail the blow that seals his doom,
And gives to infamy his mem'ry and his tomb!

Turn from the hateful scene, dear *Laura*, turn,
And thy lov'd friend with milder sorrows mourn;
Still dwell upon his fate, for ſtill thou'lt find
The contraſt lovely, and 'twill soothe thy mind.
Fall'n with the brave, e'er number'd with the slain,
His mind unwounded, calms his body's pain;
Hopeless, but not dismay'd, with fearless eye,
He reads the doom that tells him he muſt die;
Lays his brave hand upon his bleeding breaſt,
And feels his glory, while he finds his reſt.—
Then yields his transient breath which nature gave,
And sure of prouder life, o'erlooks the grave!

Sweet is the meed that waits his laurell'd bier,
'Tis valour's hope, 'tis honor's praise sincere,
'Tis friendship's manly sigh, and gentle beauty's tear. }

Bibliography of
Clio's Protest, with Other Poems

1. THE RIDOTTO OF BATH (Bath, 1771.)

THE RIDOTTO OF BATH, a Panegyrick, Written by a Gentleman, resident in that City. Being an Epistle from Timothy Screw, Under Server to Messrs. Kuhf and Fitzwater, to his brother Henry, Waiter at Almack's. (Published originally in *The Bath Chronicle*, October 10th, 1771.)

Folio broadside.

Copy in the Bath Municipal Library.

The poem is set out in a double column, beneath the title. At the foot are annotations· When *The Ridotto of Bath* was printed in *The Bath Chronicle*, certain names and words were printed with dashes and stars; as "Marshall * * * *," which was expanded to Marshall Wade" in the broadside reprint, where brief explanatory notes were added. In this form it was reprinted in the Bath edition of *The Rival Beauties*, (1773) and in *Clio's Protest, with Other Poems*, (1819).

The Bath Chronicle advertised October 17, "The Verses on the Ridotto printed in our last to be had at the printing-office 1d." *November 8th*, "Verses on the Ridotto reprinted and to be had in any number."

2. CLIO'S PROTEST (Bath, 1771.)

CLIO'S PROTEST; or, The Picture Varnished. Addressed to the Lady M—rg—r—t F—d—ce. Price 6d.

Advertised in *The Bath Chronicle* of December 5th, 1771. No copy of this can now be traced, although Mr. Walter Sichel possessed what seems to have been some pages of it.

3. THE RIVAL BEAUTIES (London, 1772.)

THE RIVAL BEAUTIES, a Poetical Contest. London. Printed for W. Griffin at Garrick's Head in Catherine-Street, Strand; and sold by R. Cruttwell in St. James's Street, Bath. Price 1s. 6d.

Quarto.

Pagination. P. [1] title; p. [ii] blank; p. [iii] Dedication; p. [iv] blank; pp. [1] and 2-4 text of *The Bath Picture*; pp. [5] and 6-17 text of *Clio's Protest*; p. [18] blank; pp. [19] and 20-25 text of *Pindar's Answer*; p. 26, blank.

The Dedication of this poem, signed by "One of a Thousand" is headed Bath, January 26, 1772.

The book contains:—

(i) *The Bath Picture*: or, a Slight Sketch of its Beauties in 1771. A Ballad. [This was printed separately, being advertised in *The Bath Chronicle* of December 5th, 1771. Price 2d.]

(ii) *Clio's Protest*; or, The Picture Varnished.

(iii) *Pindar's Answer* to the Author of *The Picture Varnished*. [This reply does not seem to have been printed separately.]

4. THE RIVAL BEAUTIES (Bath, 1773.)

THE RIVAL BEAUTIES, a Poetical Contest. Containing The Bath Picture; or, A Sketch of its Beauties in 1771. Clio's Protest; or, The Picture Varnished. And Pindar's Reply. To which is Added the Ridotto of Bath, A Panegyric. Bath. Printed by R. Crutwell, Union Passage, And Sold by All the Booksellers of that City, and by W. Griffin, Bookseller in Catherine-Street, Strand, London. MDCCLXXIII. Price One Shilling and Six-Pence.

This book (a copy of which is in the Bath Municipal Library) has not been previously recorded. It is the first book to contain *The Ridotto of Bath*.

5. CLIO'S PROTEST, WITH OTHER POEMS (London, 1819.)

CLIO'S PROTEST or, "The Picture" Varnished. With Other Poems. By the late Right Honourable R. B. Sheridan. London: Printed for Joseph Arnould, 2, Spring Gardens. 1819. Price Two Shillings and Sixpence.

Octavo, pp. viii + 52.

Contains:—*The Bath Picture, Clio's Protest, The Ridotto of Bath, Verses Addressed to Laura* (no previous publication recorded) and the Epilogue to *Semiramis*.

Longer Poems

Note

THE LOVE EPISTLES OF ARISTÆNETUS were first printed in 1771, with a Preface signed "H. S." the combined surname initials of Halhed and Sheridan. Of the twenty-six epistles the only ones here reprinted are the six which are attributed to Sheridan by Moore or Sichel.

"A FAMILIAR EPISTLE to the Author of *The Heroic Epistle to Sir William Chambers* and of *The Heroic Postscript to the Public*" was first printed in 1774; with a second edition in the same year. It was assigned to Sheridan by Thomas Linley (for which see the Introduction).

"A PORTRAIT . . . by R. B. Sheridan, Esq.," is here reprinted from John Murray's edition of *The School for Scandal* (1823) where it appears (with no real justification) as the Dedicatory Poem. It had apparently appeared surreptitiously in print, probably in some periodical, about 1810.

"VERSES TO THE MEMORY OF GARRICK, Spoken as a Monody" were first printed in 1779, with a Dedication signed "R. B. Sheridan."

R. C. R.

CONTENTS

Introduction

ACCORDING to the "Account of Richard Brinsley Sheridan, Esq.," in *The European Magazine* for February, 1782, "at the age of eighteen years, he joined with a friend in translating the Epistles of Aristænetus from the Greek." According to a well-informed biography of Sheridan in the annual *Public Characters* for 1799, "A poetical translation of Aristænetus has been attributed to him, but the share he had in that version was very limited." Beyond the fact that his friend was Nathaniel Brassey Halhed, the various enquiries of later years have not added greatly to the information that is summarised in those two concise sentences. It is certain that in November, 1770, when Halhed sent his translations to Sheridan, his collaborator had to write to a friend named Ker to buy him a copy of Aristænetus—and a Greek Grammar. In the May of the next year, the revised translation was in the hands of John Wilkie, who published it in August. Fraser Rae thought that the correspondence between the collaborators showed Sheridan's share to have been little more than the correction and polishing of phrases. Moore attributed to Sheridan two entire Epistles—the Third and the Twelfth: Mr. Sichel, making no comments upon the two selected by Moore, attributed to Sheridan three Epistles—the First, the Ninth and the Thirteenth. To these he adds one other, the Last.

But the evidence of "style" and "superiority of workmanship" on which Mr. Sichel mainly depends, is by no means decisive. He declares—"Nor is Moore at sea in attributing the Last Epistle to Sheridan alone. It is quite after his manner, and aptly named *The Rival Friends*. It seems coloured with personal feeling, and it is full of sorrow for friendship lost by rivalry, but it is not Halhed that Sheridan means, still less Matthews whom he regrets."[1] The rival friend was some mysterious person, Mr. Sichel explains, designated "K—" (possibly meaning Kearney), in some unfinished pastorals of this period. Nevertheless, Moore said very definitely that this Last Epistle was not Sheridan's, but Halhed's own:—

But by far the most interesting part of the volume is the last Epistle of the book, "From a Lover resigning his Mistress to his Friend,"—in which Halhed has contrived to extract from the unmeaningness of the original a direct allusion to his own fate and, forgetting Aristænetus and his dull personages, thinks only of himself, and Sheridan, and Miss Linley.

Thee, then, my friend,—if yet a wretch may claim
A last attention by that once dear name,—
Thee I address:—the cause you must approve;
I yield you—what I cannot cease to love.
Be thine the blissful lot, the nymph be thine:
I yield my love,—sure, friendship may be mine.
Yet must no thought of me torment thy breast;
Forget me, if my griefs disturb thy rest,
Whilst still I'll pray that thou may'st never know
The pangs of baffled love, or feel my woe.

After reading the whole of the Twenty-eight Epistles, which are written with moderate fluency, and here and there a well-turned line, there seems no reason to suggest that Sheridan did more than "correct" the versions of Halhed. The present selection is, therefore, confined to the six Epistles attributed to Sheridan by Moore and Mr. Sichel. Whereafter, one may gracefully retire before Moore.

The young authors were sanguine that their volume, which they published under the combined initials of "H. S." would bring them wealth, and demand their identity to be revealed to an admiring world. Thus Moore:—

The first account they heard of the reception of the work was flattering enough to prolong awhile this dream of vanity "It begins (writes Mr. Ker, in about a fortnight after the pub-

[1]Halhed, like Sheridan, was in love with Elizabeth Linley. The duels with Matthews were fought twelve months later than this Epistle was written.

lication) to make some noise, and is fathered on Mr. Johnson. author of the *English Dictionary*, &c. See to-day's *Gazetteer*. The critics are admirable in discovering a concealed author by his style, manner, &c."

Their disappointment at the ultimate failure of the book was proportioned, we may suppose, to the sanguineness of their first expectations. But the reluctance, with which an author yields to the sad certainty of being unread, is apparent in the eagerness with which Halhed avails himself of every encouragement for a rally of his hopes. *The Critical Review*, it seems, had given the work a tolerable character, and quoted the first Epistle. The Weekly Review in *The Public Ledger* had also spoken well of it, and cited a specimen. *The Oxford Magazine* had transcribed two whole Epistles, without mentioning from whence they were taken.[1] Every body, he says, seemed to have read the book, and one of those *hawking booksellers* who attend the coffee-houses assured him it was written by Dr. Armstrong, author of *The Œconomy of Love*. On the strength of all this he recommends that another volume of the Epistles should be published immediately—being of opinion that the readers of the first volume would be sure to purchase the second, and that the publication of the second would put it in the heads of others to buy the first. Under a sentence containing one of these sanguine anticipations, there is written, in Sheridan's hand, the word "Quixote!"

They were never, of course, called upon for the second part, and, whether we consider the merits of the original or of the translation, the world has but little to regret in the loss. Aristænetus is one of those weak, florid sophists, who flourished in the decline and degradation of antient literature, and strewed their gaudy flowers of rhetoric over the dead muse of Greece. He is evidently of a much later period than Alciphron, to

---

[1]Not all the reviews were so tolerant: "No such writer as Aristænetus ever existed in the classic æra; nor did even the unhappy schools, after the destruction of the Eastern empire, produce such a writer. It was left to the latter times of monkish imposition to give such trash as this, on which the translator has ill spent his time. We have been as idly employed in reading it, and our readers will in proportion lose their time in perusing this article."—*The Monthly Review* for December, 1771.

whom he is also very inferior in purity of diction, variety of subject, and playfulness of irony. But neither of them ever deserved to be wakened from that sleep, in which the commentaries of Bergler, De Pauw, and a few more such industrious scholars have shrouded them.

The translators of Aristænetus, in rendering his flowery prose into verse, might have found a precedent and model for their task in Ben Jonson, whose popular song, "Drink to me only with thine eyes," is, as Mr. Cumberland first remarked, but a piece of fanciful mosaic, collected out of the love-letters of the sophist Philostratus. But many of the narrations in Aristænetus are incapable of being elevated into poetry; and, unluckily, these familiar parts seem chiefly to have fallen to the department of Halhed, who was far less gifted than his coadjutor with that artist-like touch, which polishes away the mark of vulgarity, and gives an air of elegance even to poverty.

Preface

[To the Edition of 1771]

*T*HE *critics have not yet decided at what time Ariſtænetus ap-peared, or indeed whether or not he ever exiſted; for, as he is mentioned by no ancient author, it has been conjectured that there never was such a person, and that the name prefixed to the firſt Epiſtle was taken by the publisher for that of the writer. This work was never known nor heard of till Sambucus gave it to the world in the year 1566; since which time there have been several editions of it published at Paris, where the book seems to have been held in greater eſtima-tion than amongſt us. As to the real date of its composition, we have no-thing but conjecture to offer. By the twenty-sixth Epiſtle it should seem that the author lived in the time of the later emperors, when Byzanti-um was called New Rome: and therein mention is made of the panto-mime actor Caramallus, who was contemporary with Sidonius Apol-linaris.*

These Epiſtles are certainly terse, elegant, and very poetical, both in language, and sentiment; yet pleasing as they are, they have scarcely anything original in them, being a cento from the writings of Plato, Lucian, Philoſtratus, and almoſt all the ancient Greek authors, whose sentences are moſt agreeably woven together, and applied to every pas-sion incident to love. This circumſtance, though it may lessen our idea of the intention of the author, should not in the leaſt depreciate the per-formance, as it opens to us a new source of entertainment, in contem-plating the taſte of the composer in the selection of his sentences, and his ingenuity in the application of them, whilſt the authority and reputa-tion of the works from whence these sweets are extracted, adds dignity to the subject on which they are beſtowed.

Having said thus much of the original, cuſtom seems to demand some apology for the translation. And, firſt, it may to some appear a whimsical undertaking to give a metrical translation of a prosaic

137

author; but the English reader, it is to be presumed, will not find any deficiency of poetical thoughts on that account, however the diction may have suffered by passing through unworthy hands; and to such as are acquainted with that elegant luxuriance which characterizes the Greek prose, this point will not need a solution. Nor can it be deemed derogatory from the merit of our own language to affirm, that the superiority of the Greek in this respect is so forcible, that even the most trifling of these Epistles must have suffered considerably both in spirit and simplicity, if committed to the languid formality of an English prosaic translation.

The ingenious Tom Brown has translated, or rather imitated, some select pieces from this collection, but he either totally misconceived the spirit of his author, or was very unequal to the execution of it. He presents you, it is true, with a portrait of the author, and a portrait that has some resemblance to him; but it is painted in a bad attitude, and placed in a disadvantageous light. In the original, the language is neat, though energetic; it is elegant as well as witty. Brown has failed in both; and though a strict adherence to these points in a metrical translation may be esteemed difficult, yet it is hoped that the English dress in which Aristænetus is at present offered to the public, will appear to become him more than any he has ever worn in this country.

It were absurd to pretend that this translation is perfectly literal; the very genius of prose and verse forbid it; and the learned reader who shall consult the original, will find many reasons for the impropriety as well as difficulty of following the author's expressions too closely. Some things there were which it were scarce possible to handle in verse, and they are entirely omitted, or paraphrastically imitated; many passages have been softened as indelicate, some suppressed as indecent. But beside these allowable deviations, a still further licence has been taken; for where the subject would admit of it, many new ideas are associated with the original substance, yet so far affecting the author's proper style, that its native simplicity might not be obscured by their introduction. And two or three Epistles there are in this collection which must shelter themselves under the name of Aristænetus, without any other title to his protection than that of adhering to the subject of the several Epistles which they have supplanted. The only apology which can be offered for this, is an avowal that the object of this trans-

lation was not so much to bring to light the merit of an undistinguished and almost unknown ancient, as to endeavour to introduce into our language a species of poetry not frequently attempted, and but very seldom with success; that species which has been called the "simplex munditiis" in writing, where the thoughts are spirited and fanciful without quaintness, and the style simple, yet not inelegant. Though the merit of succeeding in this point should not be given to the present attempt, yet it may in some measure become serviceable to the cause, by inciting others of better taste and abilities to endeavour to redeem our language from the imputation of barbarity in this respect.

As to the many different measures which are here introduced, something besides the translator's caprice may be urged in their favour. For by a variation of metre, the style almost necessarily undergoes an alteration; and in general, the particular strain of each Epistle suggested the particular measure in which it is written. Had they been all in one kind of verse, they would have fatigued, they might have disgusted. At present, it is hoped that some analogy will be found between the mode of passion in each Epistle and the versification by which it is expressed; at the same time that a variety of metres, like a variety of prospects on a road, will conduct the reader with greater satisfaction through the whole stage, though it be short.

There remains but one thing more to be said. The original is divided into two parts; the present essay contains only the first. By its success must the fate of the second be determined.

H. S.[1]

[1]The notes here signed H.S. are reprinted from the Edition of 1771.

The Love Epistles of Aristaenetus

EPISTLE I—LAIS[1]

ARISTÆNETUS TO PHILOCALUS.[2]

BLEST with a form of heavenly frame,
    Blest with a soul beyond that form,
    With more than mortal ought to claim,
    With all that can a mortal warm,
Laïs was from her birth design'd
To charm, yet triumph o'er mankind.
There Nature, lavish of her store,
Gave all she could, and wish'd for more;
Whilst Venus gazed, her form was such!
Wondering how Nature gave so much;
Yet added she new charms, for she
    Could add—"A fourth bright grace," she said,
"A fourth, beyond the other three,
    Shall raise my power in this sweet maid."
Then Cupid, to enhance the prize,
    Gave all his little arts could reach:
To dart Love's language from the eyes
He taught—'twas all was left to teach.

---

[1]Epistle I. In this letter Aristænetus describes the beauties of his mistress to his friend. This description differs in one circumstance from the usual poetic analysis of beauty, which is this, that (if we except the epithets "ruby," "snowy," &c., which could not well have been avoided) the lady it paints would be really beautiful; whereas it is generally said, "that a negro would be handsome, compared to woman in poetical dress."—H. S.
    Attributed to Sheridan by Sichel.

[2]There is a studied propriety in the very names of the supposed correspondents in these Epistles; having in the original this peculiar beauty, that generally one, and often both of them, bear an agreeable allusion to the subject of the several letters to which they are prefixed.—H. S.

O faireſt of the virgin band!
Thou maſter-piece of Nature's hand!
So like the Cyprian queen, I'd swear
Her image fraught with life were there:
But silent all: and silent be,
That you may hear her praise from me:
I'll paint my Laïs' form; nor aid
I ask—for I have seen the maid.

Her cheek with native crimson glows,
But crimson soften'd by the rose:
'Twas Hebe's self beſtow'd the hue,
Yet health has added something too:
But if an over-tinge there be,
Impute it to her modeſty.
Her lips of deeper red, how thin!
How nicely white the teeth within!
Her nose how taper to the tip!
And slender as her ruby lip!
Her brows in arches proudly rise,
As conscious of her powerful eyes:
Those eyes, majeſtic-black, display
The luſtre of the god of day;
And by the contraſt of the white,
The jetty pupil shines more bright.
There the glad Graces keep their court,
And in the liquid mirror sport.
Her tresses, when no fillets bind,
Wanton luxurious in the wind;
Like Dian's auburn locks they shone,
But Venus wreath'd them like her own.
Her neck, which well with snow might vie,
Is form'd with niceſt symmetry;
In native elegance secure
The moſt obdurate heart to wound;
But she, to make her conqueſts sure,
With sparkling gems bedecks it round:

With gems that, ranged in order due,
Present the fair one's name to view.[1]
Her light-spun robes in every part
Are fashioned with the niceſt art,
   Tis Beauty's self before your eyes.

   How ſtately doth my Laïs go!
With ſtudied ſtep, composedly slow;
Superb, as some tall mountain fir,
Whom Zephyr's wing doth slightly ſtir:
(For surely beauty is allied
By Nature very near to Pride:)
The grove indeed mild breezes move,
But her the gentler gales of Love.
From her the pencil learns its dye—
The rosy lip, the sparkling eye;
And bids the piﬅured form assume
Bright Helen's mien, and Hebe's bloom.
But how shall I describe her breaﬅ?
   That now firﬅ swells with panting throb
To burﬅ the fond embracing veﬅ,
   And emulate her snow-white robe.
So exquisitely soft her limbs!
   That not a bone but pliant seems;
As if th' embrace of Love—so warm!
Would quite dissolve her beauteous form.
But when she speaks!—good heavens! e'en now
   Methinks I hear my fav'rite song;
E'en yet with Love's respeﬅ I bow
   To all th' enchantment of her tongue.
Her voice moﬅ clear, yet 'tis not ﬅrong;
Her periods full, though seldom long;
With wit, good-natured wit, endow'd;
Fluent her speech, but never loud.
Witness, ye Loves! witness; for well I know

[1] *With gems*, &c.] This conceit was formerly reckoned a peculiar elegance in a lady's dress.—H. S.

To her you've oft attention given;
Oft pensile flutter'd on your wings of snow
  To waft each dying sound to heaven.
  Ah! sure this fair enchantress found
The zone which all the Graces bound:
Not Momus could a blemish find
Or in her person or her mind.—
But why should Beauty's goddess spare
To me this all-accomplish'd fair?
I for her charms did ne'er decide,[1]
As Paris erſt on lofty Ide;
I pleased her not in that dispute;
I gave her not the golden fruit:
Then why the Paphian queen so free?
Why grant the precious boon to me?
Venus! what sacrifice, what prayer
  Can show my thanks for such a prize!
—To bless a mortal with a fair,
  Whose charms are worthy of the skies.

  She too, like Helen, can inspire
Th' unfeeling heart of age with fire;
Can teach their lazy blood to move,
And light again the torch of love.[2]
"Oh!" cry the old, "that erſt such charms
Had bloom'd to bless our youthful arms;
Or that we now were young, to show
How we could love—some years ago!"

  Have I not seen th' admiring throng
For hours attending to her song?

---

[1]I for her charms did ne'er decide—This alludes to the well-known contest between Juno, Venus, and Minerva, for the golden apple.—H. S.

[2]She too, like Helen, —

Οὐ Νέμεσις Τρῶας καὶ ἐϋκνήμιδας Ἀχαιοὺς
Τοιῇδ' ἀμφὶ γυναικὶ πολὺν χρόνον ἄλγεα πάσχειν·
Αἰνῶς ἀθανάτῃσι θεῇς εἰς ὦπα ἔοικεν·   Hom.

Whilst from her eyes such lustre shone
It added brightness to their own:
Sweet grateful beams of thanks they'd dart,
That showed the feelings of her heart.
Silent we've sat, with rapt'rous gaze!
Silent—but all our thoughts were praise:
Each turned with pleasure to the rest;
And this the prayer that warm'd each breast:[1]

"Thus may that lovely bloom for ever glow,
    Thus may those eyes for ever shine!
Oh may'st thou never feel the scourge of woe!
    Oh never be misfortune thine!
Ne'er may the crazy hand of pining care
    Thy mirth and youthful spirits break!
Never come sickness, or love-cross'd despair,
    To pluck the roses from thy cheek!
But bliss be thine—the cares which love supplies,
    Be all the cares that you shall dread;
The graceful drop, now glist'ning in your eyes,
    Be all the tears you ever shed.

    But hush'd be now thy am'rous song
And yield a theme, thy praises wrong:
Just to her charms, thou canst not raise
Thy notes—but must I cease to praise?
Yes—I will cease—for she'll inspire
Again the lay, who strung my lyre.
Then fresh I'll paint the charming maid,
    Content, if she my strain approves;
Again my lyre shall lend its aid,
    And dwell upon the theme it loves.

[1] We may amuse ourselves . . . by speculating whether in writing such lines as these, the young poet had not in his mind's eye the vision of the lovely Elizabeth Linley singing at one of her father's concerts.—Iolo A. Williams, *Sheridan's Plays* (1926), Introduction, p. 11.

III. L

EPISTLE III—THE GARDEN OF PHYLLION[1]

PHILOPLATANUS TO ANTHOCOME.

BLEST was my lot—ah! sure 'twas bliss, my friend,
The day—by heavens! the long live day to spend
With Love and my Limona! Hence! in vain
Would mimic Fancy bring those scenes again;
In vain delighted memory tries to raise
My doubtful song, and aid my will to praise.
In vain! Nor fancy strikes, nor memory knows,
The little springs from whence those joys arose,
Yet come, coy Fancy, sympathetic maid!
Yes, I will ask, I will implore thy aid:
For I would tell my friend whate'er befell;
Whate'er I saw, whate'er I did, I'll tell.
But what I felt—sweet Venus! there inspire
My lay, or wrap his soul in all thy fire.

Bright rose the morn, and bright remain'd the day;
The mead was spangled with the bloom of May;
We on the bank of a sweet stream were laid,
With blushing rose and lowly violets spread;
Fast by our side a spreading plane-tree grew,
And wav'd its head, that shone with morning dew.
The bank acclivous rose, and swell'd above—
The frizzled moss a pillow for my love.
Trees with their ripen'd stores, glow'd all around,
The loaded branches bow'd upon the ground;
Sure the fair virgins of Pomona's train
In those glad orchards hold their fertile reign.

[1]This is surely a most elegant descriptive pastoral, and hardly inferior to any of Theocritus. The images are all extremely natural and simple, though the expression is glowing and luxurious: they are selected from a variety of Greek authors, but chiefly from the Phædrus of Plato.—What intersertions there may be, have been before apologized for; but their detection shall be left to the sagacity or inquisition of the reader. The case is the same with the first Epistle, and indeed with most of them.— H. S.

Attributed to Sheridan by Moore. "The one Epistle that possesses much merit."— G. G. Sigmund. *Sheridan's Works* (1848.)

The fruit nectareous, and the scented bloom
Wafted on Zephyr's wing their rich perfume;
A leaf I bruised—what grateful scents arose![1]
Ye gods! what odours did a leaf disclose.
Aloft each elm slow waved its dusky top,
The willing vine embraced the sturdy prop:
And while we stray'd the ripen'd grape to find ,
Around our necks the clasping tendrils twin'd;
I with a smile would tell th' entangled fair,
I envied e'en the vines a lodging there;
Then twist them off, and sooth with am'rous play
Her breasts, and kiss each rosy mark away.
Cautious Limona trod—her step was slow—
For much she fear'd the skulking fruits below;
Cautious—lest haply she, with slipp'ry tread,
Might tinge her snowy feet with vinous red.
Around with critic glance we view'd the store,
And oft rejected what we'd praised before;
This would my love accept, and this refuse,
For varied plenty puzzled us to choose.
"Here may the bunches tasteless, immature,
Unheeded learn to blush, and well secure;
In richer garb yon turgid clusters stand,
And glowing purple tempts the plund'ring hand."
"Then reach 'em down," she said, "for you can reach,
And cull, with daintiest hand, the best of each."
Pleased I obey'd, and gave my love—whilst she
Return'd sweet thanks, and pick'd the best for me:
'Twas pleasing sure—yet I refused her suit,
But kiss'd the liberal hand that held the fruit.

Hard by the ever-jovial harvest train
Hail the glad season of Pomona's reign;
With rustic song around her fane they stand,
And lisping children join the choral band:

[1] A leaf I bruised, —Nothing can be more rural, and at the same time more forcible, than this image; where the universal fragrance of the spot is not expatiated on, but marked at once by this simple specimen.—H. S.

They busily intent now strive to aid,
Now first they're taught th' hereditary trade:
'Tis theirs to class the fruits in order due,
For pliant rush to search the meadow through:

To mark if chance unbruised a wind-fall drop,
Or teach the infant vine to know its prop.
And haply too some aged sire is there,
To check disputes, and give to each his share;
With feeble voice their little work he cheers,
Smiles at their toil, and half forgets his years.
"Here let the pippin, fretted o'er with gold,
In fost'ring straw defy the winter's cold;
The hardier russet here will safely keep,
And dusky rennet with its crimson cheek;
But mind, my boys, the mellow pear to place
In soft enclosure, with divided space;
And mindful most how lies the purple plum,
Nor soil, with heedless touch, its native bloom."

Intent they listen'd to th' instructing lord;
But most intent to glean their own reward.

Now turn, my loved Limona, turn and view
How changed the scene! how elegantly new!
Mark how yon vintager enjoys his toil;
Glows with flush red, and Bacchanalian smile:
His slipp'ry sandals burst the luscious vine,
And splash alternate in the new-born wine.
Not far the lab'ring train, whose care supplies
The trodden press, and bids fresh plenty rise.
The teeming boughs that bend beneath their freight,
One busy peasant eases of the weight;
One climbs to where th' aspiring summits shoot;
Beneath, a hoary sire receives the fruit.

Pleas'd we admir'd the jovial bustling throng,
Blest e'en in toil!—but we admired not long.
For calmer joys we left the busy scene,
And sought the thicket and the stream again;
For sacred was the fount, and all the grove
Was hallow'd kept, and dedicate to love.
Soon gentle breezes, freshen'd from the wave,
Our temples fann'd, and whisper'd us to lave.
The stream itself seem'd murm'ring at our feet
Sweet invitation from the noonday heat.
We bathed—and while we swam, so clear it flow'd,
That every limb the crystal mirror show'd.
But my love's bosom oft deceived my eye,
Resembling those fair fruits that glided by;
For when I thought her swelling breast to clasp,[1]
An apple met my disappointed grasp.
Delightful was the stream itself—I swear,
By those glad nymphs who make the founts their care,
It was delightful:—but more pleasing still,
When sweet Limona sported in the rill:
For her soft blush such sweet reflection gave,
It tinged with rosy hues the pallid wave.
Thus, thus delicious was the murm'ring spring,
Nor less delicious the cool zephyr's wing;
Which mild allay'd the sun's meridian power,
And swept the fragrant scent from every flower;
A scent, that feasted my transported sense,
Like that, Limona's sweet perfumes dispense:
But still, my love, superior thine, I swear—
At least thy partial lover thinks they are.

Near where we sat, full many a gladd'ning sound,
Beside the rustling breeze, was heard around:

[1]For when I thought—This allusion seems forced: but the ancients had an apple
which came from Cydon, a town of Crete, and was called Cydonian, that, from its size
and beautiful colour, might be said to resemble a woman's breast: and the allusion is
frequent in the old poets. In the eighteenth of these Epistles, too, we meet with the
κυδώνιον μῆλον.—H. S.

The little grasshopper essay'd its song,
As if 'twould emulate the feather'd throng:
Still lisp'd it uniform—yet now and then
It something chirp'd, and skipp'd upon the green.
Aloft the sprightly warblers fill'd the grove;
Sweet native melody! sweet notes of love!
While nightingales their artless strains essay'd,
The air, methought, felt cooler in the glade:
A thousand feather'd throats the chorus join'd,
And held harmonious converse with mankind.

Still in mine eye the sprightly songsters play,
Sport on the wing, or twitter on the spray,
On foot alternate rest their little limbs,
Or cool their pinions in the gliding streams;
Surprise the worm, or sip the brook aloof,
Or watch the spider weave his subtle woof.
We the meantime discoursed in whispers low,
Lest haply speech disturb the rural show.

Listen.—Another pleasure I display,
That help'd delightfully the time away.
From distant vales, where bubbles from its source
A crystal rill, they dug a winding course:
See! through the grove a narrow lake extends,
Crosses each plot, to each plantation bends;
And while the fount in new meanders glides,
The forest brightens with refreshing tides.
T'wards us they taught the new-born stream to flow,
T'wards us it crept irresolute and slow:
Scarce had the infant current trickled by,[1]
When lo! a wondrous fleet attracts our eye:

---

[1]Scarce had—This is an excessively pretty image. The water bailiff dug a small water-course, which came by the feet of these people in the garden; and the stream had scarce passed by them when the servants sent down several drinking vessels in the shape of ships, which held warm liquor so nicely tempered, that the coolness of the water which encompassed it in its passage, was just sufficient to render it palatable when it arrived at the port of destination.—H. S.

Laden with draughts might greet a monarch's tongue,
The mimic navigation swam along.
Hasten, ye ship-like goblets, down the vale,
Your freight a flagon, and a leaf your sail.[1]
O may no envious rush thy course impede,
Or floating apple stop thy tide-borne speed.
His mildest breath a gentle zephyr gave;
The little vessels trimly stemm'd the wave:
Their precious merchandise to land they bore,
And one by one resign'd the balmy store.
Stretch but a hand, we boarded them, and quaft
With native luxury the temper'd draught.
For where they loaded the nectareous fleet,
The goblet glow'd with too intense a heat;
Cool'd by degrees in these convivial ships,
With nicest taste, it met our thirsty lips.

Thus in delight the flowery path we trod
To Venus sacred, and the rosy god:
Here might we kiss, here Love secure might reign
And revel free, with all his am'rous train.—
And we did kiss, my friend, and Love was there,
And smooth'd the rustic couch that held my fair.
Like a spring-mead with scented blossoms crown'd,[2]
Her head with choicest wreaths Limona bound:
But Love, sweet Love! his sacred torch so bright
Had fann'd, that, glowing from the rosy light,
A blush (the print of a connubial kiss,
The conscious tattler of consummate bliss)

[1]Your freight a flagon—In the original, this luxurious image is pursued so far, that the very leaf, which is represented as the sail of the vessel, is particularized as of a medicinal nature, capable of preventing any ill effects the wine might produce.—H. S.

On this Moore comments: "As a scholar, such as Halhed could hardly have been led into the mistake, of supposing τοῦ Μηδικοῦ φυτοῦ φύλλον to mean 'a leaf of a medicinal nature,' we may, perhaps, from this circumstance not less than from the superior workmanship of the verses, attribute the whole of this Epistle and notes to Sheridan."

[2]Like a spring-mead—The word λειμών signifies a meadow: and the author takes occasion to play upon it, by saying, that Limona crowned herself with these flowers, to look like the meadow in which they grew.—H. S.

Still flush'd upon her cheek; and well might show
The choicest wreaths she'd made, how they should glow;
Might every flower with kindred bloom o'erspread,
And tinge the vernal rose with deeper red.

But come, my friend, and share my happy lot:
The bounteous Phyllion owns this blissful spot;
Phyllion, whose gen'rous care to all extends,
And most is blest while he can bless his friends.
Then come, and quickly come; but with thee bring
The nymph, whose praises oft I've heard thee sing—
The blooming Myrtala; she'll not refuse
To tread the solitude her swain shall choose.
Thy sight will all my busy schemes destroy,
I'll dedicate another day to joy,
When social converse shall the scene improve,
And sympathy bestow new charms on love.
Then shall th' accustom'd bank a couch be made;
Once more the nodding plane shall lend its shade;
Once more I'll view Pomona's jovial throng;
Once more the birds shall raise the sprightly song;
Again the little stream be taught to flow;
Again the little fleet its balm bestow;
Again I'll gaze upon Limona's charms,
And sink transported in her quiv'ring arms;
Again my cheek shall glow upon her breast;
Again she'll yield, and I again be blest.

EPISTLE IX—THE SLIP[1]

STESICHORUS TO ERATOSTHENES

A LADY walking in the street
Her lover lately chanced to meet:
But dared not speak when he came nigh,
Nor make a sign, nor wink her eye,
Lest watchful spouse should see or hear:
And servants too were in the rear.
A plea she sought to stop his walk,
To touch his hand, to hear him talk:
A plea she sought, nor sought in vain;
A lucky scheme inspired her brain.
Just as they met, she feign'd to trip,
And sprain her ankle in the slip.
The lover, ready at his cue,
Suspected what she had in view;
And as he pass'd at little distance,
Officious ran to her assistance.
Contrived her slender waist to seize,
And catch her snowy hand in his.
With unexpected raptures fill'd,
Through all their veins love instant thrill'd:
Their limbs were palsied with delight,
Which seem'd the trembling caused by fright.
Feigning condolence, he drew near,
And spoke his passion in her ear;
While she, to act the real strain,
Affects to writhe and twist with pain:
A well-concerted plan to kiss
The hand her lover touched with his:
Then, looking amorously sly,
She put it to her jetty eye;
But rubb'd in vain to force a tear
Might seem the genuine fruits of fear.

[1]Epistle IX—contains the stratagem of a lady who wanted to speak to her lover in the presence of her husband and servants.—H. S.
Attributed to Sheridan by Sichel.

EPISTLE XII—THE ENRAPTURED LOVER[1]

EUHEMERUS TO LEUCIPPUS

HITHER, ye travellers, who've known
The beauties of the Eastern zone,
   Or those who sparkle in the West:
Hither—oh, tell, and truly tell,
That few can equal, none excel,
   The fair who captivates my breast.

Survey her in whatever light—
New beauties still engage your sight:
   Nor does a single fault appear.
Momus might search, and search again,
But all his searches would be vain,
   To find occasion for a sneer.

Her height, her shape—'tis all complete;
And e'en remarkable her feet
   For taper size, genteelly slim.—
And little feet, each lover knows,
Impart a striking charm to those
   Who boast no other graceful limb.

But not her beauties only strike—
Her pleasing manners too I like:
   From these new strength my passion gains.

[1]Epistle XII—A lover here summons all the judges of beauty to decide in favour of his mistress. The libertine digression with which it concludes must be morally interpreted, as meant to show into what extravagance a man may be led by an attachment whose foundation is in vice.—H. S.

Attributed to Sheridan by Moore—"There is another Epistle, the 12th, as evidently from the pen of his friend, the greater part of which is original, and shows, by its raciness and vigour, what difference there is between 'the first sprightly runnings' of an author's own mind, and his cold, vapid transfusion of the thoughts of another. From stanza 10th to the end is all added by the translator, and all spirited—though full of a bold, defying libertinism, as unlike as possible to the effeminate lubricity of the poor sophist, upon whom, in a grave, treacherous note, the responsibility of the whole is laid.

For though her chastity be gone,
She deals deceitfully by none;
    And still some modesty remains.

And still may Pythias make pretence
To something much like innocence,
    Which forges all my chains to last:
Whate'er you give, she turns to praise;
Unlike the harlot's odious ways,
    Who sneers at presents e'er so vast.

We, like two thrushes on a spray,
Together sit, together play;—
    But telling would our pleasures wrong.—
Suffice it, Pythias will oppose
My wanton passion, till it grows
    By opposition doubly strong.[1]

Her neck ambrosial sweets exhales;
Her kisses, like Arabian gales,
    The scent of musky flowers impart.
And I, reclining on her breast,
In slumbers, happy slumbers, rest,
    Rock'd by the beating of her heart!

Oft have I heard the vulgar say,
That absence makes our love decay,
    And friends are friends but while in view:
But absence kindles my desire;
It adds fresh fuel to the fire
    Which keeps my heart for ever true.

[1]Suffice it—
        Quæ cum ita pugnaret tanquam quæ vincere nollet,
          Victa est non ægre proditione sua.—Ovid.

And oh! may faith my thanks receive,
In that it forced me not to leave
　　The fair in whom my soul is placed.
With truth my case did Homer write;[1]
For every time with new delight
　　My oft-repeated joys I taste.

Sure this is joy—true native joy
Which malice never can destroy,
　　Nor holy shackled fools receive.
Free joys! which from ourselves must flow,
Such as free souls alone can know,
　　And unchain'd Love alone can give.

But say, ye prudes! ye worthless tribe!
Who swear no gifts could ever bribe
　　Your hearts sweet virtue to forsake—
What is this treasure which ye boast?
Ye vaunt because you have not lost
　　—What none had charity to take.

Myrina carries on her back
An antidote to Love's attack;
　　Yet still at Pythias will she sneer.
And as my love is passing by,
Chrysis distorts her single eye,
　　With looks of scorn and virtuous fear.

Philinna scoffs at Pythias too,
　　—Yet she is handsome, it is true;
　　But then her heart's a heart of steel:
Incapable of all desire,
She ridicules Love's sacred fire,
　　And mocks the joys she cannot feel.

---

[1]With truth—'Ασπάσιον λέκτροιο παλαιοῦ δεσμὸν ἵκοντο. 　　—Hom. Il.—H. S.

Yet this is Virtue! woman's pride!
From which if once she ſtep aside,
    Her peace, her fame's for ever gone!
—Away; 'tis impious satyr says,
That woman's good, and woman's praise,
    Consiſt in chaſtity alone.

Can one short hour of native joy
Nature's inherent good deſtroy?
    And pluck all feeling from within?
Shall shame ne'er ſtrike the base deceiver,
But follow ſtill the poor believer,
    And make all confidence a sin?

Did gentle Pity never move
The heart once led aſtray by Love?
    Was Poverty ne'er made its care?
Did Gratuity ne'er warm the breaſt
Where guilty joy was held a gueſt?
    Was Charity ne'er harbour'd there?

Does coy Sincerity disclaim
The neighb'rhood of a lawless flame?
    Does Truth with fame and fortune fall?
Does ev'ry tim'rous virtue fly
With that cold thing, call'd Chaſtity?
    —And has my Pythias loſt them all?

No! no!—In thee, my life, my soul,
I swear I can comprise the whole
    Of all that's good as well as fair:
And though thou'ſt loſt what fools call Fame,
Though branded with a harlot's name,
    To me thou shalt be doubly dear.

Then whence these fetters for desire?
Who made these laws for Cupid's fire?
   Why is their rigour so uncommon?
Why is this honour-giving plan
So much extoll'd by tyrant man,
   Yet binding only to poor woman?

Search not in Nature for the cause;
Nature disclaims such partial laws;
   'Tis all a creature of th' imagination:
By frozen prudes invented first,
Or hags with ugliness accurst—
   A phantom of our own creation!

Two classes thus, my Pythias, show
Their insolence to scoff at you:
   First, they who've passions giv'n by Nature,
But as the task of fame is hard,
They've blest Deformity to guard
   Grim Virtue in each rugged feature.

And second, they who neither know
What Passion means, nor Love can do:
   Yet still for abstinence they preach;
Whilst Envy, rankling in the breast,
Inflames them, seeing others blest,
   To curse the joys they cannot reach.

Not but there are—though but a few!
With charms, with love—and virtue too:
   But Malice never comes from them!
With charity they judge of all,
They weep to see a woman fall,
   And pity where they most condemn.

If, Pythias, then, thou'st done amiss,
This is thy crime, and only this:
 That Nature gave thee charms to move,
Gave thee a heart to joy inclin'd,
Gave thee a sympathetic mind,
 And gave a soul attun'd to love.

When Malice scoffs, then, Pythias, why
Glistens abash'd thy tearful eye?
 Why glows thy cheek that should be gay?
For tho' from shame thy sorrows gush,
Tho' conscious guilt imprints the blush,
 By heav'ns, thou'rt modester than they.

But let them scoff, and let them sneer—
I heed them not, my love, I swear:
 Nor shall they triumph in thy fall.
I'll kiss away each tear of woe,
Hid by my breast thy cheek shall glow,
 And Love shall make amends for all.

EPISTLE XIII—THE SAGACIOUS DOCTOR[1]

Eutychobulus to Acestodorus

FORTUNE, my friend, I've often thought,
Is weak, if Art assist her not:
So equally all Arts are vain,
If Fortune help them not again:
They've little lustre of their own,
If separate, and view'd alone;
But when together they unite,
They lend each other mutual light.—
But since all symphony seems long
To those impatient for the song,
And lest my apothegms should fail,
I'll haste to enter on my tale.

Once on a time, (for time has been,
When men thought neither shame nor sin,
To keep, beside their lawful spouses,
A buxom filly in their houses,)
Once on a time then, as I said,
A hopeful youth, well-born, well-bred,
Seiz'd by a flame he could not hinder,
Was scorch'd and roasted to a cinder.
For why the cause of all his pain
Was that he fear'd all hope was vain:
—In short, the youth must needs adore
The nymph his father loved before.

---

[1]Epistle XIII—This is the story of Antiochus and Seleucus; but related in Aristæne-tus under different names. Seleucus was one of Alexander's successors in Asia, having Syria for his kingdom: he married Stratonice, daughter to Demetrius, having had, by a former marriage, a son named Antiochus. Stratonice was the most beautiful and accomplished princess of her time; and unhappily inspired her son-in-law with the most ardent passion. He fell sick, and Seleucus was in the greatest despair, when Erasistratus, one of his physicians, discovered the cause of the prince's malady, and, by his address, prevailed on the king to save his son's life, by resigning to him his wife, though he passionately loved her.—H. S.

Attributed to Sheridan by Sichel.

"His father's miſtress?"—even so,
And sure 'twas cause enough for woe.
In mere despair he kept his bed,
But feign'd some illness in its ſtead.
His father, griev'd at his condition,
Sends poſt for an expert physician.
The doctor comes—consults his pulse—
No feverish quickness—no convulse;
Observes his looks, his skin, his eye—
No symptoms there of malady;
—At leaſt of none within the knowledge
Of all the Pharmaceutic college.
Long did our Galen wond'ring ſtand,
Reflecting on the case in hand.—
Thus as he paus'd, came by the fair,
The cause of all his patient's care.—
　　Then his pulse beat quick and high;
　　Glow'd his cheek, and roll'd his eye.
Alike his face and arm confeſt
The conflict lab'ring in his breaſt.
Thus chance reveal'd the hidden smart,
That baffled all the search of art.
Still paused the doctor to proclaim
The luckily-discover'd flame:
But made a second inquisition,
To satisfy his new suspicion.
From all the chambers, every woman,
Wives, maids, and widows, did he summon;
And one by one he had them led
In order by the patient's bed.
He the meanwhile ſtood watchful nigh,
And felt his pulse, and mark'd his eye;
(For by the pulse physicians find
The hidden motions of the mind;)
While other girls walk'd by attractive,
The lover's art'ry lay inactive;
But when his charmer pass'd along,

His pulse beat doubly quick and strong.
Now all the malady appear'd;
Now all the doctor's doubts were clear'd;
Who feign'd occasion to depart,
To mix his drugs, consult his art:
He bid the father hope the best,
The lover set his heart at rest,
Then took his fee and went away,
But promised to return next day.
Day came—the family environ
With anxious eagerness our Chiron.
But he repulsed them rough, and cried,
"Ne'er can my remedy be tried."
The father humbly question'd, why
They might not use the remedy?
Th' enraged physician nought would say,
But earnest seem'd to haste away.
Th' afflicted sire more humble yet is,
Doubles his offers, pray'rs, entreaties—
While he, as if at last compell'd
To speak what better were withheld,
In anger cried, "Your son must perish—
My wife alone his life can cherish—
On her th' adult'rer dotes—and I
My rival's hated sight would fly."
The sire was now alike distrest,
To save his boy, or hurt his guest:
Long struggled he 'twixt love and shame;
At last parental love o'ercame.
And now he begs without remorse
His friend to grant this last resource;
Entreats him o'er and o'er t' apply
This hard, but only remedy.
"What, prostitute my wife!" exclaims
The doctor, "pimp for lawless flames?"—
Yet still the father teaz'd and prest;—
"O grant a doting sire's request!

The necessary cure permit,
And make my happiness complete."
Thus did the doctor's art and care
The anxious parent's heart prepare:
And found him trying long and often
The term adultery to soften.
—He own'd, "that custom, sure enough,
Had made it sound a little rough:"
"But then," said he, "we ought to trace
The source and causes of the case.
All prejudice let's lay aside,
And taking Nature for our guide,
We'll try with candour to examine
On what pretence this fashion came in."
Then much he talk'd of man's first state,
(A copious subject for debate!)
Of choice and instinct then disputes,
With many parallels to brutes;
All tending notably to prove
That instinct was the law of Love;—
In short, that Nature gave us woman,
Like earth and air, to hold in common.
Then learned authors would he quote,
Philosophers of special note,
Who only thought their dames worth feeding
As long as they held out for breeding,
And when employ'd in studious courses,
Would let them out, as we do horses.
Last follow'd a facetious query,
To rank the sex *naturæ feræ*.
    The doctor when the speech was clos'd,
Confess'd he was a little pos'd.
Then looking impudently grave,
"And how would you," said he, "behave?
Would you part freely with your wife,
To save a friend's expiring life?"
"By Jove, I'd act as I advise."

The father eagerly replies.—
"Then," cries the doctor, "I have done—
Entreat yourself to save your son.
He loves your girl—can you endure
To work the necessary cure?
If it were just that I should give
My wife to cause a friend to live,
You surely may bestow with joy
Your mistress, to preserve your boy."
He spoke with sense, he spoke with art:
Conviction touch'd the father's heart:—
"'Tis hard," he cried, "'tis passing hard,
To lose what I so much regard!
But when two dread misfortunes press,
'Tis wisdom sure to choose the less."

EPISTLE XXVIII— THE RIVAL FRIENDS[1]

NICOSTRATUS TO TIMOCRATES

TYRANT o' the heart! inconstant, faithless boy!
　　Source of these tears—as once dear source of joy!—
　　Inhuman trifler! whose delusive smile
Charms to ensnare, and soothes but to beguile—
Hence! tyrant, I renounce thy sway.—And thou,
False goddess, who prepar'st the stripling's bow,
Whose skill marks out the soft, the yielding heart,
Guides the boy's arm, and barbs the madd'ning dart,—
Thou shalt no more my midnight vows receive,
To thee no more the votive fruits I'll give,
No more for thee the festive altar raise,
Nor ever tune another note of praise.

　　This I have done.—Witness, each sacred grove!
Where wand'ring lovers sing the maid they love;
Ye awful fanes! to this false goddess rais'd,
Fanes that have oft with my free incense blaz'd;
And chiefly thou, sweet solitary bird,
Bear witness to my vows,—for thou hast heard;
And many a night hast braved the dewy wind,
To soothe, with thy soft notes, my pensive mind:
But when the churlish blast has hush'd thy lays,
Have I not filled the interval with praise—
With praise still varied to the Cyprian queen,
And sighs, the heart's best tribute, breath'd between;
Till slumb'ring Echo started from her cave,
Admiring at the late response she gave;
And thou, best warbler of the feather'd throng,
With double sweetness didst renew thy song.
—Nor were ye slow, ye gentle gales of night,
To catch such notes, and stop your silent flight,

[1]Epistle XXVIII—From a lover, resigning his mistress to his friend.—H. S.
Attributed to Sheridan by Sichel and to Halhed by Moore.

Till on your dewy wings, with morrow's rays,
To Cypria's queen ye waft the song of praise.
—In vain! officious gales;—she heeds you not;
My vows are scorn'd, and all my gifts forgot:
A happier rival muſt her power defend;—
And in that rival I have loſt a friend!

Thee, then, my friend—if yet a wretch may claim
A laſt attention by that once dear name—
Thee I address:—the cause you muſt approve;—
I yield you—what I cannot cease to love.
Be thine the blissful lot, the nymph be thine:—
I yield my love—sure friendship may be mine.
Yet muſt no thought of me torment thy breaſt;—
Forget me, if my griefs diſturb thy reſt,
Whilſt ſtill I'll pray that thou may'ſt never know
The pangs of baffled love, or feel my woe.
But sure to thee, dear charming—fatal maid!
(For me thou'ſt charm'd, and me thou haſt betray'd,)
This laſt requeſt I need not recommend—
Forget the lover thou, as he the friend.
Bootless such charge! for ne'er did pity move
A heart that mock'd the suit of humble love.—
Yet in some thoughtful hour, if such can be,
Where Love, Timocrates, is join'd with thee,
In some lone pause of joy, when pleasure's pall,
And fancy broods o'er joys it can't recall,
Haply a thought of me, (for thou, my friend,
May'ſt then have taught thy ſtubborn heart to bend,)
A thought of him, whose passion was not weak,
May dash one transient blush upon her cheek;
Haply a tear—(for I shall surely then
Be paſt all power to raise her scorn again)—
Haply, I say, one self-dried tear may fall:
One tear she'll give,—for whom I yielded all!
Then wanton on thy neck for comfort hang,
And soon forget the momentary pang;

Whilst thy fond arms—Oh down, my jealous soul!
What racking thoughts within my bosom roll!
How busy fancy kindles every vein,
Tears my burst heart, and fires my madd'ning brain.—
Hush'd be the ill-timed storm—for what hast thou,
Poor outcast wretch, to do with passion now?
I will be calm;—'tis Reason's voice commands,
And injur'd Friendship shakes her recent bands.
I will be calm;—but thou, sweet peace of mind,
That rock'd my pillow to the whistling wind;
Thou flatt'rer, Hope! thyself a cure for sorrow,
Who never show'd'st the wretch a sad to-morrow,
Thou coz'ner, ever whisp'ring at my ear
What vanity was ever pleased to hear—
Whither, ye faithless phantoms, whither flown!
—Alas! these tears bear witness ye are gone.
Return!—In vain the call! ye cannot find
One blissful seat within the sullen mind;
Ye cannot mix with Pride and Surly Care;
Ye cannot brood with Envy and Despair.

My life has lost its aim! that fatal fair
Was all its object, all its hope or care;
She was the goal to which my course was bent,
Where every wish, where every thought was sent;
A secret influence darted from her eyes,—
Each look, attraction! and herself the prize.
Concenter'd there, I lived for her alone.—
To make her glad, and to be blest, was one.

Her I have lost!—and can I blame this poor
Forsaken heart—sad heart that joys no more!
That faintly beats against my aching breast,
Conscious it wants the animating guest:
Then senseless droops, nor yields a sign of pain,
Save the sad sigh it breathes, to search in vain.

Adieu, my friend,—nor blame this sad adieu,—
Though sorrow guides my pen, it blames not you.
Forget me—'tis my prayer; nor seek to know
The fate of him whose portion muſt be woe,
Till the cold earth outſtretch her friendly arms,
And Death convince me that he can have charms.

E'en where I write, with desert views around,
An emblem of my ſtate has sorrow fourd:
I saw a little ſtream full briskly glide,
Whilſt some near spring renew'd its infant tide;
But when a churlish hand diſturb'd its source,
How soon the panting riv'let flagg'd its course!
Awhile it skulk'd sad murm'ring through the grass,
Whilſt whisp'ring rushes mock'd its lazy pace;
Then sunk its head, by the firſt hillock's side,
And sought the covert earth, it once supplied.

Introduction

ON a list of Sheridan's unpublished works, Mr. Sichel has this entry (*Sheridan*, vol. II, p. 458):—

> [?1773] "Heroic Epistle and Postscript." [Mentioned in a letter to him from Linley, evidently of this date.]

He comments elsewhere (vol. I, p. 401):—

> "Linley, who seems to have exhorted him to do justice to his talents, dropped hints that *An Heroic Epistle and Postscript* (possibly a parody of Mason) proceeded from his young friend's pen."

Since *An Heroic Postscript* "to the Public, occasioned by their favourable reception of a late *Heroic Epistle to Sir William Chambers*" was not printed till 1774, the conjectural date is incorrect. That Sheridan was supposed to have written "an answer to the celebrated *Heroic Epistle to Sir William Chambers*" is proved by the "Account of Sheridan" in *The European Magazine* for February, 1782, which (mentioning *The Epistles of Aristænetus*) added that "about the same period he printed several works, which are known only to his intimate friends; and some perhaps not even to them." It noted this "Answer" as being attributed to him "without being able either to confirm or deny the report." There is no doubt that the only poem which satisfies the descriptions given by Linley and *The European Magazine* is "*A Familiar Epistle* to the Author of *The Heroic Epistle to Sir William Chambers* and of *The Heroic Epistle to the Public*, London. Printed for J. Wilkie, 1774." It must be remembered that John Wilkie, of St. Paul's Churchyard, was then Sheridan's publisher; he had issued *The Love Epistles of Aristænetus* in August, 1771, and was to issue *The Rivals* in February, 1775. There was no more likely publisher for any work of Sheridan's. On November 17th, 1774, he wrote to Thomas Linley, that he was "just now sending to the press"[1] a book which he thought would do him some credit, "if it leads to nothing else." Evidently he had hopes that it might lead to "something else," possibly (I suggest) political patronage. "It may be observed, however, that he had not at this juncture" said *The European Magazine*, "devoted himself to the measures of opposition, or connected himself with those who are at present adverse to government."[2]

A Familiar Epistle is an examen of Mason's *Heroic Postscript to the Public*[3] as *Clio's Protest*, very much like it in style and plan, is an examen of *The Bath Picture*. It is an attack on "Patriotism," as then construed in party politics:

> The verse, tho' grac'd with Fashion's prize,
> On Party built, with Party dies;
> Thus your unfinish'd, feeble rhymes,
> Form'd as you own, to catch the times . . .
> Like insects in an early spring
> Shall just have life to buz and sting.

It reprobates the continual charge of private vice against public characters:—

[1] The several "Accounts of new Books and Pamphlets" in the periodical magazines for 1774 and 1775 do not suggest to me any other that might have been this book of Sheridan's. Mr. George W. Panter, a former President of the Bibliographical Society of Ireland, called my attention to a copy of *Nuptial Elegies* (London; G. Kearsly and J. Murray, 1774) formerly belonging to Mrs. Sheridan. But this was reviewed in *The Town and Country Magazine* for March, 1774, and could not therefore have been the book in question. Moreover, there is otherwise no reason to think that Sheridan was the author. Nor could he have been then thinking of sending to press his reply to *Taxation no Tyranny*, of which some passages survive (see Moore, *Sheridan*, p. 100) though the piece was never published. *Taxation no Tyranny* did not appear for some two or three months after this letter.

[2] But the history of Sheridan's political conversion is obscure. Although in 1775 he was opposed to Lord North, in 1770 he was one of his supporters. This is proved by a letter in his defence which Moore thought had been printed in *The Public Advertiser*, edited by Henry Sampson Woodfall. Sichel (*Sheridan*, vol. I, p. 268) shows that it did not appear in that journal, but Moore, as elsewhere, may have confused the paper with *The London Packet*, edited by William Woodfall.

[3] It had little concern with *The Heroic Epistle*, saying:
> To show we mean no hard attack,
> We have our licence to look back . . .
> And let your Postscript only be
> The touch-stone of your currency.

> They know how rare the lib'ral muse
> Will stoop to personal abuse,
> Or make the scandal of the day
> The burthen of a factious lay.

It is in the same metre as *Clio's Protest*, though a little less liberal in its double-endings. From its topical nature, a great deal of it is obscure in its allusions, but there are some pointed and lively passages:—

> All petty rogues, to prove your strength—
> You may attack with names at length;
> But when you mean to maul your betters,
> Choose Dashes, and Initial Letters.
> Thus when of Scottish Home[1] you speak,
> You name him plump, without a break:
> But a more cautious style assume
> When you attack great D * * d H * e.[2]
> Thus, slurring on poor Mallet's fame,[3]
> First boldly charge, then write the name.
> But when your satire C * s would vex
> Best note him with an F and X.[4]
> —We treat the first, as cooks are thought
> To dress small grigs, entire as caught.
> But as large eels first lose their bowels
> We gut our great names of their vowels.
> Then, roasted well on Satire's bars,
> We serve them up with forc'd-meat stars.

The Familiar Epistle ridicules the claim of its author that his *Heroic Epistle*, from its attack on the Navy-Board, forced them to conduct the great Review of the Fleet at Portsmouth in 1773:—

[1] Home, the author of *Douglas*.
[2] David Hume, the historian, his kinsman.
[3] Mallet, who anglicized his name from Malloch, poet and dramatist.
[4] "C * s F * x" in the *Heroic Epistle* denoted, of course, Charles Fox. He first met Sheridan soon after the performance of *The Rivals* (see Sichel, *Sheridan*, vol. I, p. 515) which means soon after this poem appeared.

> One single dash of Sancho's pen
> Produc'd—the Monarch—Ships—and Men!
> Wond'rous!—great England's naval line
> Call'd forth, dread bard, by one of thine!

It ends curiously, with a determination of the poet to relinquish

> .... its peevish tone,
> Tho' aim'd at *pride* and *spleen* alone.

and devote his muse to Love, to gain the smiles "of her, to whom my numbers speak," or to tell some simple tale of woe:

> While yet *she* reads, one sigh shall be
> More precious far than fame to me,
> And ending, let, uncheck'd, appear,
> The silent plaudit of a tear.

This indeed fits the mood of Sheridan in 1774. All things considered, *A Familiar Epistle* seems to have been correctly attributed to him. If it were so, it throws a new light upon his political beginnings.

PREFACE

*T*O *suppose that a Reformation can be effected, in the Political
Principles of any set of men, by the pen of a Satirist, is as vain
and ridiculous, as it would be to boast of commanding the English
navy, and directing the motions of a K—g, by a couplet. If any thing
comes peculiarly within the province of Ridicule, it is the vanity and
folly of such an attempt: and here the pen may be exercised with some
success; for tho' bad men are seldom to be ridiculed out of vices, which
are founded in the Passions,—yet, bad Authors may be brought to see
errors, which generally proceed from a disturbed Imagination; or,
what is as good, tho' they do not cease to write, they may cease to be
read. I do not mean to infer, that the Hero of this Epistle is a bad
writer; yet I do hope to convince him, that it were prudent in him, not
to rely too much on his Muse's* fixt fame; *nor,* 'till she "has nurs'd
him up to man's estate," *would I have him trust* the vigour of her
eagle wings, *in flights, to which, I fear, she will prove unequal:
Neither would I advise him, however* warm'd with memory and
public praise, to *handle his* energetic thunder *in the great Style
which he proposes. This I hope to effect from his own conviction; for it
is by no means improbable, that he may be brought to acknowledge
some little trifling disqualifications for the character he would assume
when they are laid before him with temper; though it was very natural
for him to overlook them during the fatigue of writing with such
genuine* carelessness, *and the costive pains of producing such* spon-
taneous-flowing *rhymes.—Or, if he be, indeed, the easy, genteel
Writer he affects to be, he may, perhaps, be led to respect, that the
genius which enables a man to fabricate an hundred lines,* "stans
pede in uno," *though wonderfully convenient to a polite Poet, is not
always equal to the task of* chastising a senate, stretching *folks* on
racks, *or converting them into* garbage for hell-hounds. *If he per-
sists in the attempt, he must not expect, because his* goddess of the song
continues to write *flying, that all ranks are bound to read* running.

After all, if my familiar *hints prove too weak and dull to make
good my attack, there may, from their very failure, be drawn an argument against* the careless *and* expeditious *in Poetry; for my* heroic
*Friend may be assured, that the Writer of this is as little addicted to
spend time and trouble upon trifles as himself.*

Preface

[TO THE SECOND EDITION]

*I*T *hath been very entertaining to the writer of these idle lines to have heard them commented on with great accuracy of Criticism; and as little quarter given to the Poet as he hath appeared to show to* Sancho:—*it will, doubtless, be said that he should expect no more:— however, he will take the liberty to point out to these profound Judges the line by which they should judge of their several demerits.—The first (The* HEROIC POSTSCRIPT*) is a performance confined to no particular subject: the author has, by a former Poem, established—as he himself modestly expresses it—"A Fame as fix'd as fate," and his present one was announced as superior even to that ("—paullo majora canamus"—) treating us at the same time with a specimen of the* grave *and majestic air which he intended to assume in his next.— As for these trifling comments on that performance the author can only say, that there is no one Reader of them who shall not be perfectly welcome to alter every line and expression in them, or expunge till the Poem become a non-entity:—provided only that, admitting the obvious defects of the other, he will sit down and point out those defects with truly elegant language, and in truly good verses.—When he shall have done this—the vanquished Scribler of the* Familiar Epistle *shall own him possessed of a degree of critical Assiduity and patient Dulness, which shall command his highest veneration, without one particle of Envy.*

Those who are real judges, having, no doubt, at a glance discovered what true ground for ridicule there is in Sancho's last performance, will immediately perceive that this Stricture on it, is entirely addressed to the Level of their understandings who look upon that Bard as a Genius of the first rate:—not scrupling to charge their memories with his smooth couplets with as much care and repetition as they would bestow on a bon mot of their own, or a Rondeau of Signor Mellico.

A

FAMILIAR EPISTLE

TO THE

AUTHOR

OF THE

HEROIC EPISTLE

TO

Sir WILLIAM CHAMBERS,

AND OF THE

HEROIC POSTSCRIPT

TO THE PUBLIC

A Familiar Epistle, &c.

OF all the ways a man can choose
To introduce a youthful muse,
There is not one so sure to raise
A sudden burst of public praise,
As feigning well a *Patriot's* call,
To dip the pen in party gall.
—A field so very fruitful this,
Dulness itself can't write amiss.

First they who seek satiric fame,
Must ever mark the noblest game:
Here, if they feel they've no pretence,
To urge their prey with solid sense,
They'll find a shelter in the cool
Sarcastic smile of Ridicule:
For while a Bard seems half in joke,
A deal of nonsense may be spoke;
Nor will the Critics heed a trip,
Where Irony exerts the whip;
And now and then a serious dash
Will show like knots upon the lash.

But chiefly mind, whoe'er thou art,
Who boast the Patriot Censor's part,
With unremitting hand to strike
The slavish party all alike:
No *private* virtues should abate
The rigour of thy free-born hate;
While every *private* vice may show
How well the wretch deserves the blow.

All petty rogues, to prove your strength,——
You may attack with names at length;
But when you mean to maul your betters,
Choose Dashes, ——— — — and Initial Letters.
Thus when of Scottish *Home* you speak,[1]
You name him plump, without a break;
But a more cautious style assume
When you attack great D * * d H * e :[2]
Thus slurring on poor *Mallet*'s fame,[3]
First boldly change, then write the name;
But when your satire C * s would vex,[4]
Best note him with an *F* and *X*.
——We treat the first, as cooks are thought
To dress small grigs, entire as caught;
But as large eels first lose their bowels,
We gut our great names of their vowels;
Then, roasted well on Satire's bars,
We serve them up with forc'd-meat stars.

A Poem with such helps as these,
While it is new, will always please:
The side that does not feel its malice,
Will gladly quote its lively sallies:
And if, thro' envy's current passion,
It chance to gain the stamp of fashion,
All ranks shall own 'tis shrewdly writ,
And ev'ry line shall pass for wit.
——All ranks shall own——except the few
Who give to reason, reason's due;
Who are not slaves to Passion's reign,[5]
But in the volume of the brain,
Reserve to Taste one candid page

[1] "The mighty *Home* bemir'd in prose so long."—*Her Epist.*
[2] "Let D * * d H * e from the remotest North."—*Her. Epist.*
[3] "Bids *Mallock* quit," &c.—*Her. Epist.*
[4] ——————————They circumcise C*s F*x."—*Her. Epist.*
[5] ——"Give me the man
That is not Passion's slave."—*Hamlet.*
"Within the book and volume of my brain."—*Hamlet.*

Immaculate from party rage.
—They know what springs supply the verse
Whose only aim is to asperse:
How little wit, how little sense,
Will furnish weapons for offence.
They know how much true genius scorns
To gain from Fear a crown of thorns:
They know how rare the lib'ral muse
Will stoop to personal abuse,
Or make the scandal of a day
The burthen of the factious lay.
She hates to build a single verse on
Contingencies of things or person;
Or meanly¹ catch a partial grace
From accident of time or place.
—Her province is on Fancy's pinion,
To range thro' Nature's wide dominion;
To draw her *beauties* forth to view,
And add a lustre to their hue:
To catch the pencil from her hand,
Pausing where Fate hath bade her stand,
And, with a bold, creative line,
Deserve the title of *divine*.
——For the first Muse was Nature's child,
And to a mother's weakness mild,
With filial awe she did o'erlook
Each trifling error of her book,
Transcrib'd her works with partial lays,
Concealing, where she could not praise.

¹[manly—First Edition; meanly—Errata to Second Edition.]

ENOUGH of Prologue!—For 'tis time
To check our vague, digressing rhyme,
Nor scribling on, as thoughts increase,
Neglect the Hero of our *Piece*.

To thee, whatever name you choose,
Great bantling of a nursing muse![1]
Whose dubious rhymes by turns compel us
To call thee *Sancho* and *Marcellus*[2];
To thee I turn, and mean to try
The terror of thy eagle's eye.
If, in the search, thy muse shall prove
A daughter of the thund'ring Jove,
Fit to direct the fire of youth,
And wield the stubborn bolts of truth;[3]
If such she prove—thou surely wilt,
—Confirm'd on thy heroic stilt,
Deserve both *Almon*'s glitt'ring pelf,[4]
And all the praise—thou'st giv'n thyself.
But, when she should endure the test,[5]
If, like a jade, she fall her crest;
Appear no pow'r of sacred birth,
But cloud-begot 'tween heav'n and earth,
—If this appear, do thou disown
Her sway, and quit thy vengeful throne.

In humble style, with notes annext,
Proceed we now to treat our text.—

---

[1] "The muse shall *nurse him up* to man's estate."—*Her. Post.*
[2] "I that of late Sir William's Bard, and Squire!—
Your young *Marcellus*."—*Her. Post.*
[3] "——With Truth's dread bolt."—*Her. Post.*
[4] "——Almon gave me reason for my rhyme;
————glittering orbs."—*Her. Post.*
[5] "——Hollow men, like horses, hot at hand,
Make gallant show and promise of their mettle;
But when they should endure the bloody spur,
They fall their crest."——*Jul. Cæsar.*

To show we mean no hard attack,
We wave our licence to look back:
Your first-got laurels shall escape
The terrors of a critic rape;
And let your POSTSCRIPT only be
The touch-stone of your currency.

O *Sancho*, you may well regret
The time when Justice had not set[1]
Her cruel balance, thus to check
The hope of knaves to risque their neck;
When things obtain'd a worth ideal,
And *seemings* pass'd for what was *real*.—[2]
Your verses then—smooth, clipt and trite,
False-dated,—gilt, yet still too light,[3]
Cry'd-up by those you meant to please,
Might pass on crowds with current ease:[4]
But place them where no spleen prevails,
Hung on the beam of Candour's scales,
In one, your Poem be the freight,
And let its purchase be the weight:
—I fear, in spite of all your vaunting,
There will be found a shilling wanting.

The mob assumes such impious sway,[5]
All weigh their Monarch, now, you say:
—Here, Sancho, you mistake the thing:
—They weigh his image, not their King;
And, maugre, all your trope's confusion,
I draw a different conclusion:
As copies must for ever fall
Beneath a good original,
If we, without a wish to flatter,

[1]"No senate had convey'd, &c."—*Her. Post.*
[2]"Good *seemings* then were good *realities*."—*Her. Post.*
[3]"This Poem was written last summer, &c."—Pref. to *Her. Epist.*
[4]"Or were they not, they pass'd with current ease,"—*Her. Post.*
[5]"Now, thro' the land, that impious pow'r prevails, &c.
All weigh, &c."—*Her. Post.*

Possess th' idea of the latter,
Then place an image in the scale,
No wonder that we find it fail.
Nor ought you to arraign the art
Of those who play *Cadogan*'s part;—
Your aim is one—their rebel tool
You join with shears of ridicule;
And, tho' you work with blunter nippers,
We all confess you first of clippers.
What pity, then—since one your aim—
We cannot say your *end*'s the same!
The royal Person this may stripe,
While t'other's hang'd, who hurts his type!
This gets the bays, and that a cord—
—O Justice, send the same reward!
Fannius, you add, with frowning eye,[1]
Call'd thy Heroics blasphemy:—
Believe me, Sancho, that in this
The old youth judg'd not much amiss:
For, —[2] still our figure to pursue—
Upon most glitt'ring orbs we view,
Beside the monarch of the hour,
An emblem of a greater power;
And he who proves so lost of grace,
The royal image to deface,
Would never check his ranc'rous pride
To spare the cross on t'other side.

But now, behold, our Hero own,
That all *his* glitt'ring orbs are gone[3]:—
—All, *Sancho!* No—if we may guess,
By bashful hints, what you possess,
There still remains—which few surpass—
One glitt'ring orb of—*modest brass.*

[1] "Like old young Fannius call it blasphemy."—*Her. Post.*
[2] The allusion by which Satirists of one kind are ranked as Clippers.
[3] "Sad to say! my glittering orbs are gone."—*Her. Post.*

—[1] But why this interjection here
For orbs defunct that pious fear!
Their *manes*, Sancho, cannot feel
A Scotchman's unrelenting steel:
There may be found some 'prentic'd ninny
Deprav'd enough to sweat a guinea,
But what advantage can he boast
Who grasps his steel to rob its *ghost?*

Observe!—was ever Bard so fickle?—
He leaves his scales, and takes a sickle.[2]
Like pictur'd *Time*, with scythe in hand,
Behold him take his fatal stand;
Then, with a mower's practis'd swing,
He'll cut down fools, where'er they spring;
Collect them in poetic sheaf,
— O pretty phrase for quarto leaf!—
And fairly stack the full-ear'd crop,
— Good Heav'ns, how quaint!— in *Almon's* shop.
(Thus *Phœbus*, in *Admetus'* walks,
Would reap the corn, and bind the stalks.)
Who would not think, from such a boast,
Our Bard would stoutly keep his post?
Would strain each nerve with vigour double,
'Till Dunces field lay all in stubble.
How wond'rous, then, to see him quit,
Without a stroke, this scythe of wit!
Desert his critic muse's cause,
To feed his pride with self-applause![3]
And, while he quaffs that precious slop,
Forget at once the promis'd crop!

[1]"Peace to their *manes*, may they never feel
    Some keen Scotch banker's unrelenting steel!"—*Her. Post.*
[2]"While I again the muse's sickle bring,
    To cut down Dunces, wheresoe'er they spring.
    Bind in poetic sheaves, &c. &c."—*Her. Post.*
[3]Sancho, after complimenting the wonderful powers of his muse, refers us to the Reviewers, and prettily quotes the praises he affects to despise. It is to be observed, that, whenever he speaks of himself, he does not intend the least irony.

—Thus Shenken Floyd or Patrick Bourke,
—Two lazy dogs—will quit their work,
Upon the broken gate to bask,
When Dolly brings the noon-day cask;
There cram and swill 'till mem'ry fail
And all they reap, is cheese and ale.

But O, ye knaves, whom *Sancho* hates,[1]
'Tis now the crisis of your fates!
And O, ye fools, how he will plague you;
Each line shall work you like an ague:
While moaning, groaning, pale, and trembling,
Ye both shall own them too resembling:
Nor will your fits e'er know *remission*;
—Such is his muse's expedition!—
One wond'rous letter comes in spring![2]
Twelve toiling moons a *Postscript* bring!
An hundred lines the last contains—
The *plenteous* harvest of his brains!—[3]
And if he writes as heretofore,
Next spring may yield—an hundred more!
Sure, honest Sancho, here you choose
A wrong allusion for your muse,
Her *eagle* wings!—pray what disaster[4]
Has kept the drab from flying faster?
Alas! I fear, were matters known,
And were the bird to have her own,
These wings some more ignoble fowl
Would claim;—what think you of an Owl?

Yet hold—the Lady's fame is fixt!—[5]
O Vanity, with Folly mixt!

[1] "Tremble ye fools I scorn, ye knaves I hate."—*Her. Post.*
[2] "————————————————O ego lævus
Qui purgor bilem sub verni temporis horam."—*Sanch.*
[3] "————————————the *plenteous* crop,"
We must acknowledge, contains *ten* lines more than is here mentioned.
[4] "I know the vigour of thy *eagle* wings."—*Her. Post.*
[5] "For now, my muse, thy fame is fixt as fate."—*Her. Post.*
I must repeat it, there is no irony in this:—It is the sober effusion of Vanity.

And *can* you hold a serious thought,
That with such trifles you have bought
One sprig of laurel, that shall bloom,
Instead of bramble, on thy tomb?
Believe me, Bard, as gen'rous Fate
Has fixt mortality on hate,
The Verse, tho' grac'd with Fashion's prize,
On Party built, with Party dies:
Thus your unfinish'd, feeble rhymes,
Form'd, as you own, to catch the times[1]
If foster'd by the transient rays[2]
Of Fashion, and of public Praise,
Like insects in an early spring,
Shall just have life to buz and sting;
Then proving their ignoble birth,
By dirty channels pass to earth.

Not all the truths by *Horace* writ,
(And his E P I S T L E S all had wit,
And what might best deserve the throne,
The wit they had was all *his own*)
So firm had rank'd the well-known name,
First in the page of classic fame,
As the most trifling Ode that fell
Impassion'd from his sprightly shell:[3]
Those strains he caught as Phœbus sent 'em,
Then cried,—"exegi monumentum!"[4]
I wave to mention *Virgil*'s song,—
But while our hearts to love belong,
Each youth shall study to inspire

[1]"——Let the flow of these spontaneous rhymes,
 So truly touch the temper of the times."—*Her. Post.*
[2]"Warm'd with the sun-shine of the public praise."—*Her. Post.*
[3]"O decus Phœbi, et dapibus supremi
 Grata testudo Jovis."——*Horat Od.*
[4]"Exegi monumentum ære perennius,
 Regalique situ Pyramidum altius."—*Lib. iii. Od. xxx.*
 Horace had written somewhat more than an hundred and forty lines, when he pronounced *his* "muse's fame as *fixt as Fate.*"

That love from *Ovid*'s polish'd lyre;
Nor seldom, with the same design,
Hang o'er *Tibullus*' kindred line:
While *Juvenal*, and haughty *Perseus*,
With keen *Lucilius* for the *tertius*;[1]
Mere tasks for boys, or schools for knaves,
Were better voted to their graves.—
So shall the chaste and moral lay
Of mildly melancholy *Grey*;—
So shall the simplest shepherd's tale
Which *Shenstone* told the *Leasowes*' vale;—
So shall each note of am'rous woe,
Which gentle *Hammond* taught to flow,
As best might suit the Lover's part,
Whose muse should be—a feeling heart,—
All, hurtless all, their honours wear,
—The little classics of the fair—
Gracing Fame's page without a blot,
When *Churchill* shall be quite forgot.

And what can Sancho hope to gain,
Tho' Freedom claim his *graver* strain:[2]
—With toil thou may'st become at most
A thing resembling *Churchill*'s ghost:
While wags shall own, nor sink thy merit,
They view his form, tho' not his spirit.
Then quit, at once, thy vain design,
And court the muse's smoother line:
—Or, if the fiend of baneful Spite
Alone can teach thee how to write;
If, for some crime, avenging Fate[3]
Hath curs'd thee with a tide of hate,
Whose high spring flow, with noxious force,

[1]"————secuit Lucilius urbem,
Te, Lupe, te, Muti, et genuinum fregit in illis."—*Pers.*
[2]"But if that Country claim a graver strain."—*Her. Epist.*
[3]"Nec satis apparet, cur versus, factitet: utrùm
  Minxerit in patrios cineres, aut triste bidental
  Moverit incestus:—certe *furit.*—Hor. *Ars. Poet.*

Rolls to the moon's unsteady course,
(So near to Madness is the ire
Which Envy strikes from Party fire!)
If such thy doom,—yet raise thy plan:
—Stand forth the gen'ral rod of man;
Give no distinction to thy scourge;
Thy satire's bolts impartial urge;
No more at private failures hurl'd,
But 'gainst the vices of a world.

But hold:—I'm catching *Sancho's* style;
Half light, half grave; half frown, half smile:
These vile digressions always force
One from the line of one's discourse:
Come then, my muse, let's turn about
To comment, as we first set out.

"Say first, for neither land, or sea,
Or docks, hide any thing from thee,
Say, first, what cause mov'd the grand Lord[1]
Of slumb'ring *England's* naval board,
Favour'd of Peace so long, to quit
That sleepy state? Whose prudent wit
First wish'd that flag unfurl'd
Which bears the lordship of the world?
Who first seduc'd our curious isle?
—S a n c h o—He 'twas whose baneful *guile*,
With *malice* and *revenge* inflam'd,
His K—g an *Asiatic* nam'd:
What time his *pride*, with foul disgrace,
Had cast him out from post and place;
With all his host of printer's devils,
Who durst conduct his factious evils,

[1]"A certain naval event happened just about two calendar months after the publication of the HEROIC EPISTLE. It was impossible, considering the necessary preparations, it could have been sooner. Facts are stubborn things."—Note to *Her. Post.*

Had caſt him out—encreas'd perdition!—
To dwell in endless *opposition:*
While penal laws, and Tyburn-tree,
Curb'd half his schemes of L I B E R T Y ."[1]

—Know then, ye loyal num'rous bands,
Who lately glow'd on *Portsmouth*'s sands,
Proud to behold your navy ride,
The nation's safety and its pride;
Ye Captains, Boatswains, Tarrs, and all,
Chosen to man the floating wall;
Artificers, who, day and night,
Toil'd to prepare the princely sight;
And ye, bright judges of our arms,[2]
Daughters of Beauty, whose speaking charms
Bade you forsake the favour'd earth,
To view the place of *Venus'* birth;
(While ev'ry zephyr of the main
That wanton'd in your nymph-like train,
Demanded, with a sigh of care,
Why *Amphitrite*[3] was not there)
Know all,—that this imperial shew,
(Peace to our sight, fear to our foe)
With the proud Town's enlighten'd face,
—Ow'd to a *Couplet* all its grace:
One single dash of *Sancho*'s pen,
Produc'd—the Monarch—ships—and men!
Wond'rous!—great England's naval line
Call'd forth, dread Bard, by one of thine!
S—d—h, and all the Navy-board,
Muſt own the Poet for their Lord;
Whose song, resiſtless, wields the State[4]
At will;—whose ev'ry verse is Fate!

[1] "————Milt."
[2] "With store of Ladies, whose bright eyes
Reign, influence, and judge the prize."—*Milt. Alleg.*
[3] "Hanc sequitur, *Regi Conjux maris, Amphitrite*
Casta, decens, *prolemque* udis *complexa* lacertis."—*Aurel. Gall.*
[4] "Those Ancients, whose resistless eloquence,
Wielded at will that fierce Democracy."—*Milt.*

—'Twas well his P o s t s c r i p t did not name
The luſtre of *militia* fame!
Or, in *two months*, with dire alarms,
All *Middlesex* had been in arms!
Or, had his muse condemn'd the State
Defenceless of a Sov'reign's gate,
We'd surely seen a plan, next hour,
To arm St. *James*'s like the Tower!
While T—s—d, inſtant call'd to Court,
To make the outward porch a fort,
With mortar, cannon, bomb, and shell,
Had fix'd his *ordnance* in Pall-mall!
Thence G—s—l, with a chosen band,
Well skill'd in *caſtles*[1] to command,
O'er the *Horse-guards* he might prefer,
To awe the Duns of *Weſtminſter*;
There might he reign, the Prince of *Bilks*,
And, 'ſtead of bailiffs, shoot at W—s.
If such the pow'r of *Sancho*'s pen,
—Like magic o'er the minds of men!—
Heav'n grant th' enchantment of his rhyme
May not extend to *brick* and *lime*!
Or, should he quarrel with our towns,
Our *houses*, next, may grace the Downs!
—What sport to him, to set in motion
Squares—ſtreets——and alleys, on the ocean!
While doors—floors—wainscot—pane and pannel—
Strange wreck!—come floating down the Channel.

Hold, Ridicule!—and hear our Squire
Excuse the errors of his lyre!—
—He writes—with a *spontaneous flow*,[2]
—A neat *currente calamô*—
He writes—"that he who runs may read:"—[3]

[1] *Castle*—A word of very extensive import. Vid. D—nn—g's Notes, Artic. *Two Pair of Stairs Room.*
[2] "Let the *flow* of these spontaneous rhymes."—*Her. Post.*
[3] "—That he who runs may read."—*Her. Post.*

What pity! should he not succeed!
Yet failing, let him not be vex'd,
But print—on *gingerbread*, his next:
So may—(without a moment loſt)
His little friends, with little coſt,
Buy his *hot satires* by the ounce,
And run, and read,—and eat at once!
— Thus boys for school, with book in budget,
Will chew their letters as they trudge it.[1]

---

[1]I know not whether it will be worth while to mark, seriously, any faults, in a Poem, where *carelessness* and *expedition* will be urged as a full excuse; however, as the Poet has, just before the last-quoted passage, made a point with his muse, that she should keep him within "the bounds of *Sense* and Verse," I shall take the liberty of showing to him, in Prose, a few places where she has been very remiss. A little way back, where our Bard says, "My *muse*, thy fame is fix'd as Fate," he continues his address in the *second* person, and concludes,

> "That solemn vein of irony so fine,
> Which e'en Reviewers own, adorns *thy* line,
> Would make him soon against his greatness sin,
> Desert his sofa, mount his palanquin,
> And post where'er *the goddess* led the way," &c.

Now, I beg to know who *the goddess* is? The Poet willanswer, like *Bays*, "Why the *muse*, to be sure":—then the sentence, in fact, stands,—"O muse, *thy* irony can make a King post where'er *the goddess*, that is *the muse*, that is *yourself*, led the way."—If *you* lead to Spithead, *he* must follow *her*; that is *you*.——This may be keeping in the bounds of Verse; but I am sure it leaps each "Ha ha of Common Sense."

> Ver. 91. "————————ye to whom I pay,
> Warm from the heart, *this* tributary lay:
> *That* lay shall live," &c.

Here is a strange confusion between *this* and *that:* if the Poet means to keep within the bounds of Grammar, he will make the *latter* give place to *which*.

> Verse 93. "If hireling P * * rs, in prostitution bold,
> Tell, &c."——

> "Or *They*, who honour'd by the people's choice,
> Against that people lift their rebel voice, &c."

As *They* is here the nominative case to *lift*, any school-boy would tell the writer, that the line must run, either, "Or they, who *are* honour'd"; or "—*they, honour'd* by, &c." Unfortunately, however, to make *Grammar* of this line, would be drawing it out of the bounds of *Verse*.

It may be alleged, that, in trifles, (such as the Heroic Postscript) points of this nature are to be overlook'd:——However, the direct reverse happens to be the better rule ; for, in trifles of this nature, (where there are no *very* violent flights of Imagination to draw one's attention from the inferior articles of Sense and Grammar, and where the work is not *quite* of sufficient length to make it *"fas obrepere somnum"* correctness and perspicuity are points never to be dispensed with ; much less, where the performance itself aims at being critical, and censorious.

At length view *Sancho* come to tell us,
How He resembles young *Marcellus:*
As such He'll breathe eternal spring,
And, scoffing, say—"Death, where's thy ſting?"
"*Marcellus* was not born to die:" —[1]
O Grave, where is thy victory?

Here, then, He yields the drooping nation
The comfort of his peroration:
[2]For now, that He has prov'd his force,
He means to choose a bolder course;
There ſtand prepar'd, should danger real[3]
Supplant our present woes ideal.
Be careful then, ye noble Peers,
Or *Sancho*'s muse shall *pierce your ears:*[4]
Sell on your votes to those who need 'em,
And set at auction muſty Freedom;
But in the latter be more nice,[5]
And bargain for a *double* price:
And, O ye votaries of St. *Steven,*
Preserve the scales of Juſtice even;
For, should ye sell each freehold cottage,[6]
Like *Esau,* for a mess of pottage,
With ways and means the people rob,
In bold *rebellion* 'gainſt the *mob,*—
Our Bard shall keep your spirits under

[1]"Your young Marcellus was *not born to die.*"—*Her. Post.*
Though *Sancho* modestly excepts himself from the Plebian ceremony of *dying* ; yet I
fear his date will rather be that of the *Julium Sidus,* than such as shall make us say,
   "Crescit occulto, velut arbor ævo,
      Fama *Marcelli!*"
[2]"'Tis but to try his strength that now he sports."—*Her. Post.*
[3]"If *real* danger threat fair Freedom's reign."—*Her. Post.*
[4]"I know thy strains can *pierce the ear.*"—*Her. Post.*
[5]"If hireling P * * rs, in prostitution bold,
   Sell her *as cheaply* as themselves they sold."—*Her. Post.*
Though Sancho appears here to be earnest,* yet his intention is, slily to ridicule the
system of some modern patriots, whose indignation is generally raised, not so much at
seeing Liberty bartered, as at its being forestalled at an *under* price: thus the only com-
modity they deal in often hangs on their hands, or they are obliged to part with it, as
Sancho feelingly expresses it, for a "*paltry* pay."
   [*earnest—First Edition: in earnest—Errata to Second Edition.]
[6]"——Vote the best *birthright* of her sons away."—*Her. Post.*

And bruise you with a song of thunder:[1]
Exalted on a throne of brass,
The bold *Salmoneus* he'll surpass.—
    Heavens bless us! Lord defend us[2]
    From a Poet so tremendous!

Lo! what a sudden change of style!
Black frowns dismiss the sneering smile:
Mark of *sublime*, he gives example!—
Observe—and profit by the sample:
See[3], like a lion from his den,
He roars an eight-line specimen!
O Fancy, draw the god-like figure!—
Colossus' size—or somewhat bigger!
Make both his hands the thunder brandish!
(For want of bolts—suppose the standish)
And, while his gloomy wrath is bright'ning,
Ply him with spermaceti lightning.
But, lo! a bolt of wond'rous thickness,
With words well pick'd, to show its quickness,
Comes down— *O miserere mei!*—
Souse in a line of *five spondæi!*
    Heavens bless us! Lord defend us
    From a Poet so tremendous![4]

Fly, instant fly, ye faithless crew!
—Yes—ye may fly, but He'll pursue!

---

[1]"—————————the thunder of his song."—*Her. Post.*

[2]"Vesanum tetigisse timent, fugiuntque poetam
   Qui sapiunt."—*Hor.*
To point out where Sancho stole the bold and uncommon expression with which he graces this concluding example of his *graver* style, would be referring the reader to so many of the Public Advertisers, that the detection would not be worth the trouble.

[3]"—————————————velut ursus
   Objectos caveæ valuit si frangere clathros."—*Ars. Poet.*

[4]"—————————————the thunder of his song
   Rolling in deep-ton'd energy along,
   Shall strike, with Truth's dread bolt, each miscreant's name."—*Her. Post.*
Though the first syllables of the two first feet *may* be pronounced rather shorter, yet that will be abundantly made up by the pauses, and the harshness of the rest of the line; which is altogether surprisingly well calculated—as, no doubt, the Poet intended it should be—to describe the rapid motion of a thunder-bolt.

Until each culprit on his back
He binds to little pocket rack:
There long expos'd, ye all shall feel
The torture of his quarto wheel:
While all the dogs that pass that way
Shall grin, and seize you for their prey;
Nay, pasture-beasts shall quit their herbage,
And come to pick your guts and garbage!
  Heavens bless us! Lord defend us
  From a Poet so tremendous![1]

 O how shall similes aspire
To suit this man of bolts and fire!
When striding his immortal horse
With scourge of flame He clears the course!
—O *Sancho*, let thy lucky name
Supply a hint to aid thy fame.
—Thus—when thy brother, little *Panza*[2]
(Thy peer in *steed*, tho' not in *stanza*)
Engag'd to pass the regions upper,
Astride on *Clavilino*'s crupper,
Altho' his nag ne'er mov'd a joist,—
He thought he'd gain'd a wond'rous hoist;
And when the squibs began to whiz,——
—No fire on earth e'er equall'd his![3]

 Here let us pause:—we've said enough,
If *Sancho* does not scorn rebuff:
Yet, e'er we quit the copious thesis,
—For still before our eye his piece is—
We'll just review—what store to choose in!
The diff'rent shapes we've seen his muse in.

[1]"_____*yes*, ye faithless crew,
 His muse's vengeance shall your crimes pursue,
 Stretch you on Satire's rack, and bid you lie
 Fit *Garbage* for the hell-hound Infamy."
As the elegant term *Garbage* is seldom detached from its sister-noun, I hope Sanchow
not take ill my uniting them here.
[2]As commonly written in translations for *Pança*.
[3]Vid. Don. Quixote.

III. O

Behold her first with pewter lyre,
Profess herself Sir William's Squire:
A *builder* next, in haste she marches,
With *brick* and *lime* for *marble* arches![1]
Thence in a trice we view a *reaper!*—
No Teague would do a day's work cheaper:
——A *goddess* now, with wings like *eagle*'s,
And note as *piercing* as a beagle's!
Marcellus then—no *mortal* power;
Nor born "to be cut down like flower:"
A *wet-nurse* next, with store of pap
To feed the bantling on her lap:
Last, in *Jack-Ketch*'s nobler part,
She quits the mean, too gentle cart,
Close pressing at the culprit's heels,
—With divers racks, and sundry wheels!

O Sancho, when the suff'ring nation,
Shall rouse your serious indignation;
When, bursting forth, your patriot heat
Shall bid you prove your final threat—
No more expect my humble car
Will chase your chariot thro' the war:
Alas! I fight not cap-a-pée
With figure, trope, and simile!
Your *Pegasus*, so strong and bony,
Would gallop over my poor poney!
He never eat of sacred grass,
Nor run for *fifties* on *Parnass'*:
Nor water'd at *Castalian* springs,
Nor had the loan of eagle's wings:

[1]"The muse shall deal awhile in *brick* and *lime*,
    Surpass the bold ΑΔΕΛΦΙ in design,
    And o'er the Thames fling one stupendous line—
    Of *marble* arches."—
Adelphi is graced with its proper type, to puzzle the Ladies, and display *Sancho*'s
knowledge of the Greek alphabet.

Unskill'd is he to turn and double
Thro' acres of *Pierian* ſtubble,
Where here and there a few Bay switches,
Are guarded by a thousand ditches.
My nag, unlike your high-fed prime hacks,
Would break his wind to mount your climax:
And, when in Satire's field you take him,
One line of pointed spleen would ſtake him:
Your ſteed disdains a fetter'd chime;—
Mine boggles at an awkward rhyme;
Bad grammar always made him wait;
False concord is a five-barr'd gate;
Each gap of sense, where your's would shine,
Would seem a double-ditch to mine.
—Judge how imprudent then the chase,
'Tween beaſts of such unequal race!
The one a common, jaded hack,—
The other—fit for Gods to back!

—*Ohe! jam sat!*—what scribbling rage!
—I've writ a volume for a page!
—By Heav'ns I do my spirit wrong,
To grate this scrannel-pipe so long:
Hence! hence!—I hate it's peevish tone,
Tho' aim'd at *pride* and *spleen* alone:
And, if my rhyming vein ſtill need
A song, I'll touch some gentler reed—
A reed I something know to touch;—
Whose mildly plaintive notes are such,—
They ſteal the ſting from youthful grief,
Breathe to a lover's soul relief,
Or such resign'd diſtress beſtow,
They make the suff'rer proud of woe.
—O noble trifling of the hour!
When 'scap'd from dread of Fortune's pow'r,
I loiter in some secret, rude,
Yet sometimes broken solitude,—

While, with a heart not slow to prove
My theme's delight,—I sing of love.
Not with bent brow, or raptur'd eye,
Or "thoughts commercing with the sky,"
But mildly gay, with am'rous guile
Persuading thought to wear a smile;—
Studious awhile, yet never long,
Nor rapt nor careless in my song;
Glancing at all that *Fancy* sends,
And fixing where my *heart* commends.—
Such be my walk, if *Hope* inspire
With mirthful notes to touch the lyre;
And when I've done the sprightly task,
No wreath of Laurel do I ask.—
Be there a smile upon the cheek
Of her, to whom my numbers speak;
And, while she smiles,—be mine the praise,
Without a blush, that smile to raise.
Or, if more sad my numbers flow,
To tell some simple tale of woe,
While yet *she* reads, one sigh shall be
More precious far than fame to me;
And ending, let, uncheck'd, appear
The silent plaudit of a tear.

—O ye rude souls, who never gain
A joy, but from another's pain;
Ye base, unhallow'd sons of Rhyme,
Who waste in *Satire* all your time;
Who boast no pow'r, who own no fame,
But what from dastard guilt ye claim,—
Ye little know to prize the bliss
Of such a dear reward as this;
Your hearts could ne'er the boon revere
Of such a smile, of such a tear.

FINIS

Introduction[1]

"A PORTRAIT" is not, strictly speaking, the Dedicatory Poem to *The School for Scandal*, though for over a century it has always been printed as such. It is the "copy of verses" which Sheridan, as he told his second wife, sent "with a finely bound manuscript of that comedy" to the lady whose virtues he celebrates under the name of Amoret. *A Portrait* was being circulated in MS. in less than four months, at least, after the first performance of *The School for Scandal*. The play was acted on May 8, 1777; on August 3 of the same year Lord Camden wrote to David Garrick, "By some accident you forgot to show us Sheridan's verses when you were here. Would it be too much to beg a copy?" In Boaden's *Private Correspondence of David Garrick*, another letter of August 11 from Lord Camden tells Garrick, "I have returned the verses you were so good to lend me, and, considering they are mere panegyric (the most insipid species of poetry) they are extremely good. The girls have taken a copy, perhaps without leave, but if you think Mr. Sheridan may be displeased with this liberty, it shall be burnt . . . Charles Fox dined here yesterday; he admires Sheridan's verses, and agrees with me in marking him as the first genius of these times."[2] Boaden notes that these verses were *A Portrait*, adding they "have a heavy elaborate ingenuity about them without warmth." Mr. Walter Sichel, however, pronounces them the best dedicatory poem in our language.

In the beginning the poet summons the Daughters of Calumny:

Tell me, ye prim adepts in Scandal's school,
Who rail by precept, and detract by rule,
Lives there no character, so tried, so known,

[1] Reprinted from *An Ode to Scandal*, edited by R. Crompton Rhodes (1927).
[2] Horace Walpole, hearing them recited on October 8, 1777, hoped that they would "not long retain their MS-hood."—(*Letters* X. 134.)

So deck'd with grace, and so unlike your own,
That even you assist her fame to raise,
Approve by envy, and by silence praise?
Attend!—a model shall attract your view—
Daughters of Calumny, I summon you!

The model he bids before them is "the gentle Amoret":

Adorning Fashion, unadorn'd by dress,
Simple from taste, and not from carelessness;
Discreet in gesture, in deportment mild,
No state has Amoret! no studied mien;
She frowns *no goddess*, and she moves *no queen*.[1]

The true name of Amoret, by a conceit so agreeable to the
artificial style of the poem, is not revealed until, after a dramatic
pause, the very last word of the last line. This conceit has always
been destroyed in the printed copies of the poem, where her
name is always printed beneath the title. As the poem was not
printed for more than thirty years after it was written (and then
not with Sheridan's sanction) I have dared, by slightly altering
the sub-title, to restore the artifice upon which the climax depends. This seems all the more necessary as the last line has always been misinterpreted. It has been often said, and even by
Mr. Sichel, that this last line acknowledges and celebrates her as
the inspirer of *The School for Scandal*. This cannot be sustained.
The poem invokes first, the Daughters of Calumny; second the
Muse of Poetry; and third, the gentle Amoret. After the Muse
has chanted the praise of Amoret, the Daughters of Calumny are
silenced:

And lo! each pallid hag, with blister'd tongue,
Mutters assent to all thy zeal has sung—
Owns all the colours just—the outline true;
Thee my inspirer, and my model—CREWE!

There is no reference at all in the whole poem to *The School for
Scandal*: it is not that comedy which has "cast a gloom o'er Scandal's reign," but the Portrait of Amoret, inspired by the Muse,

[1] This couplet is a parody of one in Pope's *Homer* in praise of Helen; it had perhaps no
more recondite source than a quotation in Burke's Essay on *The Sublime and Beautiful*.

and the model who sat for the Portrait is the beautiful, witty intellectual Frances Crewe—"The gentle Amoret," the only daughter of Fulke Greville, who had married John Crewe in 1775. Years afterwards, when Sheridan had forgotten these verses, their surreptitious appearance in print, probably in some periodical, reminded him that Nature had made him (as he told his second wife) "an ardent, romantic blockhead." In later years Mrs. Crewe's indiscretions were notorious. To her beauty there are many tributes besides the three portraits by Sir Joshua Reynolds. In her Diary in 1799, after her first meeting with the Sheridans, Fanny Burney wrote that "the elegance of Mrs. Sheridan's beauty is unequalled by any that I ever saw, except Mrs. Crewe's." It was a day of beautiful women, but Amoret was, as Sheridan wrote of her in his old age, "the handsomest of the set."

Mr. Sichel says that "whether these verses were as welcome to the first Mrs. Sheridan as to their recipient may be questioned, but *Pierrot*, we may be sure, could eventually explain them to her satisfaction." He had clearly no reason to explain why he considered her as his inspirer of *The School for Scandal*, for the poem said nothing of the sort. Moreover, *Pierrot* was echoing a poem of his wife's in *A Portrait*. It was (as nobody seems to have noticed) Mrs. Sheridan who gave the name of Amoret to Mrs. Crewe in her poem *Laura to Silvio*.[1] For the ultimate origin of *A Portrait* we must turn to the famous ball, given by Mrs. Crewe in 1775, of which Sheridan had sent to his wife a glowing description, praising the celebrated beauties who were there. In return she sent him this poem, *Laura to Silvio*, in which he is depicted as a young poet, undecided among so many beauties which of them he shall sing. He is now captivated by the serene and majestic Stella, then by Myra of the lustrous eyes: now by the gaiety and playfulness of Flavia, then by Jessie, "lovely in smiles, more lovely still in tears."[2]   But the loveliest of them all, as Mrs.

[1]Charles Fox also adopted the name of Amoret for Mrs. Crewe in some indifferent verses of the same year.

[2]According to Moore (who was undoubtedly correct), these ladies were: "Stella," the Marchioness of Granby (afterwards Duchess of Rutland); "Myra," the Duchess of Devonshire; "Flavia," the Countess of Jersey; "Jessie," the Countess of Craven (afterwards Margravine of Anspach).

Sheridan depicted her—and the portrait is exquisite—is Amoret:

> With gentle step and hesitating grace,
> Unconscious of her power, the fair one came;
> If while he view'd the glories of her face
> Poor Silvio doubted—who shall dare to blame?
> A rosy blush his ardent gaze reprov'd,
> The offer'd wreath she modestly declin'd. . .

At last, unable to decide, he divides his garland among them —to Myra, the rosebuds; to Stella, the glowing carnations; to Flavia, the daffodils; to Jessie, the flower called Love-in-Idleness; to gentle Amoret, Violets and Eglantine. To Laura he gives a never-fading wreath of Myrtle.

In the couplet of Sheridan then:

> Come, gentle Amoret (for 'neath that name,
> In worthier verse is sung thy beauty's fame);

the "worthier verse" is the poem, *Laura to Silvio*.

A Portrait has indeed other unnoticed allusion to Mrs. Sheridan's poem. For instance:

> On Granby's cheek might bid new glories rise,
> Or point a purer beam from Devon's eyes!

is an echo of her:

> On Myra's breast the opening rose shall blow,
> Reflecting from her cheek a livelier bloom;
> For Stella shall the bright carnation glow,
> Beneath her eye's bright radiance meet its doom.

Laura to Silvio was, in effect, a plea to Sheridan to write about his own wife, not somebody else's. *A Portrait* was the consequence, —or the inconsequence. The deftness of his allusions to the two great ladies, to Sir Joshua Reynolds, to the "all-accomplished Mrs. Greville," the mother of Mrs. Crewe, and to Mrs. Millar, the Sappho of the Garden of Bath-Easton, and to his own wife, are typical of the courtly, propitiatory manner of Sheridan. *Pierrot* could have explained, no doubt, but he did better—he anticipated.

A Portrait

FOR AMORET:

TELL me, ye prim adepts in Scandal's school,
Who rail by precept, and detract by rule,

Lives there no character, so tried, so known,
So deck'd with grace, and so unlike your own,

That even you assist her fame to raise,
Approve by envy, and by silence praise!—

Attend!—a model shall attract your view—
Daughters of Calumny, I summon you!

You shall decide if this a portrait prove,
Or fond creation of the Muse and Love.—

Attend, ye virgin critics, shrewd and sage,
Ye matron censors of this childish age,

Whose peering eye and wrinkled front declare
A fix'd antipathy to young and fair;

By cunning, cautious; or by nature, cold,
In maiden madness, virulently bold!—

Attend! ye skill'd to coin the precious tale,
Creating proof, where innuendoes fail!

Whose practis'd memories, cruelly exact,
Omit no circumstance, except the fact!—

Attend, all ye who boast—or old or young,—
The living libel of a slanderous tongue!

So shall my theme as far contrasted be,
As saints by fiends, or hymns by calumny.

Come, gentle Amoret (for 'neath that name,
In worthier verse is sung thy beauty's fame);

Come—for but thee who seeks the Muse? and while
Celestial blushes check thy conscious smile,

With timid grace, and hesitating eye,
The perfect model, which I boast, supply :—

Vain Muse! couldst thou the humblest sketch create
Of her, or slightest charm couldst imitate—

Could thy blest strain in kindred colours trace
The faintest wonder of her form and face—

Poets would study the immortal line,
And Reynolds own *his* art subdued by thine;

That art, which well might added lustre give
To Nature's best, and Heaven's superlative:

On Granby's cheek might bid new glories rise,
Or point a purer beam from Devon's eyes!

Hard is the task to shape that beauty's praise,
Whose judgment scorns the homage flattery pays!

But praising Amoret we cannot err,
No tongue o'ervalues Heav'n, or flatters her!

Yet she by Fate's perverseness—she alone
Would doubt our truth, nor deem such praise her own!

Adorning Fashion, unadorn'd by dress,
Simple from taste, and not from carelessness;

Discreet in gesture, in deportment mild
Not stiff with prudence, nor uncouthly wild:

No state has Amoret! no studied mien;
She frowns *no goddess*, and she moves *no queen*.

The softer charm that in her manner lies
Is fram'd to captivate, yet not surprise;

It justly suits th' expression of her face,—
'Tis less than dignity, and more than grace!

On her pure cheek the native hue is such,
That form'd by Heav'n to be admired so much,

The hand divine, with a less partial care,
Might well have fix'd a fainter crimson there,

And bade the gentle inmate of her breast,—
Inshrined Modesty!—supply the rest.

But who the perils of her lips shall paint?
Strip them of smiles—still, still all words are faint!

But moving Love himself appears to teach
Their action, though denied to rule her speech;

And thou who seest her speak and dost not hear,
Mourn not her distant accents 'scape thine ear;

Viewing those lips, thou still may'st make pretence
To judge of what she says, and swear 'tis sense:

Cloth'd with such grace, with such expression fraught,
They move in meaning, and they pause in thought!

But dost thou farther watch, with charm'd surprise,
The mild irresolution of her eyes,

Curious to mark how frequent they repose,
In brief eclipse and momentary close—

Ah! seest thou not an ambush'd Cupid there,
Too tim'rous of his charge, with jealous care

Veils and unveils those beams of heav'nly light,
Too full, too fatal else, for mortal sight?

Nor yet, such pleasing vengeance fond to meet,
In pard'ning dimples hope a safe retreat.

What though her peaceful breast should ne'er allow
Subduing frowns to arm her alter'd brow,

By Love, I swear, and by his gentle wiles,
More fatal still the mercy of her smiles!

Thus lovely, thus adorn'd, possessing all
Of bright or fair that can to woman fall,

The height of vanity might well be thought
Prerogative in her, and Nature's fault.

Yet gentle Amoret, in mind supreme
As well as charms, rejects the vainer theme;

And half mistrustful of her beauty's store,
She barbs with wit those darts too keen before:—

Read in all knowledge that her sex should reach,
Though Greville, or the Muse, should deign to teach,

Fond to improve, nor tim'rous to discern
How far it is a woman's grace to learn;

In Millar's dialect she would not prove
Apollo's priestess, but Apollo's love,

Grac'd by those signs, which truth delights to own,
The timid blush, and mild submitted tone:

Whate'er she says, though sense appear throughout,
Displays the tender hue of female doubt;

Deck'd with that charm, how lovely Wit appears,
How graceful Science, when that robe she wears!

With timid grace, and hesitating eye,
The perfect model, which I boast, supply:—

Such too her talents, and her bent of mind,
As speak a sprightly heart by thought refined,

A taste for mirth, by contemplation school'd,
A turn for ridicule, by candour ruled,

A scorn of folly, which she tries to hide;
An awe for talent, which she owns with pride!

Peace! idle Muse,—no more thy strain prolong,
But yield a theme, thy warmest praises wrong;

Just to her merit, though thou canst not raise
Thy feeble verse, behold th' acknowledged praise

Has spread conviction through the envious train,
And cast a fatal gloom o'er Scandal's reign!

And lo! each pallid hag, with blister'd tongue,
Mutters assent to all thy zeal has sung—

Owns all the colours just; the outline true;
Thee my inspirer; and my model—CREWE!

Introduction

AS Mr. Sichel says finely, the Monody—the Verses to the Memory of Garrick—is "in truth not so much an elegy on the life of a friend, as an epilogue to the play of Garrick's life." It was indeed, "of the theatre." Sheridan wrote it to be delivered under theatrical conditions, to be spoken from the stage of Drury Lane Theatre, as David Garrick had spoken ten years before, his Ode in Commemoration of Shakespeare. The central "property" on the stage was not, of course, as then the bust of Shakespeare, but a monumental urn to the memory of Garrick. Before it stood the reciter, Mrs. Yates, surrounded by the choir and the orchestra. It was recited for the first time at Drury Lane Theatre on March 11th, 1779, after the comedy of *The West Indian*, when according to *The Town and Country Magazine* of the time:—

The stage was disposed nearly in the form as at Oratorios, with the difference only of a vacancy being left for Mrs. Yates to speak the poem. Before the organ a monument[1] was erected .... It was generally remarked that if Mrs. Yates had not been obliged (we suppose for want of time) to read several passages, it would have had a still finer effect. However, it must be owned that she did justice to her author, as might be expected from the most pathetic speaker on the stage.[2] The Monody is divided into three parts, between each of which, and at the conclusion, airs of a solemn nature are sung by Mr.

[1]What the monument or "mausoleum" was, is not quite clear. *The Town and Country Magazine* compared it to one of its own previous illustrations, representing the Comic and Tragic Muses mourning at a tomb, on which stands a portrait of Garrick, with the winged figure of Fame overhead. Mr. Sichel says that the Monody was delivered by Mrs. Yates, "in the character of the Tragic Muse"—which, of course, she had represented during Garrick's recitations of his Shakespeare Ode in 1769.

[2]Boaden, by the way, was less complimentary to Mrs. Yates, of whom he said in his *Memoirs of Mrs. Siddons*: "Had the composition itself allowed much variety in the manner of its delivery, Mrs. Yates could not have supplied it—her style of recitation was heavy and monotonous, though musical."

Webster, Mr. Gaudry, a young lady, and Mrs. Wrighten. supported by a band of choristers.

This stress upon the theatrical purpose of the Monody is deliberate. Its delivery from the stage would at once, for many auditors, summon their recollections of Garrick's *Shakespeare Ode*, with its many-changing metres. Accordingly it is not surprising to find that "The critics have nibbled at this Monody on account of the metre not being varied, and thereby leaving too constant a monotony on the auditor's ear, which they say ought to have been relieved by a variation of measure." Thus *The Town and Country Magazine*, which shows that "the critics" had wanted, not a prolonged address in the heroic couplet, but an ode in varied measures. Moore urged that the monotony would have been diminished by a "greater variety of cadence," an occasional disturbance of the "regular footfall, so long established." But, he adds, the only licence of this kind hazarded through the poem— "All perishable"—was objected to by some of the author's critical friends who suggested that it would have been better as "All doomed to perish." Sheridan was using the conventional metre for theatrical addresses, the only accepted form for Prologues and Epilogues. He did not, it is true, use it here with the deftness and polish that he achieved in the Verses for Amoret— the so-called Dedicatory Poem for *The School for Scandal*—yet one would not deny the justness of Mr. Sichel's praise—"All the elements of Sheridan's Prologues and Epilogues characterize it —finish, fancy, grace, ingenuity, condensation." Byron, in his famous passage[1] saying that "whatever Sheridan has done, or chosen to do, has been *par excellence*, always the best of its kind," described the Garrick Monody as "the best Address" in the language. The praise would be more impressive if it could be ascertained what other "Addresses" he had in mind.

Besides the objections to its structure or its monotony of cadence, time has matured other charges against it. There is the inevitable charge of plagiarism. "Sheridan" comments Boaden in his *Life of Mrs. Siddons*, "used freely everything recollected that made for his purpose," adding that he obviously remem-

[1]Byron's *Diary*, December 18, 1813, cited by Moore, *Sheridan*, p. 684.

bered Cibber, Lloyd's *Actor*, and its paraphrase and commentary the *Rosciad* of Churchill. So, too, Moore:—

"The chief thought which pervades this poem,—namely, the fleeting nature of the actor's art and fame,—had already been more simply expressed by Garrick himself in his Prologue to *The Clandestine Marriage*:—

> The painter's dead, yet still he charms the eye,
> While England lives, his fame can never die;
> But he, who *struts his hour upon the stage*,
> Can scarce protract his fame through half an age;
> Nor pen nor pencil can the actor save;
> The art and artist have one common grave.

Colley Cibber, too, in his portrait (if I remember right) of Betterton, breaks off into the same reflection, in the following graceful passage, which is one of those instances, where prose could not be exchanged for poetry without loss:—"Pity it is that the momentary Beauties, flowing from an harmonious Elocution, cannot, like those of Poetry, be their own record; that the animated Graces of the Player can live no longer than the instant Breath and Motion that presents them, or, at best, can but faintly glimmer through the Memory of a few surviving Spectators."

This "chief thought" is, indeed, no more than a great commonplace of the theatre. It had been uttered a thousand times when players were gathered together or playing was discussed. Colley Cibber, in that unsurpassed and unsurpassable example of histrionic criticism, his Short View of the actors of his youth, had placed it in his very first page, as an epigraph (as it were) to his entire commentary. Robert Lloyd had brought *The Actor* to a full close with it:

> Relentless death untwists the mingled fame,
> And sinks the player in the poet's name,—
> The pliant muscles of the various face,
> The mien that gave each sentence strength and grace,
> The tuneful voice, the eye that spoke the mind,
> Are gone, nor leave a single trace behind.

Garrick in his Prologue to *The Clandestine Marriage*—a tribute to the memory of Quin and Mrs. Cibber—attested that it was a commonplace when he echoed Shakespeare's:—

> Life's but a walking shadow, a poore Player
> That struts and frets his houre upon the stage,
> And then is heard no more.

The charge of "plagiarism" is, therefore, unimportant. A more serious charge is the absence of personal feeling, which Moore has formulated:—

The Monody does not seem to have kept the stage more than five or six nights—nor is this surprising. The recitation of a long, serious address must always be, to a certain degree, ineffective on the stage; and though this subject contained within it many strong sources of interest, as well personal as dramatic, they were not, perhaps, turned to account by the poet with sufficient warmth and earnestness on his own part, to excite a very ready response of sympathy in others. Feeling never wanders into generalities—it is only by concentrating his rays upon one point that even Genius can kindle strong emotion; and, in order to produce any such effect in the present instance upon the audience, Garrick himself ought to have been kept prominently and individually before their eyes in almost every line. Instead of this, however, the man is soon forgotten in his Art, which is then deliberately compared with other Arts, and the attention, through the greater part of the poem, is diffused over the transitoriness of actors in general, instead of being brought strongly to a focus upon the particular loss just sustained.

The truth is, indeed, that the poem is a Monody to the Memory of Any Actor—or rather, of the actor who is the Burbage, the Betterton, the Garrick, the Irving of his generation. And therein lies its dignity and grace.

Dedication

*T*O *the* RIGHT HONOURABLE COUNTESS SPENCER, *whose approbation and esteem were justly considered by* MR. GARRICK *as the highest panegyric his talents or conduct could acquire, this imperfect tribute to his memory is, with great deference,[1] inscribed by her ladyship's most obedient humble servant.*

RICHARD BRINSLEY SHERIDAN.

March 25, 1779.

[1] The First Issue reads erroneously "difference," corrected in the Second Issue (1779).

Verses to the Memory of Garrick

SPOKEN AS A MONODY, AT THE THEATRE ROYAL IN DRURY LANE.

IF dying excellence deserves a tear,
If fond remembrance ſtill is cherish'd here,
Can we persiſt to bid your sorrows flow
For fabled suff'rers and delusive woe?
Or with quaint smiles dismiss the plaintive ſtrain,
Point the quick jeſt, indulge the comic vein,
Ere yet to buried Roscius we assign
One kind regret—one tributary line!

His fame require we aɕt a tend'rer part:
His memory claims the tear you gave his art!

The gen'ral voice, the meed of mournful verse,
The splendid sorrows that adorned his hearse,
The throng that mourn'd as their dead favourite pass'd,
The grac'd respeɕt that claim'd him to the laſt,
While Shakespeare's image from its hallow'd base
Seemed to prescribe the grave, and point the place,
Nor these,—nor all the sad regrets that flow
From fond fidelity's domeſtic woe,—
So much are Garrick's praise, so much his due,
As on this spot—one tear beſtowed by you.

Amid the hearts which seek ingenuous fame,
Our toil attempts the moſt precarious claim!
To him whose mimic[1] pencil wins the prize,
Obedient Fame immortal wreaths supplies:
Whate'er of wonder Reynolds now may raise,
Raphael ſtill boaſts contemporary praise:

[1]Magic—Murphy's transcript in his *Life of Garrick*.

Each dazzling light and gaudier bloom subdu'd,
With undiminish'd awe *his* works are view'd:
E'en Beauty's portrait wears a softer prime,
Touch'd by the tender hand of mellowing Time.

The patient Sculptor owns a humbler part,
A ruder toil, and more mechanic art;
Content with slow and tim'rous ſtroke to trace
The ling'ring line, and mould the tardy grace:
But once atchiev'd, tho' barbarous wreck o'erthrow
The sacred fane, and lay its glories low,
Yet shall the sculptur'd ruin rise to-day,
Grac'd by defeſt, and worshipp'd in decay;
Th' enduring record bears the artiſt's name,
Demands his honours, and asserts his fame.

Superior hopes the Poet's bosom fire;
Oh, proud diſtinſtion of the sacred lyre!
Wide as th' inspiring[1] Phœbus darts his ray,
Diffusive splendour gilds his vot'ry's lay.
Whether the song heroic woes rehearse,
With epic grandeur, and the pomp of verse;
Or, fondly gay, with unambitious guile,
Attempt no prize but fav'ring beauty's smile;
Or bear dejeſted to the lonely grove
The soft despair of unprevailing love—
Whate'er the theme, thro' every age and clime
Congenial passions meet th' according rime;
The pride of Glory—Pity's sigh sincere—
Youth's earlieſt blush—and Beauty's virgin tear.

Such is their meed, their honours thus secure,
Whose arts yield objeſts, and whose works endure.
The Aſtor, only, shrinks from Time's award;
Feeble tradition is his mem'ry's guard;

[1] th' aspiring—Murphy's transcript *op. cit.*

By whose faint breath his merits muſt abide,
Unvouch'd by proof—to subſtance unallied!
E'en matchless Garrick's art, to Heaven resign'd,
No fix'd effeƈt, no model leaves behind!

The *grace* of *aƈtion*, the adapted *mien*,
Faithful as nature to the varied scene;
Th' *expressive* glance, whose subtle comment draws
Entranc'd attention, and a mute applause;
Geſture that marks, with force and feeling fraught,
A sense in silence, and a will in thought;
Harmonious speech, whose pure and liquid tone
Gives verse a music, scarce confess'd its own;
As light from gems assumes a brighter ray,
And cloath'd with orient hues, transcends the day!
Passion's wild break, and frown that awes the sense,
And every Charm of gentler *Eloquence*—
All perishable! like th' eleƈtric fire,
But ſtrike the frame, and, as they ſtrike, expire;
Incense too pure a bodied flame to bear,
Its fragrance charms the sense, and blends the air.

Where, then—while sunk in cold decay he lies,
And pale eclipse for ever veils those eyes—
Where is the bleſt memorial that ensures
Our Garrick's fame?—whose is the truſt?—'Tis yours.

And O! by every charm his art essay'd
To soothe your cares!—by ev'ry grief allay'd!
By the hush'd wonder which his accents drew!
By his laſt parting tear, repaid by you!
By all those thoughts, which many a diſtant night
Shall mark his memory with a sad delight!
Still in your hearts' dear record bear his name;
Cherish the keen regret that lifts his fame;
To *you* it is bequeathed,—assert the truſt,
And to his *worth*—'tis all you can—be *juſt*.

What more is due from sanctifying Time,
To cheerful wit and many a favor'd rhyme,
O'er his grac'd urn shall bloom, a deathless wreath,
Whose blossom'd sweets shall deck the mask beneath.
For these,—when Sculpture's votive toil shall rear
The due memorial of a loss so dear—
O loveliest mourner, gentle Muse! be thine
The pleasing woe to guard the laurell'd shrine.
As Fancy, oft by Superstition led
To roam the mansions of the sainted dead,
Has view'd, by shadowy eve's unfaithful gloom,
A weeping cherub on a martyr's tomb—
So thou, sweet Muse, hang o'er his sculptur'd bier,
With patient woe, that loves the ling'ring tear;
With thoughts that mourn—nor yet desire relief;
With meek regret, and fond enduring grief;
With looks that speak—*He never shall return!*
Chilling thy tender bosom, clasp his urn;
And with soft sighs disperse th' irrev'rent dust
Which Time may strew upon his sacred bust.

Bibliography of the Longer Poems

1.—THE LOVE EPISTLES OF ARISTÆNE-TUS

THE Love Epistles of Aristænetus: Translated From The Greek Into English Metre "... Love refines The thoughts and heart enlarges; hath his seat In reason and is judicious."—Milt. Par. Lost, B.8. London: Printed for J. Wilkie, No. 71, St. Paul's Church-yard. MDCCLXXI.

8vo.

Pagination. P. [i] half-title. *The Love Epistles of Aristænetus*; p. [ii] blank; p. [iii] title; p. [iv] blank; pp. [v] & vi–xii *Preface* signed *H.S.*; pp. [xiii] & xiv–xvi; *Contents*; pp. [1] & 2–174 text; pp. [175] & [176] *Books printed for J. Wilkie.*

The Love Epistles of Aristænetus. The Second Edition Corrected. London; Wilkie, 1773, 8vo.

Fom Anderson, *Sheridan Bibliography*, p. iv.

2.—A FAMILIAR EPISTLE

A Familiar Epistle to the Author of the Heroic Epistle to Sir William Chambers and of the Heroic Postscript to the Public.

"Nunc satis est dixisse, ego mira poemata pango:
"Occupet extremum scabies: mihi turpe relinqui est."

Ars Poet.

London. Printed for J. Wilkie, No. 71, St. Paul's Church-yard. M.DCC.LXXIV.

Quarto.

Pagination. P. [i] title; p. [ii] blank; pp. [iii–iv] *Preface*; pp. [1]–35 text; p. [36] blank.

A Familiar Epiſtle. The Second Edition. London, J. Wilkie. Quarto.

[This has a new Preface substituted for that of the First Edition. The title-page is reset. Otherwise, except for two *Errata*, it is a reprint. The only copy known to me is my own.]

3.—VERSES TO THE MEMORY OF GARRICK

Verses to the Memory of Garrick. Spoken As A Monody, At The Theatre-Royal in Drury-Lane. London: Published by T. Evans in the Strand: J. Wilkie, St. Paul's Church-Yard; E. and C. Dilly, in the Poultry; A. Portal, opposite the New Church; and J. Almon, Picadilly. M.DCC.LXXIX.

4to.

Pagination. P. [1] half-title *Verses to the Memory of Garrick (Price One Shilling)*; p. [2] blank; [Frontispiece by Loutherbourg inserted]; p. [3] title; p. [4] blank; p. [5] *Dedication* dated *March* 25, 1779; p. [6] blank; pp. 7–15 Text; p. 16 blank.

[*Second Issue.*
The Second Issue is identical with the above except that the word *Deference* is corrected in the Dedication from *Difference*, as misprinted in the first issue.]

Verses to the Memory of Garrick. The Second Edition. London: 1779. 4to.

[From Sichel *Sheridan*, vol. II, p. 452. He adds there were "many more editions in the same year."]

The Airs and Chorusses in The Monody On the Death of Mr. Garrick. Set to Music by Mr. Linley.

4to.

Pagination. Pp. [i], 2-3, text; [4] blank.

[Mr. P. F. Hinton's copy. Hitherto unrecorded. No place or printer: probably sold at the Theatre.]

Fugitive Verse

Note

THE FUGITIVE VERSE has not previously been collected in any edition of Sheridan, only eight of the thirty-seven pieces now printed having appeared in *Sheridan's Complete Works* (1876). Sheridan's biographers—Moore, Rae, and Sichel—recovered twenty-five of these poems from MS.; but eight of them had previously been printed in contemporary publications, from which sources—plays, magazines, song-sheets, and memoirs—the remaining twelve pieces are also reprinted.

The Political Pasquinades are taken entirely from Moore.

R.C.R.

CONTENTS

Introduction

THROUGHOUT his life, Sheridan had a fondness for turning a verse. In his youth he contemplated a Collection of Poetry by his own hand; but this project, like so many others, never came to maturity. As a writer of *vers de Société*, or, rather, *vers du Théâtre*, he had a pretty touch, and a little more. For, as Thomas Gent wrote in his *Monody on Sheridan* (1821):—

> "In careless mood he sought the Muse's bower,
> His lyre, like that by great Pelides strung,
> The softening solace of a vacant hour,
> Its airy descant indolently rung."

After his death Thomas Moore in his *Sheridan* printed some dozen of his fugitive poems recovered from the MSS. in possession of his son Charles ; Fraser Rae recovered a few more from the same source; and from an album bequeathed by Sheridan's first wife Elizabeth to her friend Mrs. Stratford Canning; while Mr. Walter Sichel surveyed the work of his two chief predecessors, Moore and Fraser Rae, and made further additions from MSS., so that a Sheridan Anthology could be compiled from his *Sheridan* (1909). To these three sources my debt is great; and above all to Mr. Sichel, for in this Collection I have included all the poems attributed by him to Sheridan, even the few which seem to me, for reasons given, to be spurious, or at least, doubtful. There are five of these: the three songs in *The Carnival of Venice* were always accepted as Tickell's; the "Stanzas on Fire" may be George Tierney's; and the "Address to the Prince Regent" is an epigram of Rochester's, slightly adapted. To each of the poems I have added a note on the source of the text, and the reason for attribution. There was a temptation to add two songs from the so-called *Drama of Devils* which is (in fact) an immature and unfinished adaptation of Suckling's *The*

223

Goblins. But as a third, accepted by Moore as Sheridan's, is a sonnet of Sir Philip Sidney's, slightly adapted, I have resisted the temptation, since they have a curious familiarity. These, however, are printed in my account of *The Foresters*, an unfinished opera, which derived ultimately from *The Goblins*. Another song, supposedly his, from the pantomime of *Robinson Crusoe*, is printed in the discussion of that piece.

Fugitive Verse

1. MARKED YOU HER EYE OF HEAV'NLY BLUE?

MARK'D you her eye of heav'nly blue?
Mark'd you her cheek of roseate hue?
That eye, in liquid circles moving;
That cheek abash'd at Man's approving;
The *one*, Love's arrows darting round;
The *other*, blushing at the wound:

[From *The Apollo or Harmonic Miscellany* (1814), a song-book. The familiarity of these lines to Sheridan's contemporaries was no doubt due to their setting to music by Shield. It is probable that they were printed in a song-sheet about 1780, when Shield was leader of the band at the Opera House under Sheridan. The words are extracted with slight alterations, from *Clio's Protest* (1771), where they are part of the panegyric on Lady Margaret Fordyce.]

2. ANACREONTIC

I NE'ER could any luftre see
In eyes that would not look on me:
When a glance aversion hints,
I always think the lady squints.
I ne'er saw nectar on a lip,
But where my own did hope to sip.
No pearly teeth rejoice my view,
Unless a *yes* displays their hue—
The prudish lip, that *noes* me back,
Convinces me the teeth are black.
To me the cheek displays no roses,
Like that th' assenting blush discloses;

225

But when with proud disdain 'tis spread,
To me 'tis but a scurvy red.
Would she have me praise her hair?
Let her place my garland there.
Is her hand so white and pure?
I must press it to be sure;
Nor can I be certain then,
Till it grateful press again.
Must I praise her melody?
Let her sing of love and me.
If she choose another theme,
I'd rather hear a peacock scream.
Must I, with attentive eye,
Watch her heaving bosom sigh?
I will do so, when I see
That heaving bosom sigh for me.
None but bigots will in vain
Adore a heav'n they cannot gain.
If I must religious prove
To the mighty God of Love,
Sure I am it is but fair
He, at least, should hear my prayer.
But, by each joy of his I've known,
And all I yet shall make my own,
Never will I, with humble speech,
Pray to a heav'n I cannot reach.

[From Moore's *Sheridan*, pp. 130-1. This Anacreontic, written about 1770, was compressed and improved for use in *The Duenna* as Antonio's song (Act I, scene ii) Mr. Sichel (vol. I, p. 277) quotes some introductory lines reminiscent of Suckling:—

True, she is fair! I grant you that.
I wonder now you cannot move her,
Then how the devil can you love her?

Moore cites a third beginning, also from MS.:—

Go tell the maid who seeks to move
My lyre to praise, my heart to love,
No rose upon her cheek can live,
Like those assenting blushes give.]

3. THE KISS

HURRIED seal of soft affection,
   Tenderest pledge of future bliss,
   Dearest tie of soft connection,
Love's first snow-drop, virgin kiss.

Speaking silence, dumb confession,
   Passions' birth, and infant's play,
Dovelike fondness, chaste concession,
   Brightest dawn of happiest day.

[From *The Festival of Love; or, A Collection of Cytherean Poems* (1800?). This indifferent trifle is quoted by Sichel (Vol. I, p. 279) as from MS. of about 1771.]

4. I GAVE MY LOVE A BUDDING ROSE

I GAVE my love a budding rose
   My infant passion to disclose;
   And, looking in her radiant eye,
I sought to read my destiny:
She breathed upon it—it became,
Mature in form, no more the same,
As when with timid fears opprest.

I placed the rose bud on her breast.
Again she breathed in sportive play,
And wafted all the leaves away;
"And thus," she cried, "your vows of love
As passing and as light would prove
As this dispersed and faded flow'r;
One sigh expanded it to bloom,
Another sigh and it was gone,
Nor lived one transient fleeting hour."

[From *The Dramatic Works of Sheridan* (Malepeyre, Paris; 1822), a hitherto unrecorded publication, one of a series of "The British Prose Writers, with Biographical and Critical Prefaces, by J. W. Lake, Esq." The poem is entitled "Extempore Lines by the Right Honourable R. B. Sheridan. Never Before Published."
"The Life of Sheridan," signed "J. W. L.," in the first volume, includes a long letter

"by one of Sheridan's dearest and truest friends," whose anonymous writer ends:—
  "The extempore song, which has never appeared in print . . . you are very welcome
to; and as I have been favoured with some imitations and translations of it in French,
composed in a distant province, for the purpose of obtaining a prize given by an English lady for the best translation, I have sent you the copies of several, that you may
select any you deem worthy of publication."
  A French "Imitation," in seven "Stances," signed A. de S., and a "Traduction,"
by Le Baron de P— B—, follow.
  Mr. J. Rudge Harding, of Richmond, has given me these extracts from his copy
of the Malapeyre Sheridan. This "Impromptu" is quoted from Sheridan's *Dramatic
Works* (Baudry, Paris, 1828) in Sichel, vol. I, p. 279, where it is attributed to 1771-2.
There is, however, no evidence as to its date; nor, beyond Lake's correspondent, as to
its authenticity, though it seems genuine.]

5. DAMON TO DELIA

I

ASK'ST thou "how long my love shall ſtay
    When all that's new is paſt?"
How long?—Ah, Delia, can I say
How long my life will laſt?
Dry be that tear—be hush'd that sigh,
At leaſt I'll love thee till I die.

II

And does that thought afflict thee too,
    The thought of Damon's death?
That he who only lives for you,
    Muſt yield his faithful breath?
Hush'd be that sigh—be dried that tear,
Nor let us lose our Heaven here!

[From *The European Magazine* for July, 1789. Also printed in *The Town and Country
Magazine* for August, 1790. In both periodicals the title is "Stanzas, By R. B. Sheridan,
Esq.," and it is followed by "The Reply, By Mrs. Sheridan." Moore notes in the first
stanza a close resemblance to one of the madrigals of Montreuil, a French poet. Mr.
Sheridan, however, knew nothing of French, and neglected every opportunity of
learning it, till, by a very natural process, his ignorance of the language grew into
hatred of it. Besides, we have the immediate source from which he derived the thought
of this stanza, in one of the Essays of Hume ("The Epicurean") who, being a reader of
foreign literature, most probably found it in Montreuil (or in an Italian song of Menage,
from which Montreuil, who was accustomed to such thefts, most probably stole it).
The passage in Hume (which Sheridan has done little more than versify) is as follows:—

  "Why so often ask me, *How long my love shall yet endure?* Alas, my Cælia, can
I resolve the question? *Do I know how long my life shall yet endure?*"

  Mr. Hinton tells me it was printed in *An Asylum for Fugitive Pieces*. London, Debrett
1789. 12mo.]

6. DRY BE THAT TEAR

DRY be that tear, my gentlest love,
    Be hush'd that struggling sigh,
    Nor seasons, day, nor fate shall prove
More fix'd, more true than I.
Hush'd be that sigh, be dry that tear,
Cease boding doubt, cease anxious fear.—
    Dry be that tear.

Ask'st thou how long my love will stay,
    When all that's new is past?—
How long, ah, Delia, can I say
    How long my life will last?
Dry be that tear, be hush'd that sigh,
At least, I'll love thee till I die.—
    Hush'd be that sigh.

And does that thought affect thee too,
    The thought of Sylvio's death—
That he who only breath'd for you,
    Must yield that faithful breath?
Hush'd be that sigh, be dry that tear,
Nor let us lose our Heaven here.—
    Dry be that tear.

[From Moore's *Sheridan*, p. 38, transcribed from MS. As Moore noted, the opening is borrowed from Halhed's " Dwarf Elegy on a Lady of Middle Age," which begins :

    Dry be that tear, be hush'd that struggling sigh,
    Can grief revive whom Heav'n ordains to die?

The first line haunted Sheridan, who repeated it twenty years later in the *Elegy on the Death of a British Officer*, which begins:—

    "Scarce hush'd the sigh, scarce dried the ling'ring tear."

Of course, it is the previous poem with an added stanza.]

7. ON FIRE

I

IN poets all my marks you'll see,
    Since flash and smoke reveal me.
Suspect me always near Nat Lee.
    E'en Blackmore can't conceal me.

II

In Milton's page I glow by art,
    One flame intense and even:
In Shakespeare's blaze, a sudden start,
    Like Lightnings flashed from Heaven,

III

In many more, as well as they,
    Though various forms I shift,
I'm gently lambent when I'm *Gay*,
    I'm brightest when I'm *Swift*.

IV

In other forms I oft am seen,
    In breasts of young and fair,
And as the Virtues dwell within,
    You'll always find me there.

V

I with pure-piercing, brilliant gleam
    Can arm Eliza's eye.
With modest soft ethereal beam
    Sweet Mary's I supply.

[From *An Ode to Scandal* "to which are added *Stanzas on Fire*" (1819). In this Eliza and Maria are stated to be "the Ladies Eliza and Maria Birmingham, daughters of the late Earl Louth." As Mr. Sichel says, Eliza and Mary of this jeu d'esprit "may well be guessed," however (vol. I, p.315) "to have been no other than Eliza and Mary Linley." In that case, then, the probable date is 1772. Lady Elizabeth Birmingham's divorce was one of the scandals of 1778. It may be added that *The Morning Herald* attributed these verses, with the *Ode to Scandal*, to George Tierney.]

8. TO THE RECORDING ANGEL

CHERUB of Heaven, that from thy secret ſtand
    Doſt note the follies of each mortal here,
    Oh, if Eliza's ſteps employ thy hand,
Blot the sad legend with a mortal tear.

Nor, when she errs, through passion's wild extreme,
    Mark then her course, nor heed each trifling wrong;
Nor, when her sad attachment is her theme,
    Note down the transports of her erring tongue.

But, when she sighs for sorrows not her own,
    Let that dear sigh to Mercy's cause be given;
And bear that tear to her Creator's throne,
    Which gliſtens in the eye upraised to Heaven!

[From Moore's *Sheridan*, pp. 33-4. Fraser Rae cites (vol. I, p. 231) Mrs. Sheridan's original transcript which reads "Emira" to "Eliza," "not" for "nor"; and "call" for "cause." This poem is understood as a remonstrance to Miss Linley on her attachment to Captain Matthews. Moore dates it as 1770. But it seems to me that the verses had some relation to "the lecture upon decorum of conduct" which so displeased Elizabeth, and occasioned "The Grotto." The poem would therefore belong to May, 1772.]

9. THE GROTTO

I

UNCOUTH is this moss-cover'd grotto of ſtone,
    And damp is the shade of this dew-dropping tree;
    Yet I this rude grotto with rapture will own,
And, willow, thy damps are refreshing to me.

II

For this is the grotto where Delia reclined,
    As late I in secret her confidence sought;
And this is the tree kept her safe from the wind,
    As blushing she heard the grave lesson I taught.

III

Then tell me, thou grotto of moss-cover'd stone,
  And tell me, thou willow with leaves dripping dew,
Did Delia seem vex'd when Horatio was gone,
  And did she confess her resentment to you.

IV

Methinks now each bough, as you're waving, it tries
  To whisper a cause for the sorrow I feel;
To hint how she frown'd when I dared to advise,
  And sigh'd when she saw that I did it with zeal.

V

True, true, silly leaves, so she did, I allow,
  She frown'd, but no rage in her looks did I see;
She frown'd, but reflection had clouded her brow,
  She sigh'd, but perhaps 'twas in pity for me.

VI

Then wave thy leaves brisker, thou willow of woe,
  I tell thee no rage in her looks could I see;
I cannot—I will not, believe it was so,
  She was not—she could not, be angry with me.

VII

For well did she know that my heart meant no wrong,
  It sunk at the thought but of giving her pain,
But trusted its task to a faultering tongue,
  Which err'd from the feelings it could not explain.

VIII

Yet oh! if indeed I've offended the maid,
  If Delia my humble monition refuse,
Sweet willow, the next time she visits thy shade,
  Fan gently her bosom, and plead its excuse.

IX

And thou, stony grot, in thy arch may'st preserve,
    Two lingering drops of the night-fallen dew,
And just let them fall at her feet and they'll serve
    As tears of my sorrow entrusted to you.

X

Or lest they unheeded should fall at her feet,
    Let them fall on her bosom of snow, and I swear
The next time I visit thy moss-cover'd seat,
    I'll pay thee each drop with a genuine tear.

XI

So may'st thou, green willow, for ages thus toss
    Thy branches so lank o'er the slow-winding stream,
And thou, stony grotto, retain all thy moss,
    While yet there's a poet to make thee his theme.

XII

Nay more, may my Delia still give you her charms,
    Each evening, and sometimes the whole evening long,
Then, grotto, be proud to support her white arms,
    Then, willow, wave all thy green tops to her song.

[From *The European Magazine* for June, 1782, where the heading is "Verses by R. B. Sheridan, Esq., Mr. Sheridan meeting Miss Linley, now Mrs. Sheridan, at the entrance of a Grotto in the vicinity of Bath, took the liberty of offering her some advice. With which apprehending that she was displeased, he left the following lines in the Grotto the next day." Mr. Sichel prints a version, which he considers superior, from a transcript by Charles Sheridan. In this verse VI is omitted from its proper place, while verse XII is followed by a repetition of verses V, VI, and VII—apparently some accident of transcription by Charles Sheridan. In this the name of "Laura" is used instead of "Delia," and there are other minor differences. The Grotto is "supposed to have been in Spring Gardens," says Moore, a most unlikely place as this was a much-frequented public resort. The poem was written in May, 1772.]

10.   THINK NOT, MY LOVE, WHEN SECRET GRIEF

THINK not, my love, when secret grief
　　Preys on my sadden'd heart,
　　Think not I wish a mean relief,
Or would from sorrow part.

Dearly I prize the sighs sincere,
　　That my true fondness prove,
Nor would I wish to check the tear,
　　That flows from hapless love!

Alas! tho' doom'd to hope in vain
　　The joys that love requite,
Yet will I cherish all its pain,
　　With sad, but dear delight.

This treasur'd grief, this lov'd despair,
　　My lot for ever be;
But, dearest, may the pangs I bear
　　Be never known to thee!

[From Moore's *Sheridan*, p. 574. The fourth verse, slightly altered, was incorporated in Sheridan's song for *The Stranger* (1798). Mr. Sichel attributes the poem to 1772. Howard's *Beauties of Sheridan* states "this song is believed to have been addressed to Miss Linley, afterwards Mrs. Sheridan. It was set to music by her brother." Moore quotes a correspondent to *The Gentleman's Magazine* who had bought it in 1794 at "Bland's music shop in Holborn—" the copy "professing to be set to music by Thomas Wright."

Mr. P. F. Hinton tells me that this song was printed in *The London Magazine* for March, 1780, with the description, " One of the new Ballads set to Musick by Mr. Linley.   Song XI."   In this copy, verse 1, line 3 reads " Nor could I bear."]

11. TO ELIZABETH LINLEY

SHALL my Eliza to the woods and trees
    Alone communicate her tuneful lays?
Or breathe her rhyme to the unmindful breeze
And be content with Echo's idle praise?

Oh! let your Sylvio share, my gentleſt love.
Let Sylvio share each line that you rehearse.
Or will he hate flowers, elms, sweet bird and grove
    Which shall inspire the too unsocial verse.

[From Fraser Rae's *Sheridan*, vol. II, p. 113; copied from Mrs. Sheridan's album
bequeathed by her to Mrs. Canning. Mr. Sichel attributed these rather weak verses to
May, 1772.]

12. ON HIS WIFE CEASING TO SING

DOES my Eliza cease to sing,
    Or tires my love to touch the ſtring?
    Behold, she knows with equal skill,
To grace the Muse's nobler will.
Hear but her voice! amaz'd you'd swear
The soul of Music centres there!
Read but her verse, and you'll confess
Her song did raise your wonder less:
Oh! soul of harmony that knows
No touch of discord to disclose!
So well her mind and voice agree,
That every thought is melody:
While bending o'er the charmèd ſtream,
His conscious sighs approved the theme:
Nor long, nor true, he touched the lyre,
Such pleasing woe her notes inspire,
Such thoughts of joy by fortune croſt,
Such dear regret of raptures loſt,

Such eager hope of future bliss,
That melting, in a fancied kiss,
In amorous frame he lost his care,
And sought another Daphne there;
'Twas then Euterpe ceased: 'twas then
She ceased!—and stole her Brother's Pen.
Her pen is taught her notes to suit,
And prove her musically mute;
Who would not then, if Bard he were,
And knew like me, the accomplished fair,
Affirm, it was no mortal Maid
We sung, but from the Muse's shade
Euterpe: then 'twere fair to tell
How sweetly near the sacred well,
One night she chanced in softer strain
To sing of Love and Lover's pain,
Till Phœbus came the bank along,
And caught his harp to join the song.

[From Sichel's *Sheridan*, vol. I, p. 629. Elizabeth Linley's last public appearance
a singer was before March, 1773. To this year Mr. Sichel ascribes the poem. It is no
however, clear whether the title was Sheridan's—probably not.]

13. TO HYMEN

TEACH me, kind Hymen! teach—for thou
Must be my only tutor now,—
Teach me some innocent employ
That shall the hateful thought destroy,
That I this whole long night must pass
In exile from my love's embrace.
Alas! thou hast no wings, oh, Time!
It was some thoughtless lover's rhyme,
Who, writing in his Chloe's view,
Paid her the compliment through you;
For had he, if he truly loved,
But once the pangs of absence proved,

He'd cropt thy wings, and in their stead,
Have painted thee with heels of lead.
But 'tis the temper of the mind,
Where we, thy regulator find:
Still o'er the gay and o'er the young,
With unfelt steps you flit along;
As Virgil's nymph o'er ripen'd corn,
With such etherial haste was borne,
That every stock with upright head
Denied the pressure of her tread;
But o'er the wretched oh, how slow
And heavy sweeps thy scythe of woe!
Oppressed beneath each stroke they bow,
Thy course engraven on their brow.
A day of absence shall consume
The glow of youth, and manhood's bloom;
And one short night of anxious fear
Shall leave the wrinkles of a year.

For me, who, when I'm happy, owe
No thanks to fortune that I'm so;—
Who long have learned to look at one
Dear object, and at one alone,
For all the joy and all the sorrow
That gilds the day or threats the morrow;—
I never felt thy footsteps light,
But when sweet love did aid thy flight;
And, banish'd from his blest dominion,
I cared not for thy borrow'd pinion.

True, she is mine, and since she's mine,
At trifles I should not repine;
But oh! the miser's real pleasure
Is not in knowing he has treasure:
He must behold his golden store,
And feel and count his riches o'er.

Thus I, of one dear gem possess'd
And in that treasure only blest,
There every day would seek delight,
And clasp the casket every night.

[From Moore's *Sheridan*, p. 88, where it is described as having been written in 1773, soon after their marriage, during a brief absence from his cottage at East Burnham. It contains the germ of "What bard, O Time," in *The Duenna*.]

14. WHEN 'TIS NIGHT, AND THE MID-WATCH
IS COME

(For the pantomime of *Harlequin Fortunatus*.)

WHEN 'tis night, and the mid-watch is come,
    And chilling mists hang o'er the darken'd main,
    Then sailors think of their far distant home,
And of those friends they ne'er may see again:
        But when the fight's begun,
        Each serving at his gun,
Should any thought of them come o'er our mind,
    We think but, should the day be won,
How 'twill chear their hearts to hear
    That their old companion he was one.

Or, my lad, if you a mistress kind
    Have left on shore, some pretty girl and true,
Who many a night doth listen to the wind,
    And wakes to think how it may fare with you;
        O! when the fight's begun,
        Each serving at his gun,
Should any thought of her come o'er your mind,
    Think only, should the day be won,
How 'twill chear her heart to hear
    That her own true sailor he was one.

[From *The Beauties of Sheridan*, p. 49. This song, unknown to Mr. Sichel, was known to Moore, although he quoted only one couplet. It is recorded by Mr. Williams (*Seven XVIII Century Bibliographies*) as printed in *Songs in the Glorious First of June* (1794) with Sheridan's name as author, and reprinted in *Songs in Cape Vincent* (1797). Neither of these occasional entertainments was printed in full. *Harlequin Fortunatus*, an alteration of Woodward's pantomime, is ignored by Genest, but it was supposedly acted at Drury Lane in the early months of 1780. *Aris's Gazette* of that year announced the performance at the Theatre, Birmingham, of *An Interlude* "written by R. B. Sheridan, Esq. Taken from the pantomime of *Fortunatus* representing the Storming and Taking of Fort Omoa. In which will be introduced songs by Mr. Linley." There can be no reason to doubt, therefore, that Sheridan and Linley wrote *When 'tis Night* for a patriotic interlude in *Fortunatus* and used it afterwards in *The Glorious First of June* and *Cape St. Vincent.*]

15. CHEARLY, MY HEARTS, OF COURAGE

CHEARLY, my hearts, of courage true!
 The hour's at hand to try your worth;
 A glorious peril waits for you,
And valour pants to lead you forth;
Mark where the enemy's colours fly, boys;
There some shall conquer, and some must die, boys;
  But that appals not you or me,
  For our watch-word it shall be,
"Britons, strike home!"

Chorus

"Britons, strike home! revenge your country's wrong!"

When rolling mists their march shall hide,
 At dead of night a chosen band,
List'ning to the dashing tide,
 With silent tread shall print the sand:
Then where the Spanish colours fly, boys,
We'll scale the walls, or bravely die, boys;
  For we are Britons bold and free,
  And our watch-word it shall be,
"Britons, strike home!" &c.

The cruel Spaniard, then too late,
    Dismay'd, shall mourn th' avenging blow,
Yet, vanquish'd, meet the milder fate
    Which mercy grants a fallen foe.
Thus shall the British banners fly, boys,
On yon proud turrets rais'd on high, boys;
    And while the gallant flag we see,
    We'll swear our watch-word still shall be,
"Britons, strike home!" &c.

[From *The Beauties of Sheridan*, pp. 49-50. This song is not recorded by Mr. Sichel. This song was also from *Harlequin Fortunatus*.

Since writing the former note, I have discovered both " Chearly My hearts " and " When 'tis night " in *The Lady's Magazine* Supplement for 1779, which shows that *Fortunatus ; or, the Wishing Cap*, with the new interlude of Fort Omoa, was played for the first time at Drury Lane on January 3rd, 1780. Mr. P. F. Hinton adds that *The London Magazine* for February, 1780, prints both of them as " Corrected Copies of the Songs sung in the Pantomime called *Harlequin Fortunatus*, and said to be written by Mr. Sheridan."

" When 'tis night " was sung by Bannister and " Chearly, my hearts " by Vernon, both in the character of Sailors.]

16. WE TWO, EACH OTHER'S ONLY PRIDE

(From *The Foresters*, an unfinished opera.)

WE two, each other's only pride,
    Each other's bliss, each other's guide,
    Far from the world's unhallow'd noise,
Its coarse delights and tainted joys,
Through wilds will roam and deserts rude—
For, Love, thy home is solitude.

There shall no vain pretender be,
To court thy smile and torture me,
No proud superior there be seen,
But nature's voice shall hail thee, queen.

With fond respect and tender awe,
I will receive thy gentle law,
Obey thy looks, and serve thee still,
Prevent thy wish, foresee thy will,
And, added to a lover's care,
Be all that friends and parents are.

[From Moore's *Sheridan*, p. 237. *The Foresters* was never acted, though frequently
paragraphed as about to be represented in 1780 and thereabouts. This is the only
song which has survived, although it can hardly be doubted that others had been
written. Even so optimistic a genius as Sheridan would scarcely venture to speak of
an opera as "almost complete" when in fact, he has written only one song and a few
pages of dialogue. Moore described this song as "for grace and tenderness, not unworthy of the hand that produced *The Duenna*."]

17. LINES BY A LADY OF FASHION

THEN, behind, all my hair is done up in a plat,
And so, like a cornet's, tuck'd under my hat.
Then I mount on my palfrey as gay as a lark,
And, follow'd by John, take the dust in High Park.
In the way I am met by some smart macaroni,
Who rides by my side on a little bay pony—
No sturdy Hibernian, with shoulders so wide,
But as taper and slim as the ponies they ride;
Their legs are as slim, and their shoulders no wider,
Dear sweet little creatures, both pony and rider!

But sometimes, when hotter, I order my chaise,
And manage, myself, my two little greys.
Sure never were seen two such sweet little ponies,
Other horses are clowns, and these macaronies,
And to give them this title, I'm sure isn't wrong,
Their legs are so slim, and their tails are so long.
In Kensington Gardens to stroll up and down,
You know was the fashion before you left town,—
The thing's well enough, when allowance is made
For the size of the trees and the depth of the shade,

III. R

But the spread of their leaves such a shelter affords
To those noisy, impertinent creatures called birds,
Whose ridiculous chirruping ruins the scene,
Brings the country before me, and gives me the spleen.

Yet, tho' 'tis too rural—to come near the mark,
We all herd in *one* walk, and that, neareſt the Park,
There with ease we may see, as we pass by the wicket,
The chimneys of Knightsbridge and—footmen at cricket.
I muſt tho', in juſtice, declare that the grass,
Which, worn by our feet, is diminished apace,
In a little time more will be brown and as flat
As the sand at Vauxhall or as Ranelagh mat.
Improving thus faſt, perhaps, by degrees,
We may see rolls and butter spread under the trees,
With a small pretty band in each seat of the walk,
To play little tunes and enliven our talk.

[From Moore's *Sheridan*, pp. 176-7. Several ideas were transferred from this poem to
The School for Scandal; one may discern the origin of Mrs. Pursy puffing round the
Ring "with her hair plaited up behind like a drummer's," of Lady Betty Curricle
"taking the dust in Hyde Park," and (of course) of Sir Benjamin Backbite's epigram on
the ponies. The fragment was obviously unrevised, for the idea of Sir Benjamin's "impromptu" is twice developed. It was probably composed at the end of 1776. The use
of the seventeenth-century form "High Park" for "Hyde Park" as by Etherege, is
curious.]

18. TO LAURA

NEAR Avon's ridgy bank there grows
   A willow of no vulgar size,
That tree firſt heard poor Silvio's woes,
And heard how bright were Laura's eyes.

Its boughs were shade from heat and show'r,
   Its roots a moss-grown seat became;
Its leaves would ſtrew the maiden's bow'r,
   Its bark was shatter'd with her name!

Once on a blossom-crowned day
Of mirth-inspiring May,
Silvio, beneath this willow's sober shade
In sullen contemplation laid,

Did mock the meadow's flowery pride,—
   Rail'd at the dance and sportive ring;—
The tabor's call he did deride,
   And said, *it was not Spring*.

He scorn'd the sky of azure blue,
   He scorn'd whate'er could mirth bespeak;
He chid the beam that drank the dew,
   And chid the gale that fann'd his glowing cheek.
Unpaid the season's wonted lay,
For still he sigh'd, and said, it *was* not *May*.

Ah, why should the glittering stream
   Reflect thus delusive the scene?
Ah, why does a rosy-ting'd beam,
   Thus vainly enamel the green?
To me nor joy nor light they bring
I tell thee, Phœbus, *'tis not Spring*.

"Sweet tut'ress of music and love,
   Sweet bird, if 'tis thee that I hear,
Why left you so early the grove,
   To lavish your melody here?
Cease, then, mistaken thus to sing,
Sweet nightingale! it *is* not *Spring*.

"The gale courts my locks but to tease,
   And, Zephyr, I call'd not on thee;
Thy fragrance no longer can please,
   Then rob not the blossoms for me:
But hence unload thy balmy swing,
Believe me, Zephyr, 'tis *not Spring*.

"Yet the lily has drank of the show'r,
  And the rose 'gins to peep on the day;
And yon bee seems to search for a flow'r,
  As busy as if it were May:—
In vain, thou senseless flutt'ring thing,
My heart informs me, *'tis not Spring.*"

May pois'd her roseate wings, for she had heard
  The mourner, as she pass'd the vales along;
And, silencing her own indignant bird,
  She thus reprov'd poor Silvio's song.

"How false is the sight of a lover;
How ready his spleen to discover
  What reason would never allow!
Why,—Silvio, my sunshine and show'rs,
My blossoms, my birds, and my flow'rs,
  Were never more perfeĉt than now.

"The water's refleĉtion is true,
The green is enamell'd to view,
  And Philomel sings on the spray;
The gale is the breathing of spring,
'Tis fragrance it bears on its wing,
  And the bee is assur'd it is *May.*"

"Pardon" (said Sylvio with a gushing tear)
"*'Tis Spring,* sweet Nymph, *but Laura is not here.*"

[From Moore's *Sheridan*, pp. 147-149. Moore describes these verses as written in the spring of 1777, and sent to his wife, then staying at Bath, with a letter telling her about "some splendid party, at which he had lately been present where all the finest women of the world of fashion were assembled." Mr. Sichel, although elsewhere adopting this date, says that the occasion of this letter was a celebrated *fête* given by Mrs. Crewe in 1775. However, that may be, to the verses "To Laura," Mrs. Sheridan responded with verses "To Silvio," echoes of which are to be found in Sheridan's poem, "A Portrait."

19. THE GONDOLIER'S SONG

(From *The Carnival of Venice.*)

I

SOON as the busy Day is o'er,
  And Evening comes with pleasant shade,
We Gondoliers from shore to shore,
Merrily ply our jovial trade.

And while the Moon shines on the Stream,
  And as soft music breathes around;
The feathering oar returns the gleam,
  And dips in concert to the sound.

II

Down by some Convent's mould'ring walls
  Oft we hear the enamoured Youth;
Softly the watchful Fair he calls,
  Who whispers vows of Love and Truth.

And while the Moon [&c.]

III

And oft where the Rialto swells,
  With happier pairs we circle round;
Whose secret sighs fond Eccho tells,
  Whose murmur'd vows she bids resound.

And while the Moon [&c.]

IV

Then joy's the Youth, that Love conceal'd,
That fearful Love must own its sighs.
Then smiles the Maid, to hear reveal'd
How more than ever she complies.

And while the Moon [*&c.*]

[From *Songs in the Carnival of Venice* (1781). In this year Sheridan's brother-in-law Tickell brought out at Drury Lane an opera called *The Carnival of Venice*. Mrs. Crouch in her *Memoirs* said, "Many songs in this piece so perfectly resembled in poetic beauty those which adorn *The Duenna* that they declare themselves to be offspring of the same Muse." Moore, quoting this passage, said he did not know on what grounds the conjecture was founded, but Mr. Sichel selects three songs as Sheridan's, without producing any further evidence than Mrs. Crouch's. It must, however, be remembered that as Miss Phillips, she had played Emily in the first representation of *The Carnival of Venice*. Nevertheless, I see no reason that they should not have been Tickell's own. The pamphlet of Songs in the comic opera of *The Carnival of Venice* was printed in 1781, without the name of publisher, printer, or author. Apparently, however, it was sold at the theatre. As to this particular "Gondolier's Song," Moore definitely denied that Sheridan could ever have written the "four pretty lines" which form the chorus, as he had "no feeling for natural scenery"—not a very substantial argument. The song was sung by Bannister as Lucio, the third and fourth verses being omitted in representation.]

20. BY ADVERSE FATE

(From *The Carnival of Venice*.)

BY adverse Fate when Beauty sighs,
A mingled claim our bosoms prove;
'Tis Virtue grac'd with gentler ties,
'Tis Pity soften'd into Love.

Blest, doubly blest, his transport glows,
Whose Pity can each joy refine;
When from that God-like source it flows,
The generous passion is divine.

[From *Songs in The Carnival of Venice* (1781). Mr. Sichel has selected this as "beginning in the style of *The Duenna*." It was sung by Dubellamy as Melvil.]

21. THE GENTLE PRIMROSE

(From *The Carnival of Venice*.)

I

THE gentle Primrose of the vale,
Whose tender bloom rude winds assail,
Droops its meek leaves, and scarce suſtains
The night's chill snow and beating rains.

II

'Tis paſt—the morn returns—sweet Spring
Is come—and hills and valleys sing.
But low the gentle Primrose lies,
No more to bloom, no more to rise.

[From *Songs in the Carnival of Venice* (1781). This song is described by Mr. Sichel (vol. I, p. 443) as the best in this comic opera, adding that in it "Mrs. Sheridan, I think must have had a hand." Which seems no great argument for Sheridan's authorship! It was sung by Mrs. Crouch as Emily.]

22. IF FORTUNE

I

IF Fortune to thee treasures gave,
Each debt of mine thou'dſt gladly pay,
And nothing for thyself would save
Nor deem thy bounty thrown away.

II

Cruel Eliza! would this ease
My burdens, or make me more free
When the wish only does increase
The debt of love I owe to thee?

[From Fraser Rae's *Sheridan* (vol. II, p. 115), where it is transcribed from Mrs. Sheridan's album, bequeathed to Mrs. Stratford Canning. Mr. Sichel dates it "?1783."]

23. AS SHEPHERDS THROUGH THE VAPOURS GREY

AS shepherds thro' the vapours grey
  Behold the dawning light,
  Yet doubt it is the rising day,
Or meteor of the night;

So varying passions in my breaſt,
  Its former calm deſtroy——
By Hope and Fear at once oppress'd,
  I tremble at my joy!

[From Howard's *The Beauties of Sheridan*, previously printed as "by R. B. Sheridan, Esq.," in *The Poetical Register* for 1808-9. (London. Rivington. 1812.)]

24. EPITAPH ON BROOKS

ALAS! that Brooks, returned to duſt
  Should pay at length the debt that we,
  Averse to parchment, mortgage, truſt,
Shall pay, when forced, as well as he.

And die so poor, too! He whose trade
  Such profits cleared by draught and deed,
Though pigeons called him murmuring Brooks
  And dipped their bills in him at need.

At length his laſt conveyance see,
  Each witness mournful as a brother,
To think that this world's mortgagee
  Muſt suffer judgment in another!

Where no appeals to court can reſt,
  Reversing a Supreme decree,
But each decision ſtands expressed
  A final precedent *in re*.

[From *Recollections of the Last Half Century by the Rev. J. Richardson*. Brooks was the founder of Brooks's, the famous Club which Sheridan joined in 1780, shortly after his election to Parliament. Brooks was a money-lender with many clients among the members. Mr. Sichel dates the epitaph as 1780.]

25. ON TWO DEAD SPEAKERS

MOURN, mourn, St. Stephen's Choirs, with ceaseless
  grieving
  Two kindred spirits from the senate fled,
In the same chair we heard them both lie living,
 On the same day we see them both lie dead.

Sure in one grave they ought to lie together,
 Then in their praise should fiction's self be loath;
The stone that says a civil thing of either,
 May praise impartially, and lie for both.

[From Fraser Rae, who heads this epitaph (as if part of the original MSS.):— "Lord Grantley and the Rt. Hon. C. W. Cornwall, who had both been speakers of the House of Commons, died at the same time (January, 1789) and were both equally eminent for political integrity and personal veracity.]

26. ELEGY ON THE LAMENTED DEATH OF AN AVADAVAT

I

WHY trickles the tear from Elizabeth's eye?
 Why thus interrupted her elegant chat?
 Ah! bootless that tear and bootless that sigh,
They cannot revive your poor Avadavat.

II

Each bird that is born of an egg has its date,
 No power can lengthen its days beyond that;
Then let us submit to the dictates of Fate,
 And no longer lament the poor Avadavat.

III

Some comfort it is that no violent death,
  Assailed it from shooter, from birdlime or cat,
But a common disorder arrested its breath.
  'Twas the *husk* served its writ on the Avadavat.

IV

The prisoner insolvent who dies in the Fleet
  From death gets his Habeas as Wilkes did from Pratt,
When caged up for life, no joys could be sweet
  And this was the case of the Avadavat.

V

And now it has flown to new scenes of delight,
  Where Venus's pigeons long cooing have sat.
While Lesbia's sparrow from envy moults white
  And the Muses all chirp to the Avadavat.

VI

Astonished they list to its musical throat
  And Euterpe in vain tries a sharp or a flat:
In vain! for from H E R the sweet bird caught its note
  Who excels every Muse, as her Avadavat.

[From Fraser Rae's *Sheridan*, vol. II, pp. 121, 122, transcribed from Mrs. Sheridan's Album bequeathed to Mrs. Canning. Avadavats were tiny singing birds, mentioned in *The School for Scandal* by Joseph Surface as among the trifling presents he had received from Sir Oliver. The mention of "Lesbia's sparrow" is not altogether happy in its playfulness, for Sheridan was here no Catullus, although the verses are reasonably deft. Mr. Sichel dates this poem alternately as ?1777 and ?1786, but his evidence supports the later year.]

27. ON THE DEATH OF ELIZABETH SHERIDAN

I

NO more shall the spring my lost treasure restore,
    Uncheered, I shall wander alone,
    And, sunk in dejection, for ever deplore
The sweets of the days that are gone.
While the sun, as it rises, to others shines bright,
    I think how it formerly shone;
While others cull blossoms, I find but a blight,
    The sweets of the days that are gone.

II

I stray where the dew falls, through moon-lighted groves,
    And list to the nightingale's song ;
Her plaints still remind me of long-vanished loves,
    And the sweets of the days that are gone.
Each dew-drop that steals from the dark eye of night
    Is a tear for the bliss that is flown
While others cull blossoms, I find but a blight
    And I sigh for the days that are gone.

[From *The Reminiscences of Michael Kelly* (1826) Vol. II, pp. 290-1. Kelly found this ballad at Sheridan's house, under a table on a half-sheet of paper in his handwriting. "On my return home, the words seemed to me beautiful and I set them to music. It is, of all my songs, my greatest favourite, as the poetry always brings to my mind the mournful recollection of past days. It was also a great favourite with Mr. Sheridan, and often has he made me sing it to them." Kelly does not describe them as an elegy on Mrs. Sheridan, or as composed soon after her death in 1792, though such (as Mr. Sichel argues) seems to have been the case.]

28. FROM EVERY LATENT FOE

(A Verse for the National Anthem.)

FROM ev'ry latent Foe,
And the Assassin's Blow
God save the King.
O'er him Thine Arm extend,
For Britain's sake defend,
Our Father, Prince and Friend,
God save the King.

[From a broadside of additional verses to the National Anthem, "Richard Brinsley Sheridan's, Esq. celebrated additional verse to the old popular Anthem of God Save the King to which are respectively added 20 others, by an Irishman in London." This verse was improvised by Sheridan, and forthwith played and sung at Drury Lane Theatre after Hadfield's attempt to assassinate King George III in 1800.]

29. MELANCHOLY, FRIEND TO GRIEF

MELANCHOLY, friend to Grief,
Ever o'er my spirit reign,
To my sorrows bring relief
And thyself inspire my strain.

When thy sadness can impart
All its healing, soft'ning powers,
Then thy tears are to the heart
Like the falling dew to flowers.

Happy he whose peaceful day
In retirement gently flows
From the busy world away
All the balmy calm he knows.

Then he hopes alone in thee
Some relief from care to find,
Seeking no society
But his memory or mind.

[From Fitzgerald's *Lives of the Sheridans*, vol. I, p. 211. Sichel describes this song as from a piece apparently intended to be called *The Governor* (vol. I, p. 7) and quotes (very judiciously) only the first and second verses. "Balmy calm" is a vile phrase, and the last verses seem to be an unrevised draft.]

30. ON LADY ANNE HAMILTON'S DOG

MY name is Albion—Lady dear,
Accept my service tendered here,
For know, I've laid my plan
So gentle, kind and good to be,
That in your favour soon you'll see
Your rival, Lady Anne.

I'll love your friend, I'll bite your foe,
I'll guide your steps where'er you go;
Where'er you choose your seat,
There at your feet I'll rest reclined,
'Twill please the wise and good to find
That Albion's at your feet.

[From Sichel's *Sheridan*, vol. I, p. 316. These album-verses from the Sheridan MSS.
are dated 1806.]

31. ON LADY ANNE HAMILTON

PRAY how did she look? Was she pale, was she wan?
She was blooming and red as a cherry—poor Anne.

Did she eat? Did she drink? Yes, she drank up a can,
And ate very near a whole partridge—poor Anne.

Pray what did she do? Why, she talked to each man
And flirted with Morpeth and Breanebie—poor Anne.

Pray how was she drest? With a turban and fan,
With ear-rings, with chains, and with bracelets—poor Anne.

And how went she home? In a good warm sedan
With a muff and a cloak and a tippet—poor Anne!

[From Sichel's *Sheridan*, vol. I, p. 317, transcribed from MS. formerly belonging
to the Countess of Bessborough. "It must have been dashed off after a party," says
Mr. Sichel.]

32. LINES BY A LADY ON THE LOSS OF HER TRUNK

HAVE you heard, my dear Anne, how my spirits are sunk?
　　Have you heard of the cause? Oh, the loss of my *Trunk*!
　　From exertion or firmness I've never yet slunk;
But my fortitude's gone with the loss of my *Trunk*!
Stout Lucy, my maid, is a damsel of spunk;
Yet she weeps night and day for the loss of my *Trunk*!
I'd better turn nun, and coquet with a monk;
For with whom can I flirt without aid from my *Trunk*!

Accurs'd be the thief, the old rascally hunks,
Who rifles the fair, and lays hands on their *Trunks*!
He, who robs the King's ſtores of the leaſt bit of junk,
Is hang'd—while he's safe, who has plunder'd my *Trunk*!

There's a phrase amongſt lawyers, when *nunc*'s put for *tunc*;
But, tunc and nunc both, muſt I grieve for my *Trunk*!
Huge leaves of that great commentator, old Brunck,
Perhaps was the paper that lin'd my poor *Trunk*!
But my rhymes are all out;—for I dare not use ſt—k;
'Twou'd shock Sheridan more than the loss of my *Trunk*.

[From Moore's *Sheridan*, from MSS.]

33. I HAVE A SILENT SORROW HERE

(From *The Stranger*.)

I HAVE a Silent Sorrow here,
　　A Grief I'll ne'er impart;
It breathes no Sigh, it sheds no Tear,
　　But it consumes my heart!
This cherish'd woe, this loved despair,
　　My lot for ever be;
So, my Soul's Lord, the pangs I bear
　　Be never known by thee!

And when pale characters of Death
Shall mark this alter'd Cheek;
When my poor wasted trembling breath
My Life's last hope would speak;
I shall not raise my Eyes to Heav'n,
Nor mercy ask for me;
My Soul despairs to be forgiven,
Unpardon'd, Love, by thee!

[From a music sheet, "The Favourite Song, sung by Mrs. Bland in *The Stranger*. The words by R. B. Sheridan, Esqre., the Air by her Grace the Dutchess of Devonshire," printed by Longman Clementi & Company (1798?). In the printed book of *The Stranger*, by Benjamin Thompson (1800), it is stated for the words of this song, "the translator is indebted to R. B. Sheridan, Esq., M.P." Sheridan's share in *The Stranger* was otherwise small.]

34. YES, YES, BE MERCILESS, THOU TEMPEST DIRE!

(From *Pizarro*.)

I

YES, yes, be merciless, thou Tempest dire!
Unaw'd, unshelter'd, I thy fury brave,
I'll bare my bosom to thy forked fire,
Let it but guide me to Alonzo's grave!

O'er his pale corse then, while thy lightnings glare,
I'll press his clay-cold lips, and perish there.

But thou wilt wake again, my boy;
Again thou'lt rise to life and joy——
Thy father never!——
Thy laughing eyes will meet the light,
Unconscious that eternal night
Veils his for ever!

II

On yon green bed of moss there lies my child,
  Oh! safer lies from these chill'd arms apart;
He sleeps, sweet lamb! nor heeds the tempeſt wild,
  Oh! sweeter sleeps than near this breaking heart.

Alas! my babe, if thou would'ſt peaceful reſt,
Thy cradle muſt not be thy mother's breaſt.

Yet thou wilt wake again, my boy;
Again thou'lt rise to life and joy——
    Thy father never!————
Thy laughing eyes will meet the light,
Unconscious that eternal night
    Veils his for ever!

[From *Pizarro* (1799). Also issued about the same time as a song-sheet in Kelly's *Music to Pizarro*. Mr. Sichel prints (*Sheridan*, vol. II, p. 279), from the Sheridan MSS., "an alternative song . . . in a sort of blank verse intended to be transformed to rhyme "

On a sad bed of leaves and moss my child is laid,
Yet better than this chill'd bosom, for
Thou sleep'st my babe, nor heed'st the tempest wild
This bosom is no couch for peace or thee.
Alas! Alas! my babe, if thou wouldst rise,
Seek any cradle but thy mother's breast.

This is, however, obviously the first rough draft of the first six lines in stanza II.]

35. THE WALSE

WITH tranquil step, and timid, downcast glance,
Behold the well-pair'd couple now advance.
In such sweet posture our first Parents mov'd,
While, hand in hand, through Eden's bowers they rov'd;
Ere yet the Devil, with promise foul and false,
Turn'd their poor heads and taught them how to *Walse*.
One hand grasps hers, the other holds her hip—
For so the Law's laid down by Baron Trip.

[From Moore's *Sheridan*, p. 708. It had been repeated to Moore, he says, by the author in a ball-room. The Waltz was introduced into England in 1812, but was strongly reprobated, since the older country-dances had permitted no greater intimacy than the holding of hands. The books of airs called Waltzes published from about 1800 were adapted to country dances, and not to the Waltz. "Baron Trip," says Moore, "whose name suits so aptly as a legal authority on the subject of Waltzing, was, at the time these verses were written, well-known in dancing-circles." Leonard's *Book of Light Verse* (1910) prints from an unstated source, another version of this trifle:—

> Behold with downcast eyes and modest glance,
> In measured step, a well-dress'd pair advance,
> One hand on hers, the other on her hip,
> For thus the law's ordained by Baron Trip.
> 'Twas in such posture our first parents moved
> When hand-in-hand through Eden's bowers they roved;
> Ere yet the Devil, with practice foul and false,
> Turned their poor heads and taught them how to waltz.

Since Moore printed his version from a rough draft, Leonard's version seems authentic and superior—except for the unlucky displacement of a couplet, which makes nonsense of the whole!]

36. THE WALTZ

WHILE arts improve in this aspiring age,
Peers mount the coach-box, horses mount the stage,
And waltzing females with unblushing face
Disdain to dance but in a man's embrace,
While arts improve and modesty is dead,
Sound sense and taste are like our bullion, fled.

[From Fraser Rae's *Life of Sheridan*, vol. II, p. 210, quoted from "a Scrap-book of Thomas Grenville's at Stowe." Sichel quotes it under the title of "The Waltz, An Apostrophic Poem," by misunderstanding Rae's reference to Byron's celebrated attack (1812) on the newly-introduced dance. His conjectural date (1800?) is also incorrect. "Horses mount the stage" is a reference to the equestrian drama, formerly peculiar to Astley's Amphitheatre, which was inaugurated by Colman's *Blue-Beard* on February 18, 1811, "when a whole troop of horses made their first appearance in character at Covent Garden."]

37. AN ADDRESS TO THE PRINCE REGENT

IN all humility we crave
Our Regent may become our slave,
And being so, we trust that H E
Will thank us for our loyalty.
Then, if he'll help us to pull down
His Father's dignity and Crown,
We'll make him, in some time to come,
The greatest Prince in Christendom.

[From Moore's *Sheridan*, p. 654, where it is dated 1811. This ironical epigram condenses, as Mr. Sichel puts it, "the first article of faith of the great Revolutionary families." It was written during the controversy on the powers of the Regent. Sheridan, however, has little claim to it. It merely altered Rochester's "Commons Petition to King Charles II. :—

"In all humanity we crave
Our Sovereign must be our slave, &c."]

Political Pasquinades

MOORE discovered among the papers of Sheridan a string of political pasquinades "written at various dates, chiefly by Sheridan," but owing some of its numbers to Tickell and Lord John Townshend. They were little more than the Limericks of their era, written, it seems, to the air of a ballad beginning:

> Mistress Arne, Mistress Arne
> It gives me con*carn*—

Already, when Moore wrote "Time," as he said, had "removed their venom, and with it a great deal of their wit," so that they were even then like "dried snakes, mere harmless objects of curiosity." Even their authorship does not seem to be at all certain, since the one on Lord Mountmorres, which Moore gives definitely to Townshend, Mr. Sichel gives as definitely to Sheridan, for the curious reason that "there are numbers of similar ones among his own papers, and a few in the Holland House MSS." Their annotation would be a curious exercise, and scarcely worth the labour it would demand:

I

> Johnny W—lks, Johnny W—lks,
> Thou greatest of bilks,
> How chang'd are the notes you now sing!
> Your fam'd Forty-five
> Is Prerogative,
> And your blasphemy, "God save the King,"
> Johnny W—lks,
> And your blasphemy, "God save the King."

II

Jack Ch—ch—ll, Jack Ch—ch—ll,
The town sure you search ill,
Your mob has disgraced all your brags;
When next you draw out
Your hospital rout,
Do, prithee, afford them clean rags,
Jack Ch—ch—ll,
Do, prithee, afford them clean rags.

III

Captain K—th, Captain K—th,
Keep your tongue 'twixt your teeth,
Lest bed-chamber tricks you betray;
And, if teeth you want more,
Why, my bold Commodore,—
You may borrow of Lord G—ll—y,
Captain K—th,
You may borrow of Lord G—ll—y.

IV

[1]Joe M—wb—y, Joe M—wb—y,
Your throat sure must raw be,
In striving to make yourself heard;
But it pleased not the pigs,
Nor the Westminster whigs,
That your knighthood should utter one word,
Joe M—wb—y,
That your knighthood should utter one word.

"This stanza and the next were by Lord John Townshend.—Moore."

V

M—ntm—res,—M—ntm—res,
Whom nobody for is,
And *for* whom we none of us care;

From Dublin you came—
It had been much the same
If your lordship had stayed where you were,
M—ntm— res,
If your lordship had stayed where you were.

VI

Lord O— gl—y, Lord O—gl—y,
You spoke mighty strongly—
Who you *are*, tho', all people admire!
But I'll let you depart,
For I believe in my heart,
You had rather they did not inquire,
Lord O— gl— y,
You had rather they did not inquire.

VII

Gl— nb— e, Gl—nb—e,
What's good for the scurvy?
For ne'er be your old trade forgot—
In your arms rather quarter
A pestle and mortar,
And your crest be a spruce gallipot,
Gl—nb—e,
And your crest be a spruce gallipot.

VIII

Gl—nb—e, Gl—nb— e,
The world's topsy-turvy,
Of this truth you're the fittest attester;
For, who can deny
That the low become high,
When the king makes a lord of Silvester,
Gl— nb— e,
When the king makes a lord of Silvester?

IX

Mr. P—l, Mr. P—l,
In return for your zeal,
I am told they have dubb'd you Sir Bob
Having got wealth enough
By coarse Manchester stuff,
For honours you'll now drive a job,
Mr. P—l,
For honours you'll now drive a job.

X

Oh poor B—ks, oh poor B—ks,
Still condemn'd to the ranks,
Not e'en yet from a private promoted;
Pitt ne'er will relent,
Though he knows you repent
Having once or twice honestly voted,
Poor B—ks,
Having once or twice honestly voted.

XI

Dull H— l— y, dull H—l—y,
Your auditors feel ye
A speaker of very great weight,
And they wish you were dumb,
When, with ponderous hum,
You lengthen the drowsy debate,
Dull H—l—y,
You lengthen the drowsy debate.

"There are about as many more of these stanzas," adds Moore, "written, at different intervals, according as new victims, with good names for rhyming, presented themselves—the metre being a most tempting medium for such lampoons. There is, indeed, appended to one of Sheridan's copies of them, a long list (like a Table of Proscription), containing about fifteen other names marked out for the same fate; and it will be seen by the following specimen that some of them had a very narrow escape:

Will C—rt—s . . . . .
V—ns—t—t, V—ns—t—t,— for little thou fit art.
Will D—nd—s, Will D—nd—s,— were you only an ass.
L—ghb—h,— thorough.
Sam H—rsl—y, Sam H—rsl—y, . . . coarsely.
P—ttym—n,—speak truth if you can."

It would not be worth adding to this collection of "dried snakes" any specimens from *The Rolliad*,[1] although it may be denied that Sheridan's disclaimer to any share in the authorship covered some of the later contributions. But this negative evidence scarcely warrants any new "attributions."

---

[1] It was about this time [1785] that, in the course of an altercation with Mr. Rolle, the member for Devonshire, Mr. Sheridan took the opportunity of disavowing any share in the political satires then circulating, under the titles of *The Rolliad* and the *Probationary Odes*. "He was aware," he said, "that the Honourable Gentlemen had suspected that he was either the author of those compositions, or some way or other concerned in them; but he assured him, upon his honour, he was not—nor had he ever seen a line of them till they were in print in the newspaper."—Moore, *Sheridan*, p. 107.

Bibliography of Fugitive Verse

[A S the source of each poem has been given in the notes, this bibliography excludes the various periodical publications, biographies, etc. Where the Songs are from plays, they are discussed bibliographically under their respective titles in the present edition.]

The Life Of The Right Honourable Richard Brinsley Sheridan. Containing a Comprehensive Review of his Abilities, as a Poet, a Statesman, an Orator, and a Dramatiſt. With the Remarks of Pitt, Fox, and Burke, On his moſt Celebrated Speeches, and Many Curious Anecdotes on his Parliamentary, Literary and Private Career. Never Before Published; Including his Monody on Garrick, Verses to Miss Linley, and a Collection of his Fugitive Poetry. John Fairburn [1816?]
8vo.

[I have not seen this book, which apparently contains the first attempt to collect the fugitive verse. My note is derived from *The Booklover's Leaflet*, No. 202. Pickering and Chatto. It is there dated " Circa 1816." Anderson, *Sheridan Bibliography*, p. ix, gives a short title reference to a "Second Edition [1816?] 8vo" of this book.]

A Collection of Poems, moſtly original, by Several Hands. Dublin: Printed for the Editor, By M. Graisberry. MDCCL-XXXIX.

[I am indebted to Mr. Iolo A. Williams for the title of this book, from a copy in the possession of Mr. Edward Gathorne-Hardy. It seems to be the first book (apart from periodicals) to contain "The Grotto" (No. 9). This collection has not previously been recorded in the Sheridan bibliographies.]

The Beauties of Sheridan, consiſting of Selections from his Poems, Dramas, and Speeches. By Alfred Howard, Esq., London. Printed by T. Davison. For Thomas Tegg, No. 73, Cheapside ; H. Griffin and Co., Glasgow ; and J. Cumming, Dublin [1834?].
24mo. Pp. 214.

[I am indebted to Mr. M. Willson Disher for a copy of this book, apparently the first (apart from periodicals and music-sheets) to contain the Songs in *Harlequin Fortunatus* (Nos. 14 and 15). Anderson, *Sheridan Bibliography*, p. iii, dates it "[1834?]."

Prologues and Epilogues

Note

SHERIDAN'S PROLOGUES AND EPI-
LOGUES have not been collected previously. Mr.
Sichel's bibliography (*Sheridan*, vol. II, p. 454) enumerated
eleven, to which are now added the Epilogues to *Edward and
Eleanora* and *The Fair Circassian*. This section does not include
those for Sheridan's own plays printed elsewhere with the texts.
What is supposed by Mr. Sichel to be an Epilogue to *The Tempest*
is shown here to be wrongly assigned, and a note is included upon
some lost or incomplete pieces.

R.C.R.

CONTENTS

Epilogue to *Edward and Eleanora*[1]

Written by R. SHERIDAN, Esq.

Spoken by MRS. MATTOCKS

YE wedded critics,[2] who have mark'd our tale,
How say you? Does our plot in nature fail?
May we not boaſt that many a modern wife
Would lose her own, to save a husband's life?
Would gladly die—O monſtrous and ill-bred,
There's not a husband here but shakes his head!
But you, my gall'ry friends[3]—Come, what say you?
Your wives are with you—shake their noddles too.
Above there—hey, lads[4]—You'll not treat us so—
You side with us?—They grin, and grumble No!
Yet hold——tho' these plain folks traduce their doxies,
Sure we have Eleanoras in the boxes?
Inhuman beaux! why that ill-natur'd sneer?
What, then you think there's no such idiot here?
There are, no doubt, tho' rare to find I know,
Who could lose husbands, yet survive the blow;
Two years a wife—view Lesbia sobbing, crying,
Her chair is waiting—but my lord is dying;
Preparing for the worſt! she tells her maid,
To countermand her points and new brocade;
For O! if I should lose the beſt of men,
Heav'n knows when I shall see the club again.
"So, Lappet, should he die while I am out,
You'll send for me to lady Baſto's rout;
The doctor said he might hold out till three,

[1] The footnotes that follow are Sheridan's. [2] To the Pit.
[3] To the First Gallery. [4] Second Gallery.

But I han't spirits for the Coterie!"
Now change the scene—place madam in the fever,
My lord for comfort at the Scavoir Vivre;
His valet enters—shakes his meagre head,
"Chapeau—what news?"——"Ah,! Sir, me lady dead."
"The deuce!—'tis sudden, faith—but four days sick!
Well, seven's the main—(poor Kate)—eleven's a nick."
But hence reflections on a senseless train,
Who, lost to real joy, should feel no pain;
'Mongst Britain's daughters still can Hymen's light
Reveal the love which charm'd your hearts to-night,
Shew beauteous martyrs—who would each prefer
To die for him who long has liv'd for her;
Domestic heroines—who, with fondest care,
Outsmile a husband's grief—or claim a share;
Search where the rankling evils most abound,
And heal with cherub-lips the poison'd wound.
Nay, such bright virtues in a royal mind
Were not alone to Edward's days confin'd,
Still, still, they beam around Britannia's throne,
And grace an Eleanora of our own.

[From *The Town and Country Magazine* for April, 1775.
Edward and Eleanora, acted at Covent Garden on March 18th, 1775, was altered
by Thomas Hull from James Thomson's tragedy. Mrs. Mattocks, who spoke the
Epilogue, played Daraxa, an Arabian Princess. The Coterie and the Scavoir Vivre
were two of the most fashionable clubs of the time—the night-clubs of the period.
Contemporary allusions to them are numerous. On May 18th, 1775 "The noblemen
and gentlemen of the Scavoir Vivre Club" gave a masquerade of unusual splendour.
The Coterie also gave magnificent entertainments; its quadrille-tables, frequented by
the noblewomen of the time, were often mentioned. In 1771 there was printed a
satirical pamphlet, with the title:—
    "*The Coterie Recommended:* or, the Pleasure of the Beau Monde Vindicated: in an
Oration made before that honourable and truly laudable Society on the 4th of April
[1771] being the Anniversary of its Institution: By the Hon. Mr. Sham'em. (8vo.
Gardner)."]

Epilogue to *Semiramis*

Written by R. B. SHERIDAN, Esq.

Spoken by MRS. YATES.

DISHEVELL'D ſtill, like Asia's bleeding queen,
Shall I with jeſts deride the tragic scene?
No, beauteous mourners!—from whose downcaſt eyes—
The Muse has drawn her nobleſt sacrifice!
Whose gentle bosoms, Pity's Altars,—bear
The cryſtal incense of each falling tear!—
—There lives the Poet's praise—no critic art
Can match the comment of a feeling heart!
When gen'ral plaudits speak the Fable o'er,—
Which mute attention had approv'd before,
Tho' ruder spirits love th' accuſtom'd jeſt,
Which chases sorrow from the vulgar breaſt,
Still hearts refined their sadden'd tint retain,—
—The sigh is pleasure, and the jeſt is pain!—
—Scarce have they smiles to honour Grace or Wit,
—Tho' Roscius spoke the verse himself had writ.
Thus, thro' the time when vernal fruits receive
The grateful show'rs that hang on April's eve,
Tho' ev'ry coarser ſtem of foreſt birth
Throws with the morning beam its dews to earth,
—Ne'er does the gentle Rose revive so soon—
But bath'd in Nature's tears, it droops till noon.
O could the Muse one simple moral teach!
From scenes like these, which all who heard might reach!
—Thou child of Sympathy—who'er thou art,
Who, with Assyria's Queen, haſt wept thy part—
Go search, where keener woes demand relief,
Go—while thy heart yet beats with fancy'd grief;

Thy lips still conscious of the recent sigh,
The graceful tear still ling'ring in thy eye—
Go—and on *real* misery bestow
The bless'd effusion of fictitious woe!—
So shall our muse, supreme of all the nine,
Deserve, indeed, the title of—*Divine!*—
Virtue shall own her favour's from above,
And Pity—greet her—with a sister's love!

[From the First Edition of *"Semiramis*. A Tragedy . . . by George Edward Ayscough, Esq. 1776." *The Whitehall Evening-Post* commented on the first production—"The Epilogue was remarkable for its beauty. It began with the same idea which John Hume has with great simplicity and force held out in the epilogue to *Douglas*, but pursued it with a strain of chaste imagery and fine poetry which we do not remember to have heard equalled but in an Epilogue by the same writer. We mean Sheridan's Epilogue to the Comedy of *The Rivals*." Mrs. Yates played Semiramis, "Asia's bleeding Queen," at the first performance at Drury Lane on December 12th, 1776. Ayscough's play was adapted from Voltaire.]

Prologue to *Sir Thomas Overbury*

Written by R. BRINSLEY SHERIDAN *Esq.*

Spoken by MR. HULL.

TOO long the Muse, attach'd to regal show,
Denies the scene to tales of humbler woe;
Such as were wont, while yet they charm'd the ear,
To steal the plaudit of a silent tear;
When Otway gave domestic grief its part,
And Rowe's familiar sorrows touch'd the heart.

A scepter'd traitor, lash'd by vengeful fate,
A bleeding hero, or a falling state,
Are themes (tho' nobly worth the classic song)
Which feebly claim your sighs, nor claim them long;
Too great for pity, they inspire respect,
Their deeds astonish rather than affect;
Proving how rare the heart that woe can move,
Which reason tells us we can never prove.

Other the scene, where sadly stands confest
The private pang that rends the suff'rer's breast;
When sorrow sits upon a parent's brow,
When fortune mocks the youthful lover's vow,
All feel the tale, for who so mean but knows
What father's sorrows are? what lover's woes?

On kindred ground our bard his fabric built,
And plac'd a mirror there for private guilt;
Where, fatal union! will appear combin'd
An angel's form, and an abandon'd mind;

Honour attempting passion to reprove,
And friendship struggling with unhallow'd love.

Yet view not, critics, with severe regard
The orphan-offspring of an orphan-bard;
Doom'd, while he wrote, unpitied to sustain
More real mis'ries than his pen could feign.
Ill-fated Savage! at whose birth was giv'n
No parent but the Muse, no friend but heav'n!
Whose youth no brother knew, with social care
To soothe his suff'rings, or demand to share;
No wedded partner of his mortal woe,
To win his smile at all that fate could do;
While at his death, nor friend's, nor mother's tear,
Fell on the track of his deserted bier.

So pleads the tale,[1] that gives to future times
The son's misfortunes, and the parent's crimes;
There shall his fame (if own'd to night) survive,
Fix'd by the hand that bids our language live.

[From *The Town and Country Magazine* for February, 1777. *Sir Thomas Overbury*,
altered by William Woodfall from Savage's play, was acted at Covent Garden on
February 1st, 1777. Hull acted the Earl of Northampton.]

[1] The Life of Richard Savage, written by Dr. Samuel Johnson.—Original footnote.

Epilogue to *The Fatal Falsehood*

Written by R. B. SHERIDAN, Esq.; and spoken by MR. LEE
LEWIS, in the Character of an enraged Author.

UNHAND me, gentlemen, by Heaven, I say,
I'll make a ghost of him who bars my way.
                              [*Behind the Scenes.*
Forth let me come—A Poetaster true,
As lean as Envy, and as baneful too;
On the dull audience let me vent my rage,
Or drive these *female* scriblers from the stage:
For scene or history, we've none but these,
The law of Liberty and Wit[1] they seize
In Tragic—Comic—Pastoral—they dare to please.
Each puny Bard must merely burst with spite,
To find that women with such fame can write:
But, oh! your partial favour is the cause,
Who feed their follies with such full applause;
Yet still our tribe shall seek to blast their fame,
And ridicule each fair pretender's aim;
When the dull duties of domestic life,
Wage with the Muse's toils eternal strife.

What motley cares *Corilla's* mind perplex,
While maids and metaphors conspire to vex!
In studious deshabille behold her sit,
A letter'd gossip, and a housewife wit;
At once invoking, tho' for different views,
Her gods, her cook, her milliner, and muse,

[1]Surely this is a misprint for "the law of liberty and writ," echoing Polonius in
Hamlet—"the best actors in the world, either for Tragedie, Comedy, History,
Pastorall . . . . . for the law of writ, and the liberty, these are the only men." Or was
it a half-pun?

Round her strew'd room, a frippery chaos lies,
A chequer'd wreck of *notable* and *wise*;
Bills, books, caps, couplets, combs, a vary'd mass,
Oppress the toilet, and obscure the glass;
Unfinish'd here an epigram is laid,
And there, a mantua-maker's bill unpaid;
Here new-born plays fore-taste the town's applause,
There, dormant patterns pine for future gauze;
A moral essay now is all her care,
A satire next, and then a bill of fare:
A scene she now projects, and now a dish,
Here's Act the First—and here—Remove with Fish.
Now while this eye in a fine phrenzy rolls,
That, soberly casts up a bill for coals;
Black pins and daggers in one leaf she sticks,
And tears and thread, and balls and thimbles mix.

Sappho, 'tis true, long vers'd in epic song,
For years esteem'd all household studies wrong;
When dire mishap, though neither shame nor sin,
Sappho herself, and not her Muse, lies in.
The virgin Nine in terror fly the bower,
And matron Juno claims despotic power;
Soon Gothic hags the classic pile o'erturn,
And caudle-cup supplants the sacred urn;
Nor books, nor implements escape their rage,
They spike the ink-stand, and they rend the page;
Poems and plays one barbarous fate partake,
Ovid and Plautus suffer at the stake,
And Aristotle's only sav'd—to wrap plumb cake.

Yet, shall a *woman* tempt the Tragic Scene?
And dare—but hold—I must repress my spleen;
I see your hearts are pledg'd to her applause,
While Shakespeare's Spirit seems to aid her cause;
Well pleas'd to aid—since o'er his sacred bier

A female hand did ample trophies rear,
And gave the greenest laurel that is worshipp'd there.

[From *The Lady's Magazine* for December, 1779, in which month it appeared also in *The Town and Country Magazine*. *The Fatal Falsehood* was acted at Covent Garden on May 6th, 1779. Hannah More, the author, seems to have asked Sheridan to write an Epilogue to her previous tragedy *Percy*, and received from him a consent which came to nothing. At that time, (1777) he was continually being solicited for Prologues or Epilogues. Jephson wanted him to write one for *The Law of Lombardy*. The Epilogue for *The Fatal Falsehood* might have been written for any play by a "female author"; it is one of the best things Sheridan ever wrote. The description of Corilla's toilet, a perfect picture of the "blue stocking" of the day, is as consummate in its finish as the neatest raillery of Pope. In Sheridan's rough draft for this Epilogue, says Mr. Sichel (*Sheridan*, vol. I, p. 542), "there were no less than one hundred and forty-five unrhymed, unrhythmical lines, most of them discarded, before the admired description of Corilla's toilet begins. It well exemplifies his uncouth and bewildering way of shaping verses. . . . Satirising affectation, for instance, he treats us to the following disjointed farrago:

A less substantial, but more lovely, cargo there
Is the loving(?) voice of th' accomplished Fair—
Not swayed by malice nor by surly zeal,—
The rougher sciences are ne'er of use—
Nor proud ambition, nor uncouth policy,
Nor slighted vows, nor solitary woe, ...
As in a Turtle with an eagle's wing,
As well may build a Chinese Temple on a base of stone."

The interest of this quotation is that it finally proves that these were the verses Sheridan had not finished in January, 1779, when he wrote Garrick that "idle as such employment is, I have been diverted from it by one thing or other more idle even than rhyming." He added, "I mean to be vastly civil to female talent of all sorts, and even to the affectation of it where the person is very handsome (for the grace of Venus which passes all understanding, atones for an abundance of frailty)." The desire "to be vastly civil to female talent" lingered rather heavily in the closing couplets, which were obviously a compliment to Mrs. Montagu's *Essay on the Writings and Genius of Shakespeare*. But the picture of Corilla's toilet is superb in balance and cadence, grace and wit.

It should be noted that the germ of this Epilogue is to be found as the description of a military lady's toilet in *The Camp* (Act II, scene iii), in a lost passage recovered by me. Apparently when Sheridan wrote the Epilogue, he deleted this passage from the prompt-book, but its presence is a great argument in favour of his authorship of *The Camp*.]

Prologue to *The Miniature Picture*

Written by R. B. SHERIDAN, Esq.

CHILL'D by rude gales, while yet reluctant May
   Withholds the beauties of the vernal day,
   As some fond maid, whom matron frowns reprove,
Suspends the smile her heart devotes to love,
The Season's pleasures too delay their hour,
And Winter revels with protracted pow'r;
Then blame not, Critics, if thus late we bring
A Winter's Drama,—but reproach—the Spring.
What prudent Cit dares yet the season trust,
Bask in his whisky, and enjoy the dust?
Hors'd in Cheapside, scarce yet the gayer Spark
Atchieves the Sunday triumph of the Park;
Scarce yet you see him, dreading to be late,
Scour the New-road, and dash through Grosvenor-gate;
Anxious—yet timorous too—his steed to show,
The hack'd Bucephalus of Rotten-row!
Careless he seems, yet, vigilantly sly,
Woos the stray glance of ladies passing by,
While his off heel, insidiously aside,
Provokes the caper which he seems to chide,
Scarce rural Kensington due honour gains,
The vulgar verdure of her walks remains!
Where white-rob'd Misses amble two by two,
Nodding to booted Beaux—"How do? How do?"
With generous questions that no answer wait—
"How vastly full! A'n't you come vastly late?
I'n't it quite charming? When do you leave town?
A'n't you quite tir'd? Pray can we set you down?"

These suburb pleasures of a London May,
Imperfect yet, we hail the cold delay;
But if this plea's denied, in our excuse
Another still remains you can't refuse;
It is a lady writes—and hark!—a noble Muse!
But see a Critic starting from his bench—
"A noble Author?"—Yes, Sir, but the Play's not French:
Yet if it were, no blame on us could fall,
For we, you know, must follow Fashion's call,
And true it is, things lately were *en train*
To woo the Gallic Muse at Drury Lane;
Not to import a troop of foreign elves,
But treat you with French actors—in ourselves:
A friend we had, who vowed he'd make us speak
Pure flippant French—by contract—in a week.
Told us 'twas time to study what was good,
Polish, and leave off being understood;
That crouded audiences we thus might bring
To Monsieur Parsons, and Chevalier King:
Or should the vulgar grumble now and then,
The Prompter might translate—for country gentlemen.
Straight all subscribed—Kings, Gods, Mutes, Singer, Actor,—
A Flanders figure-dancer our contractor.
But here, I grieve to own, tho't be to you,
He acted—e'en as most contractors do;
Sold what he never dealt in, and th' amount
Being first discharged, submitted his account:
And what th' event? Their industry was such,
Dodd spoke good Flemish, Bannister bad Dutch.
Then the rogue told us, with insulting ease,
So it was foreign, it was sure to please:
Beaux, wits, applaud, as fashion should command,
And Misses laugh—to seem to understand—
So from each clime our clime may something gain;
Manhood from Rome, and sprightliness from Spain;
Some Russian Roscius next delight the age,
And a Dutch Heinel skate along the stage.

Exotic fopperies, hail! whose flatt'ring smile
Supplants the sterner virtues of our isle!
Thus, while with Chinese firs and Indian pines
Our nurseries swarm, the British oak declines:
Yet, vain our Muse's fear—no foreign laws
We dread, while native beauty pleads our cause:
While you're to judge, whose smiles are honours higher
Than verse should gain, but where those eyes inspire.
But if the men presume your pow'r to awe,
Retort their churlish senatorial law;
This is *your* house,—and move—the gentlemen withdraw:
Then they may vote, with envy never ceasing,
Your influence has increas'd, and is increasing;
But there, I trust, the resolution's finish'd;
Sure none will say—it ought to be diminish'd.

[From *The Annual Register for* 1780. *The Miniature Picture* by the Countess of Craven (afterwards Margravine of Anspach), was acted at Drury Lane on May 24th, 1780, although it was not printed (apparently) till 1781. (But see the Bibliography.) The first thirty lines of this Prologue were afterwards made frugally to serve as the Prologue to *Pizarro,* with this added couplet:

> Should our Play please—and you're indulgent ever
> Kindly decree, "'tis better late than never."]

Epilogue to *The Fair Circassian*

Written by a Friend.

Spoken by Miss FARREN.

OF late at Westminster,[1] in order due,
A gracious speech first made, debates ensue.
Ere then, in this *full house*, our author's fate
Becomes the subject of your warm debate—
Ere yet you opposition-criticks rise
To move for censures, and refuse supplies;
Or partial friends pour down corrupt applause,
By *orders* pension'd in the author's cause,
From either party—none will sure impeach
My sovereign title to pronounce the speech.

Through me the muse her *loyal subjects* greets—
Tho' I speak standing, and you keep your seats—
Pleas'd that so full a house attends the summons—
Pit—Box—and Gallery—Peers and faithful Commons—
With deep concern she bids me here relate
What dangers threaten the dramatic state—
What hosts of foes her tottering realms invade,
By fashion muster'd, and by folly paid:
While *Taste*, her old ally, unmov'd we see,
And *Spleen* preserves an *arm'd neutrality*.
See first come on—all arm'd in whalebone hoops—
The tuneful leaders of the Italian troops.
Long have they wag'd—too oft with conquest crown'd—
The doubtful conflict betwixt sense and sound.

[1]The first night's representation happened on the opening of Parliament.—Original footnote.

Allied with these—in hoſtile bands advance
The light-heel'd legions of invading France.
To point her thunders on our British coaſt,
Year after year, has been vain Gallia's boaſt.
Their troops embark—the bold attempt is plann'd—
Their *heroes threaten*—and their *dancers land.*—
These only put their threats in execution,
And lay all London under contribution.
Immortal chiefs! who on one leg can do
What yet no warrior has atchiev'd on two.
Like Rome's proud viĉtor, in their fierce attack,
They come, they see, they conquer, and—go back.
And, modern Jasons, as of old in Greece,
Sail home triumphant with the golden fleece.

Before such dangers shall we proſtrate fall?
Or, like true Britons, boldly brave them all?
If fairly led, we'll bid their hoſt defiance,
Dissolv'd a late *unnatural alliance*;
Our leader too shall now assiſtance lend,
Not promise succours, and delay to send:
But chiefly *here*—our hopes and courage lie
In *you*, our trueſt friend and beſt ally—
Support our Bard to-night, and on his part
Receive the *tribute* of a grateful heart—
Thro' me receive, and here again I'll meet ye,
Aĉt as ambassadress, and sign the treaty.

[From *The Lady's Magazine* for December, 1781. The attribution of this Epilogue
to Sheridan is due to Mr. I. A. Williams in an article in *The London Mercury* for
August, 1924. In this he quoted a letter (in the possession of Mr. Herbert E.
Norris, of Cirencester) without place or date from S. J. Pratt, the author of *The Fair
Circassian*, to "R. B. Sheridan, Esq., Norfolk Street." He begins by thanking
Sheridan for the manner in which the tragedy was "got up," and ends with a postscript mentioning that he proposes to dedicate it to the Prince of Wales, whom "one
may suppose will be a Hamet." This proves that the tragedy was *The Fair Circassian*,
—the dedication of which to the Prince of Wales, remarks that, "at this bright and
unprejudiced crisis of your life, the precepts of Omar and the practice of Hamet, as
drawn by Hawkesworth, and dramatised by the author of this tragedy, will win upon
your attention." In the course of the letter, Pratt say, "the press stands still for the
Epilogue, of which I have got a copy, and wait only to know whether I may join the

name of its excellent author or only say in my printed Tragedy, by a friend." Sheridan's name appeared in none of the three editions of *The Fair Circassian,* whose Epilogue was printed anonymously. Mr. Williams adds: "After the Dedication follows a Preface, at the end of which come the following sentences:

The liberal, perhaps the unequalled support which the managers have afforded by the scenery, the interesting manner in which Mr. Linley has set the Epithalamium, the taste of Mr. De Loutherberg, and the splendour which the performers have thrown over the characters by their excellent representation, demand and receive the most warm and pointed expressions of gratitude. There remains but one tribute of justice more, and *that* is due to Mr. Sheridan, whose attention has, on this occasion, been friendship, and whose assistance must always be fame.

So that it will be seen that, though (owing no doubt to Sheridan's wish) Pratt did not particularise Sheridan's assistance, he did, in a general way, acknowledge it.

"The printed play has two Prologues (printed at the beginning), and one Epilogue (printed at the end). The first Prologue is 'By a Friend,' and the second 'By Miss [Anna] Seward.' The Epilogue is simply described as 'Spoken by Miss Farren," without any hint as to its author's identity—which would lead one—other things being equal—to suppose that Pratt himself wrote it. However, in the light of the letter now in Mr. Norris's possession, it seems pretty clear that this Epilogue must be by Sheridan, who probably did not wish his name to be associated with it, authors being somewhat nice about acknowledging trifles of this kind. Moreover the style is much in favour of my supposition, as is the matter—especially the parliamentary simile, for Sheridan was fond of political jokes, and had comparatively recently (September 12, 1780) been returned to Parliament as member for Stafford. The fact that Pratt, in his letter, suggested the phrase 'By a Friend,' may suggest, perhaps, that the first Prologue, and not the Epilogue, was Sheridan's work. But I do not think this confusion is likely, especially as the first Prologue is a much less lively piece of work than the Epilogue."

Perhaps the reason that Sheridan concealed his authorship is to be found in the mention of the French dancers. In the summer of 1781, Vestris, "le Dieu de danse," paid his first visit to London with his son Auguste, and they returned to Paris with £20,000,—paid them by the proprietors of the Opera House, one of whom was Sheridan. In "the great tragick ballet of *Jason and Medea,* composed by the celebrated Noverre," the elder Vestris had his greatest part—"his forcible manner of characterising the passions in the part of Jason first distinguished him as an actor superior to all his contemporaries," said *The London Magazine* for April, 1780.]

Epilogue for a Benefit Play

IN this gay month, when through the sultry hour
The vernal sun denies the wonted show'r,
When youthful spring usurps maturer sway
And pallid April steals the blush of May,
How joys the rustic tribe to view display'd
The lib'ral blossom and the early shade!
But ah! far other air our soil delights,
Here "charming weather" is the worst of blights,
No genial beams rejoice our rustic train;
Their harvest's still the better for the rain!
To summer suns our groves no tribute owe,
They thrive in frost, and flourish best in snow,
While other woods resound the feather'd throng,
Our groves, our woods, are destitute of song:
The thrush, the lark, all leave our mimic vale,
No more we boast our Christmas nightingale,
Poor Rossignol—the wonder of his day,
Sang through the winter, but is mute in May.
Then bashful spring, that gilds fair nature's scene,
O'ercasts our lawns, and deadens ev'ry green,
Obscures our sky, embrowns the wooden shade,
And dries the channel of each tin cascade.
Oh, hapless we, whom such ill-fate betides,
Hurt by the beam which cheers the world besides!
Who love the ling'ring frost, nice chilling show'rs,
While Nature's *Benefit*—is death to ours,
Who, witch-like, best in noxious mists perform,
Thrive in the tempest and enjoy the storm.
Oh, hapless we! unless your generous care
Bid us no more lament that Spring is fair,
But plenteous green from the dramatic soil,
The vernal harvest of our winter's toil,

For April suns to us no pleasure bring:
Your presence here is all we feel of Spring;
May's riper beauties here no bloom display,
Your fostering smile alone proclaims it May.

[From Moore's *Life*, p. 247; Moore says, "though apparently finished, this Epilogue has not, as far as I can learn, appeared in print, nor am I at all aware for what occasion it was intended."

Those who are acquainted with old theatrical customs will however at once see that this Epilogue was spoken in April or May—when the actors took their annual "benefits," each having a day set aside for a performance whose profits went to him. A fine spring meant an empty playhouse, and an empty pocket. Mr. Sichel has unfortunately misunderstood this entirely by assigning this Epilogue, whose specific occasion is unknown, to a revival of *The Tempest* in the season of 1776-1777 at Drury Lane, when Sheridan first entered into management. This was given, not at the beginning of the season (as Mr. Sichel says), but in the middle, on January 4. This circumstance alone is decisive. But Mr. Sichel, who obviously understands the allusions to May as merely symbolical, discovers that there is a reference to Garrick's retirement in the remark about "our Christmas nightingale, poor Rossignol." But alas for this pretty fancy! Rossignol was a person of some note in his day, but although a century has passed since Moore printed this Epilogue, nobody has recognised his name. He was ... an imitator of bird-cries! On the second performance of *The Rivals*, this comedy was followed at Covent Garden by an opera called *The Druids*, with the additional performance of Signor Rossignol "being his tenth appearance here."

In 1783 in London and Westminster, among the entertainers of "Mr. Breslaw's Italian Company" was "the famous Rossignol from Naples, who will imitate various birds to the astonishment of the audience." He had several copyists, some of whom borrowed not only his "business" but also his name—"the English Rossignol" in 1783, and "Sieur Rossignol jun." in 1790. It has always seemed to me that in *The Critic* there *is* an unsuspected hit at their type of performance. When Tilburina says:

> Now, too, the feather'd warblers tune their notes
> Around and charm the listening grove—The lark!
> The linnet! chaffinch! bullfinch! goldfinch! greenfinch!

the obvious "business" was to give "off" the same cry for each bird (an old promptbook I once saw marked them all "cuckoo"). When Rossignol died I do not know, but the Epilogue seems to have been written soon afterwards.

He was living in 1796, when he was engaged at Plymouth Theatre by John Bernard, who wrote in his *Retrospections* (vol. II, p. 323):

"This person was the most wonderful of all the species which in my experience have flooded the Stage. His ability lay not in simply imitating the human voice, (the common province of ventriloquists, and the most attainable,) but those of all birds and beasts, and all noises whether natural or mechanical. It was difficult to say which was most to be admired in his organ—its astounding power, or its minute liquidity; for he could give you as correct an idea of the sawing of a huge piece of timber, as of the song of a linnet.

"His entertainment was divided into three parts, with two appropriate scenes, which he carried with him: the first represented an aviary and menagerie, in which he personated the keeper, and as he approached every animal or bird, gave its distinct growl or whistle; the next was the interior of a workshop, in which he pretended to be making a box, and imitated the sounds of all the implements employed. These were rendered characteristic by his dress, and somewhat humorous by his broken-English exclamations.]

Epilogue for an Unknown Play

To be spoken by a Woman of Fashion.

[A Fragment.]

THERE are some fragments of an Epilogue, apparently
intended to be spoken in the character of a Woman of
Fashion, which give a lively notion of what the poem
would have been, when complete.   The high carriages that had
just then come into fashion are thus adverted to:—

My carriage stared at!—none so high or fine—
Palmer's mail-coach shall be a sledge to mine.

.   .   .   .

No longer now the youths beside us stand,
And talking lean, and leaning press the hand;
But, ogling upward, as aloft we sit,
Straining, poor things, their ancles and their wit,
And, much too short the inside to explore,
Hang like supporters half way up the door.

The approach of a "veteran husband," to disturb these flirta-
tions and chase away the lovers, is then hinted at:—

To persecuted virtue yield assistance,
And for one hour teach younger men their distance,
Make them, in very spite, appear discreet,
And mar the public mysteries of the street.

The affectation of appearing to make love, while talking on
indifferent matters, is illustrated by the following simile:—

So when dramatic ſtatesmen talk apart,
With praſtis'd geſture and heroic ſtart,
The plot's their theme, the gaping galleries guess,
While Hull and Fearon think of nothing less.

The following lines seem to belong to the same Epilogue:—

The Campus Martius of St. James's Street,
Where the beau's cavalry pace to and fro,
Before they take the field in Rotten Row;
Where Brooks's Blues and Weltje's Light Dragoons
Dismount in files, and ogle in platoons.

[From Moore's *Life*, pp. 245-6. Since Hull and Fearon were members of the Covent
Garden company, the Epilogue may have been intended for that theatre. The date
must have been within a reasonable time of August, 1784, when the first of "Palmer's
mail-coaches" ran from London to Bristol. "Brooks's" and "Weltje's" (which Moore
misprints "Weltze's") were two of the most fashionable clubs of the time. Such clues
as to the occasion are meagre, especially as there is some doubt as to whether these
fragments all belong to the same Epilogue.

However, in 1786 Sheridan promised Burgoyne a Prologue for his new play, but
when the letter arrived which was supposed to contain it, the paper was found to be
blank. Mr. Sichel gives this anecdote on the authority of a letter from Mrs. Tickell;
he does not identify the play, though it was undoubtedly *The Heiress*. For this
comedy, the Prologue was written by General Fitzpatrick, while—as the author says
in his Preface to the printed play—he was forced "by an accident" to piece together
the Epilogue very hastily. The circumstances are a little obscure, but it seems clear
that what went astray was not the Prologue but the Epilogue, which was eventually
spoken by Miss Farren who played a Woman of Fashion, Lady Emily. (The custom
was for an actor to speak the Prologue, an actress the Epilogue.) Accordingly, this
may be a fragment of the lost Epilogue to *The Heiress*, and have nothing to do with
Covent Garden. If this surmise is correct, the complete prologue will not be discovered in any periodical, if incorrect, it may.

There seems no likelihood of discovering another epilogue, about which Moore
continues:—

He had also begun another Epilogue, directed against female gamesters, of
which he himself repeated a couplet or two to Mr. Rogers a short time before his
death, and of which there remain some few scattered traces among his papers:—

A night of fretful passion may consume
All that thou hast of beauty's gentle bloom,
And one distemper'd hour of sordid fear
Print on thy brow the wrinkles of a year.

.   .   .   .

Great figure loses, little figure wins.

.   .   .   .

Ungrateful blushes and disorder'd sighs,
Which love disclaims nor even shame supplies.

.   .   .   .

Gay smiles, which once belong'd to mirth alone,
And starting tears, which pity dares not own.

Mr. Sichel (*Sheridan*, vol. I, p. 545) sees in this fragment "a side-glance at the Duchess of Devonshire and her sister," those unrepenting gamblers. He quotes another passage:

> The loveliest energies of Beauty's Life,
> Perversely wasted in the meanest strife,
> To see quick blushes and disordered sighs,
> Which Love disowns, nor even shame supplies;
> —Sighs that were once the breath of Love alone
> And starting tears which Pity dare not own.

Another Prologue, unknown to Mr. Sichel, or any other of Sheridan's biographers or bibliographers, was written in 1777, to be spoken by Lee Lewis in the character of Harlequin. It was written "To the Memory of Harry Woodward," who died in April, 1777; Boaden preserves a fragment of it in his *Memoirs of Mrs. Siddons* (vol. I, p. 107):—

"Lee Lewes, in default of a better, had destined himself some way to succeed Woodward, and Sheridan, to whom everybody now turned as the rising muse, honoured his benefit with a few lines, which he spoke in the character of Harlequin, to the memory of Woodward:—

> "But hence with tragic strains, unless to mourn
> That LUN and MARPLOT here shall ne'er return;
> The comic muse, who still with anxious pride
> The claim of motley Pantomime denied,
> Now humbly hangs o'er Woodward's recent bier,
> Sees the fantastic mimic mourner there,
> Yet deigns to join in grief, and sheds a kindred tear.

"In reference to an art, which hurries faster than any other into oblivion, I snatch with pride every votive garland of poetic flowers, and bid them, I hope not vainly, to bloom a little longer over departed genius."]

Bibliography of the Prologues and Epilogues

[THIS list is restricted to the First Editions of plays by other authors. It is most likely that all these were originally printed as broadsides, though no copies have survived, or (at least, to my knowledge) have been recorded.]

1. EDWARD AND ELEANORA (1775.)

Edward and Eleanora: A Tragedy, Acted at the Theatre-Royal in Covent-Garden. Altered from James Thomson. And now adapted to the English Stage by Thomas Hull. London. J. Bell. 1775.

[Octavo. Not recorded by Sichel or Williams. I have not recently examined a copy, having used the first Irish edition, *Edward and Eleanora*. Dublin. W. Spotswood. MDCCLXXV. 12mo.—Also not recorded.]

2. SEMIRAMIS (1776.)

Semiramis: A Tragedy: As it is Acted At The Theatre Royal in Drury-Lane. By George Edward Ayscough, Esq. London: Printed for J. Dodsley, In Pall-Mall. M.DCC.LXXVI.

8vo. pp. viii + 76.

3. SIR THOMAS OVERBURY (1777.)

Sir Thomas Overbury: A Tragedy. Altered from the Late Mr. Richard Savage. As now performing at the Theatre-Royal in Covent-Garden. London. Printed by William Woodfall; And sold by Francis Newbery. The Corner Of St. Paul's Church-Yard. M. DCC.LXXVII. [Price, One Shilling and Six-Pence.]

8vo. Pp. viii+84.

[Some copies read "Printed by William Woodfall For Francis Newbery," and add, after the price, "Entered at Stationer's Hall." These must be a second issue.]

SHERIDAN'S PLAYS AND POEMS
290 SHERIDAN'S PLAYS AND POEMS

4. THE FATAL FALSEHOOD (1779.)

The Fatal Falsehood: A Tragedy. As It Is Acted At The Theatre-Royal, In Covent-Garden. By The Author of Percy. London: Printed For T. Cadell, In The Strand, M. DCC. LXXIX. (Price One Shilling And Six Pence.)

8vo. Pp. viii+84.

5. THE MINIATURE PICTURE (1781.)

The Miniature Picture: A Comedy. In Three Acts: Performed At The Theatre-Royal Drury-Lane. London: Printed for G. Riley, Bookseller, at the City Circulating Library, St. Paul's Church-yard. M.DCC.LXXXI. 8vo. Pp. 92.

Pagination. Half-title: recto, The Miniature Picture: A Comedy. Price One Shilling and Six-Pence. verso: blank. Pp. [i]—[x] title, etc.; pp. [9] +10-87, text; p. [88] "Books Printed for G. Riley."

[This curious pagination makes me suspect a previous issue; it was apparently caused by the reprinting of the prefatory matter with the addition of an "Advertisement" which complains of the bad acting. This suspicion, I feel, would be confirmed by an inspection of the copy in the Henry H. Huntington Library, California; this formerly belonged to John Larpent, the Reader of Plays for the Lord Chamberlain, who licensed a *printed* copy on May 22nd, 1780, two days before the performance at Drury Lane.]

6. THE FAIR CIRCASSIAN (1781.)

The Fair Circassian. A Tragedy. As Performed At The Theatre-Royal, Drury-Lane, By the Author Of Sympathy, A Poem. London: Printed For R. Baldwin, No. 47, Pater-Noster Row: MDCCLXXXI. *Half title*. The Fair Circassian. A Tragedy. [Price 1s. 6d.]

8vo. pp. xii+80.

[Not recorded by Sichel. The identification of the anonymous Epilogue as Sheridan's is due to Mr. Iolo A. Williams, who discovered it after he had published his Sheridan Bibliography.]

Miscellanea and Apocrypha

Note

THIS survey of the Miscellaneous and Apocryphal Works deals with *Affectation* and *The Foresters*, two unfinished plays—with *The Storming of Fort Omoa*, and *The Glorious First of June*, two unpublished interludes—with *Robinson Crusoe*, an unpublished pantomime—with the unpublished alteration of *The Tempest*—with seven plays in which Sheridan is supposed to have collaborated—with the political parodies bearing the titles of Sheridan's plays, and with several lesser topics.

R.C.R.

CONTENTS

Unfinished Plays

AFFECTATION, A COMEDY

"**M**R. SHERIDAN has made considerable progress with his new comedy of *Affectation*, which will succeed the opera of Mr. Tickell, the parts of which are already distributed." So said *The Morning Post* of November 6th, 1781. "Mr. Tickell's Opera," *The Carnival of Venice*, was duly performed on December 13th, but it was not succeeded by *Affectation*. As *The European Magazine* for February, 1782, in its "Account of Sheridan," said "though we are frequently informed that an opera called *The Foresters* and a Comedy called *Affectation* are soon to be produced, we have expected them so long, that we now have no reliance on any assurances that can be given respecting these pieces." This leaves no doubt that these were the two unnamed plays mentioned in *The London Magazine* for November, 1778, which stated in a "Memoir of Sheridan" that "it is said he has a comedy and a comic opera nearly ready for the stage." Even as late as April, 1795, as Mr. Sichel discovered from contemporary announcements, he was still reported as having "nearly ready for the stage" the same two pieces. About the same period Queen Charlotte enquired, after a command performance of *The School for Scandal*, when his pen was to give them another play. He replied that he was writing a comedy, which he expected very shortly to finish. It was Michael Kelly, hearing the story next day, who gave the reason, as he tells in his *Reminiscences*, that Sheridan never finished *Affectation*.

"You will never write again," said Kelly. "You are afraid to write."

Sheridan fixing his "penetrating eye" on Kelly, asked, "Of whom am I afraid?"

"You are afraid of the author of *The School for Scandal*."

Although the reports that Sheridan was writing his new comedy of *Affectation* cover a period of twenty years the fragments which survive are, as it were, watermarked 1778. There are touches of the camp jargon:

A true trained wit lays his plan like a general—foresees the circumstances of the conversation—surveys the ground and contingencies—detaches a question to draw you into the palpable ambuscade of his ready-made joke.

I made regular approaches to her by sonnets and rebusses —a rondeau of circumvallation—her pride sapped by an elegy and her reserve surprised by an impromptu—proceeding to storm with Pindarics, she, at last, saved the further effusion of ink by a capitulation.

It was this affectation that Sheridan ridiculed in *The Camp*:

this madness has infected the whole road from Maidstone to London; the camp jargon is as current all the way as bad silver; the very postillions that drive you talk of their cavalry, and refuse to charge on a trot up the hill, the turnpikes seem converted into redoubts, and the dogs demanded the countersign of my servants, instead of the tickets: then when I got to Maidstone, I found the very waiters had got a smattering of tactics, for inquiring what I could have for dinner, a cursed drill waiter, after reviewing his bill of fare with the air of a field-marshal, proposed an advanced party of soup and bouille to be followed by the main body of ham and chickens, flanked by a fricasee, with sallads in the intervals, and a corps de reserve of sweetmeats and whipt syllabubs to form a hollow square in the centre.

So, too, there is much in the mood and style of *The Critic*. Mr. Puff's account of "the full accomplishment of modern gallantry" is anticipated:—

What are the affectations you chiefly dislike?

There are many in this company, so I'll mention others.—

To see two people affecting intrigue, having their assignations in public places only; he, affecting a warm pursuit, and the lady, acting the hesitation of retreating virtue—Pray, ma'am, don't you think, &c.—while neither party have words between 'em to conduct the preliminaries of gallantry, nor passion to pursue the object of it.

A plan of public flirtation—not to get beyond a profile.

A man intriguing, only for the reputation of it—to his confidential servant: "Who am I in love with now?"—"The newspapers give you so and so—you are laying close siege to Lady L. in *The Morning Post*, and have succeeded with Lady G. in *The Herald*—Sir F. is very jealous of you in *The Gazetteer*.—"Remember to-morrow, the first thing you do, to put me in love with Mrs. C."

"I forgot to forget the billet-doux at Brooks's."—"By-the by, an't I in love with you?"—"Lady L. has promised to meet me in her carriage to-morrow; where is the most public place?"

It seems, indeed, as if Sheridan began to work upon *Affectation* as soon as *The School for Scandal* was performed, but put it aside while engaged upon *The Camp* and *The Critic*. Either the reports that he had "nearly finished" this comedy were ridiculously exaggerated, by himself as by others, or the piece must have existed in a more developed form than these jottings. But Michael Kelly, who was one of his closest friends and associates, ended the list of Sheridan's plays by saying that "he began an opera called *The Foresters*, and had written an act or two of a comedy which he had never finished."

Moore, in printing the extracts, wrote:—

"But, of all Mr. Sheridan's unfinished designs, the Comedy which he meditated on the subject of *Affectation* is that of which the abandonment is most to be regretted. To a satirist, who would not confine his ridicule to the mere outward demonstra-

tions of this folly, but would follow and detect it through all
its windings and disguises, there could hardly perhaps be a
more fertile theme. Affectation, merely of *manner*, being itself
a sort of acting, does not easily admit of any additional colour-
ing on the stage, without degenerating into farce; and, accordingly, fops and fine ladies—with very few exceptions—
are about as silly and tiresome in representation as in reality.
But the aim of the dramatist, in this comedy, would have been
far more important and extensive;—and how anxious he was
to keep before his mind's eye the whole wide horizon of folly
which his subject opened upon him, will appear from the following list of the various species of Affectation, which were
written by him on the inside cover of the memorandum-book,
that contains the only remaining vestiges of this play:—

> An Affectation of Business.
>   of Accomplishments.
>   of Love of Letters and Wit
>   Music.
>   of Intrigue.
>   of Sensibility.
>   of Vivacity.
>   of Silence and Importance.
>   of Modesty.
>   of Profligacy.[1]
>   of Moroseness.

In this projected comedy he does not seem to have advanced
as far as even the invention of the plot, or the composition of a

---

[1]The germ of *Affectation* is to be found, I think, in Sheridan's adaptation of *The
Goblins* (circa 1772) the so-called *Drama of Devils*. Pamphiles, a soldier, is brought be-
fore Pevidor, the Devil-Judge, in a place which is feigned to be Hell. Pamphiles is directed
to speak "affectedly." His crime is the Affectation of Profligacy:
Pevidor. Indeed! what was thy employment then, friend?
Pamphiles. Hunting—
Pevidor. 'Tis false.
Pamphiles. Hunting women's reputations.
Pevidor. What, thou wert amorous?
Pamphiles. No, on my honour, sir, but vain, confounded vain—the character of bring-
ing down my game was all I wished, and, like a true sportsman, I would have given my
birds to my pointers.
Pevidor. This crime is new—

single scene. The memorandum-book alluded to—on the first leaf of which he had written in his neatest hand (as if to encourage himself to begin) "Affectation"—contains, besides the names of three of the intended personages, Sir Babble Bore, Sir Peregrine Paradox, and Feignwit, nothing but unembodied sketches of character, and scattered particles of wit, which seem waiting, like the imperfect forms and seeds in chaos, for the brooding of genius to nurse them into system and beauty."

"In this work," Moore adds, "as well as in *The School for Scandal*, he was desirous of making the vintage of his wit as rich as possible, by distilling into it every drop that the collected fruits of his thought and fancy could supply. Some of the jests are far-fetched, and others, perhaps, abortive —but it is pleasant to track him in his pursuit of a point, even when he misses. The very failures of a man of real wit are often more delightful than the best successes of others—the quicksilver, even in escaping from his grasp shines; *it still eludes him, but it glitters still*."

Moore's memoranda are given, as he printed them, "with no other difference, than that of classing together those that have relation to the same thought or subject."

Character.—Mr. Bustle.

A man who delights in hurry and interruption—will take any one's business for them—leaves word where all his plagues may follow him—governor of all hospitals, &c.—share in Ranelagh —speaker every where, from the Vestry to the House of Commons—"I am not at home—gad, now he has heard me and I must be at home."—"Here am I so plagued, and there is nothing I love so much as retirement and quiet."—"You never sent after me. —Let servants call in to him such a message as "Tis nothing but the window-tax,' he hiding in a room that communicates.—A young man tells him some important business in the middle of fifty trivial interruptions, and the calling in of idlers, such as fidlers, wild-beast men, foreigners with recommendatory letters, &c.—answers notes on his knee, 'and so your uncle died?'—for your obliging enquiries—and left you an orphan—to cards in the evening."

"Can't bear to be doing nothing."—"Can I do anything for any body any where?"—"Have been to the Secretary—written to the Treasury."—"Must proceed to meet the Commissioners, and write Mr. Price's little boy's exercise."—The most active idler and laborious trifler.

He does not in reality love business—only the appearance of it. "Ha! ha! did my Lord say that I was always very busy?—What, plagued to death?"

Keeps all his letters and copies—"Mem. to meet the Hackney-coach Commissioners—to arbitrate between &c. &c."

Contrast with the man of indolence, his brother.—"So, brother, just up! and I have been &c. &c."—one will give his money from indolent generosity, the other his time from restlessness—"'Twill be shorter to pay the bill than look for the receipt."—Files letters, answered and unanswered—"Why, here are more unopened than answered!"

He regulates every action by a love of fashion—will grant annuities though he doesn't want money—appear to intrigue, though constant, to drink, though sober—has some fashionable vices—affects to be distressed in his circumstances, and, when his new vis-a-vis comes out, procures a judgment to be entered against him—wants to lose, but by ill-luck wins five thousand pounds.

One who changes sides in all arguments the moment any one agrees with him.

An irresolute arguer, to whom it is a great misfortune that there are not three sides to a question—a libertine in argument; conviction, like enjoyment, palls him, and his rakish understanding is soon satiated with truth—more capable of being faithful to a paradox[1]—"I love truth as I do my wife; but sophistry and paradoxes are my mistresses—I have a strong domestic respect for her, but for the other the passion due to a mistress."

One, who agrees with every one, for the pleasure of speaking

[1]This surely must characterise Windham.—*Sichel*.

their sentiments for them— so fond of talking that he does not contradict only because he can't wait to hear people out.

A tripping casuist, who veers by others breath, and gets on to information by tacking between the two sides— like a hoy, not made to go straight before the wind.

The more he talks, the farther he is off the argument, like a bowl on a wrong bias.

———

"What are the affectations you chiefly dislike?"

There are many in this company, so I'll mention others.—To see two people affecting intrigue, having their assignations in public places only; he, affecting a warm pursuit, and the lady, acting the hesitation of retreating virtue—'Pray, ma'am don't you think, &c.'—while neither party have words between 'em to conduct the preliminaries of gallantry, nor passion to pursue the object of it.

A plan of public flirtation—not to get beyond a profile.

———

Then I hate to see one, to whom heaven has given real beauty settling her features at the glass of fashion, while she speaks——not thinking so much of what she says as how she looks, and more careful of the action of her lips than of what shall come from them.

A pretty woman studying looks and endeavouring to recollect an ogle, like Lady ——, who has learned to play her eyelids like Venetian blinds.[1]

An old woman endeavouring to put herself back to a girl.

———

A true trained wit lays his plan like a general—foresees the circumstances of the conversation—surveys the ground and contingencies—detaches a question to draw you into the palpable ambuscade of his ready-made joke.

———

A man intriguing, only for the reputation of it—to his confidential servant: "Who am I in love with now?"—"The news-

[1]This simile is repeated in various shapes through his manuscripts—"She moves her eyes up and down like Venetian blinds"—"Her eyelids play like a Venetian blind," &c. &c.—*Moore.*

paper give you so and so—you are laying close siege to Lady L. in *The Morning Post*, and have succeeded with Lady G. in *The Herald*—Sir F. is very jealous of you in the *Gazetteer*."—"Remember to-morrow, the first thing you do, to put me in love with Mrs. C."

"I forgot to forget the billet-doux at Brooks's."—"By the bye, an't I in love with you?"—"Lady L. has promised to meet me in her carriage to-morrow—where is the most public place?"

"You were rude to her!"—"Oh no, upon my soul, I made love to her directly."

An old man, who affects intrigue, and writes his own reproaches in *The Morning Post*, trying to scandalise himself into the reputation of being young, as if he could obscure his age by blotting his character—though never so little candid as when he's abusing himself.

———

'Shall you be at Lady———'s?—I'm told the Bramin is to be there, and the new French philosopher."—"No—it will be pleasanter at Lady ———'s conversazione—the cow with two heads will be there.'

———

"I shall order my valet to shoot me the very first thing he does in the morning."

———

"You are yourself affected and don't know it—you would pass for morose."

He merely wanted to be singular, and happened to find the character of moroseness unoccupied in the society he lived with.

He certainly has a great deal of fancy and a very good memory, but with a perverse ingenuity he employs these qualities as no other person does— for he employs his fancy in his narratives and keeps his recollections for his wit—when he makes his jokes you applaud the accuracy of his memory, and 'tis only when he states his facts, that you admire the flights of his imagination.

———

A fat woman trundling into a room on castors—in sitting can only lean against her chair—rings on her fingers, and her fat arm

ſtrangled with bracelets, which belt them like corded brawn—
rolling and heaving when she laughs with the rattles in her
throat, and a moſt apopleƈtic ogle—you wish to draw her out,
as you would an opera-glass.

A long lean man, with all his limbs rambling—no way to reduce him to compass, unless you could double him like a pocket
rule—with his arms spread, he'd lie on the bed of Ware like
cross on a Good Friday bun—ſtanding ſtill, he is a pilaſter without a base— he appears rolled out or run up againſt a wall—so
thin, that his front face is but the moiety of a profile—if he ſtands
cross-legged, he looks like a caduceus, and put him in a fencing
attitude, you would take him for a piece of chevaux-de-frise—to
make any use of him, it muſt be as a spontoon or a fishing-rod—
when his wife's by, he follows like a note of admiration—see
them together, one's maſt, and the other all hulk—she's a dome
and he's built like a glass-house— when they part, you wonder to
see the ſteeple separate from the chancel, and were they to embrace, he muſt hang round her neck like a skein of thread on a
lace-maker's bolſter—to sing her praise you should choose a
rondeau, and to celebrate him you muſt write all Alexandrines.

I wouldn't give a pin to make fine men in love with me—every
coquette can do that, and the pain you give these creatures is very
trifling. I love out-of-the-way conqueſts; and as I think my at-
traƈtions are singular, I would draw singular objeƈts.

The loadſtone of true beauty draws the heavieſt subſtances—
not like the fat dowager, who frets herself into warmth to get the
notice of a few *papier mâché* fops, as you rub Dutch sealing-wax
to draw paper.

If I were inclined to flatter I would say that, as you are unlike
other women, you ought not to be won as they are. Every woman
can be gained by time, therefore you ought to be by a sudden impulse. Sighs, devotion, attention weigh with others; but they are
so much your due that no one should claim merit from them. . . .

You should not be swayed by common motives—how heroic
to form a marriage for which no human being can guess the in-

ducement—what a glorious unaccountableness! All the world will wonder what the devil you could see in me; and, if you should doubt your singularity, I pledge myself to you that I never yet was endured by woman; so that I should owe every thing to the effect of your bounty, and not by my own superfluous deserts make it a debt, and so lessen both the obligation and my gratitude. In short, every other woman follows her inclination, but you above all things, should take me, if you do not like me. You will, besides, have the satisfaction of knowing that we are decidedly the worst match in the kingdom—a match, too, that must be all your own work, in which fate could have no hand, and which no foresight could foresee.

A lady who affects poetry.—"I made regular approaches to her by sonnets and rebusses—a rondeau of circumvallation— her pride sapped by an elegy, and her reserve surprised by an im- promptu—proceeding to storm with Pindarics, she, at last, saved the further effusion of ink by a capitulation."

Her prudish frowns and resentful looks are as ridiculous as 'twould be to see a board with notice of spring-guns set in a high- way, or of steel-traps in a common—because they imply an in- sinuation that there is something worth plundering where one would not, in the least, suspect it.

The expression of her face is at once a denial of all love-suit, and a confession that she never was asked— the sourness of it arises not so much from her aversion to the passion, as from her never having had an opportunity to show it.—Her features are so un- fortunately formed that she could never dissemble or put on sweetness enough to induce any one to give her occasion to show her bitterness.—I never saw woman to whom you would more readily give credit for perfect chastity.

Lady Clio. "What am I reading"?—"have I drawn nothing lately?—is the work-bag finished?—how accomplished I am!— has the man been to untune the harpsichord?—does it look as if I had been playing on it?

"Shall I be ill to-day?—shall I be nervous?"—"Your La'ship was nervous yesterday."—"Was I?—then I'll have a cold—I haven't had a cold this fortnight—a cold is becoming—no—I'll not have a cough; that's fatiguing—I'll be quite well."—"You become sickness—your La'ship always looks vastly well when you're ill."

"Leave the book half read and the rose half finished—you know I love to be caught in the fact."

One who knows that no credit is ever given to his assertions has the more right to contradict his words.

He goes the western circuit, to pick up small fees and impudence.

A new wooden leg for Sir Charles Easy.

An ornament which proud peers wear all the year round—chimney-sweepers only on the first of May.

In marriage if you possess anything very good, it makes you eager to get everything else good of the same sort.

The critic when he gets out of his carriage should always recollect, that his footman behind is gone up to judge as well as himself.

She might have escaped in her own clothes, but, I suppose, she thought it more romantic to put on her brother's regimentals.

THE FORESTERS

(And the Adaptation of The Goblins)

THE masque or comic opera of The Foresters was reported as being "nearly ready for the stage" as frequently as Affectation, and over the same long period. Richard Tickell mentioned it in a preface he wrote for The Rivals, not, of course, for publication, but as a sort of humorous anticipation of what would be written by Editors of, say, the present century.

"With Fox and a few others of lesser note, Sheridan formed as desperate and profligate a gang as ever disgraced a civilized country. They were guilty of every species of enormity, and went so far as even to commit robberies on the highway, with a degree of audacity that could be equalled only by the ingenuity with which they escaped conviction. Sheridan, not satisfied with eluding, determined to mock, the justice of his country, and composed a Masque called The Foresters, containing a circumstantial account of all the robberies he had committed, and a good deal of sarcasm on the pusillanimity of those whom he had robbed, and the inefficiency of the penal laws of the kingdom. This piece was acted at Drury Lane Theatre with great applause, to the astonishment of sober persons, and the scandal of the nation."

This humorous perversion does convey (so far as one may gather from the surviving fragments) some idea of the tone and nature of The Foresters. But only a single song has been preserved "We two each other's only pride," unless (as is likely) he intended to introduce "Dry be that tear" from another discarded opera which has been called A Drama of Devils. This earlier piece has no title on the manuscript but the description, "A Wild Drama," yet it is only reasonable to regard it as the first draft of The Foresters.

In this first draft the chief personages are a band of outlaws who, under the name and disguise of Devils, terrorise a village adjoining the forest which they haunt. The name of the robber chief is Pevidor: the heroine is called Reginella, whom Mr.

Sichel compared to Miranda. It is curious that nobody has followed a clue which is cited by Mr. Sichel from *The Gentleman's Magazine* for January, 1840. This states that "Sheridan left an unfinished sketch which remodelled *The Goblins* by Suckling, and adapted that comedy to the modern stage." If the pursuit had commenced in so obvious a place as the familiar *Companion to the Playhouse* (1764), it would have been at once discovered, under *The Goblins* that Suckling "in the execution of his Design, followed the footsteps of Shakespear, of whom he was a close admirer, his Reginella being an open imitation of Miranda in *The Tempest*, and his Goblins (though only Thieves in Disguise) yet seem to have been copied from the same play."

The Drama of Devils is in short, an immature attempt to adapt *The Goblins*. As an Edition of Suckling, the first for many years, appeared in 1770, 12mo, it is possible that some of the dialogue dates from that period, though the incorporation of the song "Dry be that tear" suggests a later time. But there are two songs, not by Suckling, which have a curiously Elizabethan ring. They are all sung by the Foresters in their assumed character of Devils:

Catch

In the earth's centre let me live,
There, like a rabbit will I thrive,
Nor care if fools should call my life infernal:
While men on earth crawl lazily about,
Like snails upon the surface of the nut,
We are, like maggots, feasting in the kernel.

Catch

'Tis woman after all
Is the blessing of this ball,
'Tis she keeps the balance of it even.
We are devils, it is true,
But had we women too,
Our Tartarus would turn to a Heaven!

A third song, described by Moore, as "evidently the germ" of "Here's to the Maiden of Bashful Fifteen," was intended to alter a song of Suckling's with a similar refrain. It shows that, for once, the origin of this famous drinking-song is correctly alleged.

Glee

What's a woman good for?
Rat me, sir, if I know.

. . . .

She's a savour to the glass,
An excuse to make it pass.

. . . .

There is yet another song which Moore did not doubt as being Sheridan's, but it was discovered to be merely a sonnet of Sir Philip Sidney's in his *Arcadia*, slightly altered. It is sung by a huntsman with his lute to awaken Reginella, the Malvina of *The Foresters*, to whom perhaps it would have been sung by her romantic lover, the Captain of the Foresters.

Oh yield, fair lids, the treasures of my heart,
  Release those beams, that make this mansion bright,
From her sweet sense, Slumber! though sweet thou art,
  Begone, and give the air she breathes in light.

Or while, oh Sleep, thou dost those glances hide,
  Let rosy slumbers still around her play,
Sweet as the cherub Innocence enjoy'd,
  When in thy lap, new-born, in smiles he lay.

And thou, oh Dream, that com'st her sleep to cheer,
  Oh take my shape, and play a lover's part;
Kiss her from me, and whisper in her ear,
  Till her eyes shine, 'tis night within my heart.[1]

---

[1]Moore notes, "I have taken the liberty here of supplying a few rhymes and words that are wanting in the original copy of the song. The last line of all runs thus in the manuscript: *Till her eye shines I live in darkest night*—which, not rhyming as it ought, I have ventured to alter as above." This tell-tale line is Sidney's. Sigmund, in his Edition of *Sheridan*, (1848), gives the sonnet from *Arcadia* (Book III):

  Look up, faire liddes, the treasure of my heart,
  Preserve those beames, this ages only light;

There is nothing, indeed, to show at what time Sheridan relinquished the adaptation of *The Goblins*. I surmise, however, that it was when he discovered that in the trial-scene in Hell, which he developed from Suckling, there was the germ of a comic idea which he sought to exploit as the main theme of *Affectation*. Thereupon he transformed his plot by abandoning the idea of devils or goblins, and making his personages simply foresters, or rather outlaws and freebooters. Moreover, he succumbed to the influence of Ossian, not merely in the use of such names as Oscar and Malvina, Morven and Colona, but, says Mr. Sichel, "the high-flown apostrophes of Ossian swell its language."

But Sheridan was obviously dissatisfied with this fantastical nomenclature, and noted on the fly-leaf, "*Vide* Petrarch's *Laura*," from which, it seems, he intended to borrow other names. The draft of *The Foresters*, as it survives, is not very interesting. In one scene two brothers Nico and Lubin are introduced, "both equally enamoured of the fair Malvina, yet preserving their affection unaltered towards one another." Moore gives yet another hint of the autobiographic fallacy—that it would seem to recall the rivalry of Richard and Charles Sheridan for Elizabeth Linley if— he adds, it were not for the exceeding *niaiserie* of the dialogue (the third speaker is Oscar, Malvina's father):—

Nico. I should have been sooner; but Lubin would stay to make himself fine—though he knows he has no chance of appearing so to Malvina.

Lubin. No, in truth—Nico says right—I have no more chance than himself.

> To her sweet sence, sweet sleepe, some ease impart,
> Her sence too weake to beare her spirits might.
> And while, O Sleepe, thou closest up her sight,
> (Her sight, where Love did forge this fairest dart)
> O harbour all her parts in easefull plight:
> Let no strange dreame make her faire body start.
> But yet, O dreame, if thou wilt not depart,
> In this rare subject from thy common right;
> But while thyself in such a seate delight,
> Then take my shape, and play a lover's part;
> Kiss her from me, and say unto her sprite
> Till her eyes shine, I live in darkest night.

Oscar. However, I am glad to see you reconciled, and that you live together, as brothers should do.

Nico. Yes, ever since we found your daughter cared for neither of us, we grew to care for one another. There is a fellowship in adversity that is consoling; and it is something to think that Lubin is as unfortunate as myself.

Lubin. Yes, we are well matched—I think Malvina dislikes him, if possible more than me, and that's a great comfort.

Nico. For my part, I should certainly hang myself, only I think that Lubin should swing first.

Lubin. We often sit together, and play such woeful tunes on our pipes, that the very sheep are moved at it.

Oscar. But why don't you rouse yourselves, and since you can meet with no requital of your passion, return the proud maid scorn for scorn.

Nico. Oh mercy, no—we find a great comfort in our sorrow—don't we, Lubin?

Lubin. Yes, if I meet no crosses, I shall be undone in another twelvemonth—I let all go to wreck and ruin.

Oscar. But suppose Malvina should be brought to give you encouragement.

Nico. Heaven forbid! that would spoil all.

Lubin. Truly I was almost assured within this fortnight that she was going to relax.

Nico. Ay, I shall never forget how alarmed we were at the appearance of a smile one day.

Where Moore sees only *niaiserie*, Mr. Sichel discerns more justly in this comic dolorousness an anticipation of a humorist of a much later era, W. S. Gilbert.

But *The Foresters* survives in too fragmentary a state to be more than a curious memorial of lost hopes. May one see in the loves of Zelie and Hassarac in *The Forty Thieves* the last, thin, forlorn echo of Malvina and her rescuer, the Captain of the Freebooters? It may be so, for Sheridan was very tenacious of his ideas. In Mr. Sichel's words, *The Foresters* was "a sentimental journey that failed."

Unpublished Interludes

THE STORMING OF FORT OMOA, 1780

AN INTERLUDE IN *Harlequin Fortunatus*

ON August 30th, 1780, according to *Aris's Gazette* of the time a performance of *The Tempest*, with songs by the younger Linley, was given at the New Street Theatre (now the Royal), Birmingham, "By particular Desire of the Noblemen and Gentlemen of the Bean Club," the famous old Warwickshire Tory Club. It was followed by

"An Interlude, written by R. B. Sheridan, Esq., taken from the Pantomime of 'Fortunatus,' representing the Storming and Taking of Fort Omoa. In which will be introduced Songs by Mr. Linley. To conclude with the song of 'Rule Britannia.'"

This advertisement was long a puzzle to me, and no biography of Sheridan, no theatrical memoir which came my way, contained any reference to this Interlude of *The Storming of Fort Omoa*.

The London Gazette of the time, however, eventually explained the event with which the Interlude was concerned. The Secretary of War, Lord George Germaine, issued from Whitehall, on December 18, 1779, a despatch from Captain Dalrymple, of the Loyal Irish Volunteers, dated from San Fernando de Omoa on October 21, 1779, narrating the capture of the fortification Porto Omoa, there described as "the key to the Bay of Honduras, where the register ships and treasure are sent to from Guatimala in time of war." In this despatch Dalrymple mentioned

an instance of an elevated mind in a British tar, which amazed the Spaniards, and gave them a very high idea of British valour. Not contented with one cutlass, he had scrambled up the walls with two, and meeting a Spanish officer without arms, who had been roused out of his sleep, had the generosity not to take any advantage; but, presenting him with one of his cutlasses, told him, "You are now on a footing with me." It further appears that the countersign of the day was "Britons strike home."

When, however, this was discovered, the rest of the enquiry offered no difficulty. *Harlequin Fortunatus* would, as a pantomime, be revived about Christmas. It was not then surprising, after a long pursuit through various uninformative periodicals, at last to discover from *The Lady's Magazine* that on January 3, 1780, "was revived at Drury Lane Theatre the old and formerly favourite pantomime called *Fortunatus or the Wishing-Cap*, with "the addition of three new scenes representing the assault and capture of Fort Omoa in the Bay of Honduras." The account continued:—

"A grand scene, so designed as to exhibit the inside of the Fort, with the guns mounted, the exterior of one of the bastions, with the fosse and counterscarp, and the harbour and British fleet, at one view is first discovered.—By the happy contrivance of this scene (which is a fresh and powerful proof of Mr. de Loutherbourg's great genius and abilities as an artist) the audience see the mode of defence used by the besieged, and the British tars in the act of scaling the walls of the Fort at the same time. The assistants proving successful as to the outworks, which they carry, the scene changes to the interior of the fort, in which is represented the singular instance of an English seaman's bravery, recited in Capt. Dalrymple's dispatch from Omoa,—a Spaniard without arms being furnished with a cutlass by a sailor, who afterwards conquers him and then spares his life. This over, the scene changes again and the surrender of the Fort in form by the Spanish governor's delivery of the keys of it is exhibited. After which the whole entertainment finishes with Mr. Vernon's singing of 'Rule Britannia,' assisted by Mr. Gaudry, and the chorus supported by most of the singing performers of the theatre. Preparatory to the exhibition of the new scenes, Mr. Bannister and Mr. Vernon have each a song; Mr. Vernon's, having for its burthen, 'Britons, strike home!' was received with loud and universal applause."

These songs (to be found in this edition among the Fugitive Verse) were "The Midnight Watch" and "Chearly, my hearts of courage true."

Michael Kelly tells in his *Reminiscences* that Sheridan, coming one day to a rehearsal of a pantomime at the theatre, found everything in confusion, because no time had been allowed for the carpenters to set a scene. It was suggested to him that a song would give them sufficient opportunity. So then and there, says Kelly, "he sat down at the prompter's table on the stage and wrote on the back of the playbill the beautiful ballad of 'The Midnight Watch,' which was set to music by his father-in-law, Mr. Linley, in a style which established it as one of the most beautiful specimens of pure English melody." Kelly heard this anecdote from Sheridan's stage-manager, Thomas King, the original Sir Peter Teazle, but he said in error that it was written for Sheridan's pantomime of *Robinson Crusoe* (1781). The ballad became very popular; it was repeated in two other patriotic interludes (both never printed), which Sheridan wrote and produced at Drury Lane Theatre, *The Glorious First of June* (1794) and *Cape St. Vincent or British Valour Triumphant* (1797).

Except for these introductory ballads, and the closing song, the Interlude was entirely pantomime, that is, dumb-show. Sheridan's scenario is not likely to be recovered.

THE GLORIOUS FIRST OF JUNE, 1794

(and Cape St. Vincent, 1797)

ALTHOUGH in 1794 Sheridan was immersed in politics, says Moore:
"He had also on his mind the care of his new Theatre, which opened on the 21st of April, with a prologue, not by himself, as might have been expected, but by his friend General Fitzpatrick. He found time, however, to assist in the rapid manufacture of a little piece called *The Glorious First of June*, which was acted immediately after Lord Howe's victory, and of which I have found some sketches in Sheridan's hand-writing,—though the dialogue was no doubt supplied (as Mr. Boaden says) by Cobb, or some other such *pedissequus* of the Dramatic Muse. This piece was written, rehearsed, and acted within three days. The first operation of Mr. Sheridan towards it was to order the mechanist of the theatre to get ready two fleets. It was in vain that objections were started to the possibility of equipping these paste-board armaments in so short an interval—Lord Chatham's famous order to Lord Anson was not more peremptory. The two fleets were accordingly ready at the time, and the Duke of Clarence attended the rehearsal of their evolution. This mixture of the cares of the Statesman and the Manager is one of those whimsical peculiarities that made Sheridan's own life so dramatic, and formed a compound altogether too singular ever to occur again."

Of Sheridan's scenario, Moore quoted this extract:—

SCENE I.—Miss *Leake*—Miss *Decamp*—*Walsh*
Short dialogue—Nancy persuading Susan to go to the Fair, where there is an entertainment to be given by the Lord of the Manor—Susan melancholy because Henry, her lover, is at sea with the British Admiral—*Song*—Her old mother scolds from the cottage—her little brother (*Walsh*) comes from the

house, with a message—laughs at his sister's fears and sings
—*Trio*.

Scene II—*The Fair*

Puppet-show—dancing bear—bells—hurdy-gurdy—recruiting party—song and chorus.

Ballet—D'Egville

Susan says she has no pleasure, and will go and take a solitary walk.

Scene III—*Dark Wood*

Susan—gipsy—tells her fortune—recitative and ditty.

Scene IV

Sea-Fight—hell and the devil!

Henry and Susan meet—Chorus introducing burden, "Rule Britannia."

Michael Kelly, in his *Reminiscences*, gives this account:

"On the 2nd of July [1794] a new musical piece was produced, entitled *The Glorious First of June!* written by Mr. Cobb, for the benefit of the widows of the brave men who fell on that day. It was well suited to the purpose, and was a sequel to *No Song, No Supper*, it was all got up in three days. Mr. Joseph Richardson wrote an elegant Prologue on the occasion, which was spoken, with great feeling by John Kemble. The piece concluded with a grand fight, and a sumptuous *fête*, in honour of our glorious victory. Storace and myself gave it some new songs; but the music was chiefly old. I had to represent the character of Frederick; and as I was much employed in writing the music, I begged Mr. Sheridan (who wrote a good many speeches for it), to make as short a part for me, and with as little speaking in it as possible. He assured me he would. In the scene in which I came on, to sing a song (written by Cobb) 'When in war on the ocean we meet the proud foe,' there was a cottage in the distance, at which (the stage direction said) I was to look earnestly, for a moment or two, and the line which I then had to speak was this:—

"*There stands my Louisa's cottage; she must either be in it or out of it.*

"The song began immediately, and not another word was there in the whole part. This sublime and solitary speech produced a loud laugh from the audience. When the piece was over, Mr. Sheridan came into the green-room, and complimented me on my quickness, and being so perfect in the part which he had taken so much pains to write for me; which, he said, considering the short time I had to study it, was truly astonishing. He certainly had the laugh against me, and he did not spare me."

The entertainment was not printed[1], but a book of Songs was issued. These were written by several hands, among them the Duke of Leeds, Lord Mulcaster, and Mrs. Robinson. Sheridan's contribution to the songs seems to have been limited to the inclusion of the two nautical songs he had written fourteen years before for the pantomime of *Harlequin Fortunatus*. Three years later, this entertainment was altered to serve in the celebrations of the victory of Cape St. Vincent.

[1]The MS. of *The Glorious First of June*, belonging to the Lord Chamberlain's Office, endorsed by the Reader of Plays, John Larpent, is now in the Henry E. Huntington Library, California (*See* Allardyce Nicoll. *XVIII Century Drama*, 1750-1800).

BIBLIOGRAPHY

Songs, Duetts, Choruses, &c. In a New And Appropriate Entertainment, Called *THE GLORIOUS FIRST OF JUNE*. Performed, For the First Time, By His Majesty's Servants, At the Theatre-Royal, Drury-Lane. For the Benefit of the Widows and Orphans of the brave Men who fell in the late Engagements under Earl Howe. London: Printed by C. Lowndes, No. 66, Drury-Lane. Next the Stage-Door, And Sold In The Theatre. Price Sixpence.

8vo.

Pagination. P. [1] Title; p. [2] blank; [3] *Persons Represented*; pp. [5] and 6-15 Text; p. [16] blank.

Songs, Duetts, Chorusses, &c. in an Occasional Entertainment called Cape St. Vincent, or British Valour Triumphant. Altered from a Dramatical Performance performed in 1794. And acted by Their Majesty's Servants at The Theatre Royal Drury Lane. London: C. Lowndes 1797.

8vo.

[Not recorded by Sichel.]

Some Supposed Collaborations

ACCORDING to Mr. Walter Sichel, Sheridan "shared in the adaptation of," "contributed to," "assisted in the preparation of," "gave some touches to," or "helped in the arrangement of," some ten plays performed under his management at Drury Lane. About this fact, expressed in terms so general, there would be no reasonable doubt, since in the course of a management that extended over thirty years, he must have given advice and assistance to numerous authors whose plays he produced. As the manager he accepted a certain responsibility— an "Editorial" responsibility is the convenient metaphor. His contemporaries expected him to revise, or cause to be revised, the plays he presented,—even in despite of their authors. For instance, in his first season at Drury Lane, *The London Magazine* declared that *The Milesian*, a comic opera by Isaac Jackman, could have been a better piece "if Mr. Sheridan was not so idle, nor the author so obstinate." But advice, assistance, and correction of this sort do not constitute collaboration: the study of them belongs to the life of Sheridan as a theatrical manager, rather than as a dramatic author. It is clear that the "Privy Council" or "Cabinet" of Drury Lane Theatre (as they were called) must have given their assistance in a great number of instances: Mrs. Sheridan acted as a reader of plays; in 1779 Sheridan told Holcroft to send to her the MS. of an afterpiece in which he was interested, Dibdin's *The Shepherdess of the Alps*. It was probably Mrs. Sheridan, and not her husband, who collaborated in 1786 with Burgoyne in adapting *Richard Cœur de Lion* from the French. To her; to Richard Tickell; and, in later years, to Tom Sheridan, he seems to have delegated many of his duties as a theatrical manager. But it would be interesting to know whether he prepared for the stage the comedy of *The Fathers* in 1778, when this lost play of Henry Fielding's had been recovered "in a tatter'd manuscript." An Advertisement to the printed play[1] acknowledges the "kindeſt assiſtance" which he had shown to "the fragment"and attributes "much of the applause with which it had been received" to Garrick's Prologue and Epilogue, and to "the very liberal and friendly assiſtance of Mr. Sheridan." This comedy has escaped Mr. Sichel; but it might be surmised that it contains more of Sheridan's work than is to be found in six pieces of which he gives details: *The Carnival of Venice* (1781), *Harlequin Hurly-Burly* (1785), *The Heiress* (1786), *Richard Cœur de Lion* (1786), *The Doctor and the Apothecary* (1788), and *Thelypthoros* (1790). However, since Sheridan as a song writer comes under the view of the present Edition, some notes on these pieces may be desirable, if only as a stimulus to further enquiry. Although the pieces have not yet passed beyond the footnote ſtage in Sheridan's bibliography, there is an increasing tendency to regard them as plays in which Sheridan definitely collaborated. It seems to me, however, that any more profound research on my part would have been a chase of the Will o' the wisp. But others may disagree.

---

[1]The Fathers; or, The Good-Nature'd Man. A Comedy. As it is Acted at the Theatre Royal in Drury Lane, London. Printed for T. Cadell, in the Strand MDCCLXXVIII. (Price One Shilling and Six-Pence). 8vo.

THE CARNIVAL OF VENICE, 1781

"TICKELL . . . wrote several plays, two of which are familiar, *The Carnival of Venice* (1781), for which Sheridan wrote the songs; and *The Camp* (1778), which was attributed to Sheridan, but of which in fact he was mainly a reviser."—Sichel, *Sheridan*, vol. I, p. 443.

Elsewhere (vol. II, p. 459) Sichel limits Sheridan's contribution to "three songs."[1] His ultimate authority is a conjecture by Mrs. Crouch (*Memoirs*, vol I, pp. 107-109) who, as Miss Phillips, played Emily in the original representation. Moore, who declined otherwise to record an opinion, denied firmly that Sheridan could ever have written one of the three specified songs, "The Gondolier's Song." And Mrs. Crouch judged on "style."

It is not easy to see *why* Sheridan should have written these songs, especially at a time when he was notoriously neglecting the theatre for his political career. They were not, one surmises, beyond the skill of Tickell. Contemporary reviews universally ascribed the opera to him, and they were commonly well-informed: "This Opera is said to be the production of the ingenious author of *Anticipation*, *The Wreath of Fashion*, *the Poetical Epistle from Charles Fox to Jack Townshend*, and other publications of acknowledged merit and great popularity," said *The Lady's Magazine* for December, 1781. *The European Magazine* for January, 1782, described it as "A Comic Opera by Mr. Tickell."

The "several plays," which Tickell is supposed to have written, reduce themselves in fact to *The Carnival of Venice*, since his only other dramatic exercise was to alter Allan Ramsay's opera, *The Gentle Shepherd*, for the production at Drury Lane on October 30, 1781. The songs from this alteration are believed to have been printed; but since the compilation of the *Biographica Dramatica* no copy of them seems to have been recorded. How-

---

[1]These are reprinted in the Fugitive Verse of the present edition.

ever, the only new song, in *The Gentle Shepherd*, according to *The Lady's Magazine*, was one beginning:

> When laſt the wind unroofed the barn,
> When laſt the fire burnt up the yarn,
> When Wattie laſt was sore affright,
> And wander'd in the snow a' night,
> You, Goody, you,
> I tell you true,
> You got the blame of a' fell out,
> And ilk one dreads ye a' about.

This gives but little to work upon as to his capacity as a dramatic song writer.

The Carnival of Venice, aɛted at Drury Lane on Oɛtober 21ſt, 1781, was never published, though the songs were:

Songs, Duos, Trios, Chorusses, &c. in the Comic Opera of the Carnival of Venice, as it is performed at the Theatre Royal in Drury Lane. London: MDCCLXXXI. [Price Sixpence] 8vo.

Pagination. P. [1] Title; p. [2] Blank; p. [3] *Dramatis Personæ*; p. [4] Blank; pp. 5-27, Text; p. 28 Blank.

[The Songs should have an engraved half-title with the imprint "London; 1781." The book has no name of printer or publisher, but *The Gazetteer* advertised on December 21st, 1781, "Books of the Songs in the Opera to be had at the Theatre." The Music was printed:

The Carnival of Venice . . . A Comic Opera. For the Voice and Harpsichord. London: Printed for S. A. & P. Thompson [1782?].]

HARLEQUIN HURLY-BURLY, 1785

"SHERIDAN . . . contributed some touches to the panto-mime of *Harlequin Hurly-Burly* in 1785."—Sichel, *Sheridan*, vol. II, p. 459.

These touches were inconsiderable, if they amounted to no more than the song which Mr. Sichel mentions (obscurely and casually) as being sent to Mrs. Tickell from Chatsworth, where the Sheridans were staying. "Mrs. Bouverie, too, had forwarded a song, really written by Sheridan, for a pantomime, *The Hurly-Burly*" (vol. I, p. 612). What song it was I do not know. Allardyce Nicoll, *XVIII Century Drama*, 1750-1800 records "*Hurly Burly; or the Fairy of the Well*. By James Cobb. 8vo [1785]" and mentions that Cobb's collaborator was Thomas King. Boaden calls *Harlequin Hurly-Burly* "the running pantomime of the season": it was produced either late in December, 1785, or early in January, 1786.

THE HEIRESS, 1786

"IN a letter of 1785, Mrs. Tickell says about Sheridan's corrections of Burgoyne's *The Heiress*—'I am sure I can see the hand of a master in several tints? Eh? Is it not so?'— And she speaks elsewhere of its *Sheridanisms*—Sichel, *Sheridan*, vol. I, p. 22.

Burgoyne's preface to *The Heiress* speaks of an accusation by certain "daily prints," that he was guilty of "a species of plagiarism." Obviously, he was charged with imitating, among others, Sheridan: in reply to which he quotes the famous sentence in the Preface to *The Rivals* about "faded ideas that float in the fancy like half-forgotten dreams." This can only be interpreted as a direct denial of Mrs. Tickell's supposition, which may, after all, have been derived from the "daily prints." It must, however, be supposed that Sheridan wrote, or started to write, an Epilogue for *The Heiresss* of which some fragments survive, being discussed in the present edition as the "Epilogue for an Unknown Play." But the evidence seems to contradict any rumour that Sheridan helped in *The Heiress* beyond such advice as manager would give to author, and friendly dramatist to friendly dramatist.

RICHARD CŒUR DE LION, 1786

"TO *Richard Cœur de Lion*, a romantic operetta ... Sheridan seems to have supplied both songs and ideas; and Tickell too, seems to have made suggestions."—Sichel, *Sheridan*, vol. I. p. 34.

Michael Kelly, who saw the performance at Drury Lane at the desire of Mrs. Sheridan, says (*Reminiscences*, vol. I, p. 293) "General Burgoyne had translated it, and Mrs. Sheridan adapted it to the English Stage." *The Thespian Dictionary* says that "in adapting this opera from the French of Sedaine, Burgoyne was 'assisted by other authors.'" Boaden, in his *Life of Mrs. Jordan* (vol. I, p. 96), says "the vast popularity of Sedaine's *Richard Cœur de Lion* in Paris set both our theatres to work to prepare it for the English Stage. Macnally undertook it for Mr. Harris, and Burgoyne for Sheridan. The latter, with great happiness, introduced Richard's Queen in the situation of Blondel." Although this is loosely worded, it *may* mean that Sheridan was the originator of a change in the plot, which is explained by the preface to the published Edition—"No adventitious matter has been introduced: some liberty, however, has been taken in effecting the principal incident of the piece, the discovery of Richard's confinement being now given to Matilda instead of Blondel."

As for the songs, they have no great merit, but this is the neatest of them:

> The God of Love a bandeau wears:
> Wou'd you know what it declares?
> And why his eyes are clouded?
> 'Tis to show us that his pow'r
> Is ne'er so fatal, ne'er so sure,
> As when in darkness shrouded.

The music by Grètry was adapted by Thomas Linley. The *Songs, Chorusses &c* were published in 1786, 8vo; the play, "*Richard Cæur de Lion*, An Historical Romance," was also printed, 1786; 8vo. and 12mo. It was acted and printed anonymously: the first Edition I have seen with an author's name is:—

Richard Cæur de Lion An Historical Romance. By Lieut.-General Burgoyne. Dublin: For William Jones. No. 86, Dame Street. MDCCXCIV.

12mo. pp. 48.

THE DOCTOR AND THE APOTHECARY, 1788

"AMONG the pieces submitted to him [in 1788] was a musical piece, which the writer may be allowed to mention, since its hero is a namesake. Its title is *The Doctor and Apothecary*. It was translated by Sheridan's friend Cobb, from the German of the Viennese Baron Dittersdorf"—Sichel, *Sheridan*, vol. I, p. 198. "He assisted . . . apparently in Cobb's *The Doctor and Apothecary*."—*ibid*. Vol. II, p. 454.

Michael Kelly, who played Carlos, in this operatic farce, said (*Reminiscences*, Vol. I, p. 312)—"Mr. Cobb, the late secretary of the East India Company, was adapting, with Storace, Baron Didersdorf's *Doctor and Apothecary*. They wished to consult me upon the kind of songs I should wish to have written for me."—*The European Magazine* for October, 1788, describes it as "a musical farce taken from the German of Stephani by Mr. Cobb." —the share of Dittersdorf, a well-known amateur violinist, being probably confined to the music. It is quite possible that Sheridan was consulted about the adaptation; but as none of the characters has a name remotely resembling his own, it is also possible that Mr. Sichel is confusing it with some other piece.

The piece was published as *The Doctor and the Apothecary*, 1788, 8vo, as also were the *Songs*, 1788, 8vo. There appears no reason to associate the name of Sheridan with it, except as manager of the theatre.

THELYPTHOROS (?1790)

"*THELYPTHOROS; or, Wives at Will,* a manuscript play (B.M. Add. MS. 2308) contains many corrections in Sheridan's manner. The play itself, however, was by Pilon, and was acted at Covent Garden in 1781. Its revival may have been intended at some later date at Drury Lane, as the corrections are said to be in Tom Sheridan's hand, which would have been impossible for some nine years later."—Sichel, *Sheridan,* vol. I, p. 55.

There is no suggestion that Sheridan had any share in Pilon's original farce, never published, entitled *Thelypthora; or, More Wives than One,* acted at Covent Garden on March 8th, 1781. Its theme is thus summarized: "The entire structure of the drama is founded upon Madan's *Thelypthora,* the absurd doctrines of which, so far as they concern plurality of wives, it exposes to ridicule . . . one of the leading maxims is that seduction of a virgin constitutes marriage with her."—*The London Magazine* for March, 1781.

Tom Sheridan, born in 1775, became under-manager at Drury Lane in 1801. He wrote *The Russians,* acted at Drury Lane in 1813. As there is no evidence that a revival of *Thelypthoros* was ever contemplated, its connection with Sheridan, on the grounds of corrections made in a handwriting that resembles his son's, is unusually tenuous.

THE STRANGER, 1798

"THE theatrical season of 1798 introduced to the public the German drama of *The Stranger*, translated by Mr. Thompson, and (as we are told by this gentleman in his preface) altered and improved by Sheridan. There is reason, however, to believe that the contributions of the latter to the dialogue were much more considerable than he was perhaps willing to let the translator acknowledge. My friend Mr. Rogers has heard him, on two different occasions, declare that he had written every word of *The Stranger* from beginning to end; and, as his vanity could not be much interested in such a claim, it is possible that there was at least some virtual foundation for it."

Thus Moore in his *Sheridan*. But . . . why should Sheridan conceal his authorship of *The Stranger* and vaunt his adaptation of *Pizarro*? Is it possible, indeed, that Rogers was confusing the two, the second of which Moore was so anxious to repudiate for him? It is clear, however, that *The Stranger* stands on a different footing from the other pieces in which Sheridan is supposed to have collaborated.

It was with *The Stranger* that, as the wits said, the English Stage first "ran stark German." Since the Restoration, the one dominant foreign dramatic influence had been that of France, and though in the previous decade certain plays of Goethe, Schiller, and Kotzebue had been translated, they were virtually no more than literary precursors. Frederick Reynolds declared that "even Otway had never surpassed the pathos of Kotzebue in *The Stranger*," and James Boaden demanded, "What signifies the reasoning, where every heart is touched and every eye is suffused with tears?" "A few weeks before the Battle of Waterloo," said George Daniel, the Duke of Wellington was so deeply affected by the representation of *The Stranger* that he wept. On the other hand Canning and his fellows mocked merrily at the whole German School in their travesty, *The Rovers; or, the Double Arrangement*, in which they made sport of Sheridan's song "I have a Silent Sorrow here."

The Stranger was translated by Benjamin Thompson of Nottingham, and altered for the stage by Sheridan. Two other translators had submitted versions of Kotzebue's *Menschenhass und Reue* to the Theatres Royal, George Papendick to Covent Garden and Schink to Drury Lane. They both seem to have used the original title of *Misanthropy and Repentance*, but after the success of Thompson's rendering, and before his piece was printed, each of them published his own version under the title of *The Stranger*. Schink accused Sheridan of appropriating his entire play: but his alteration of *Misanthropy and Repentance* was greatly inferior to Thompson's, which had been submitted to Sheridan through his associate Edward Grubb. As none of the translators had the sanction of Kotzebue in their undertaking, none of them had any moral claim to consider it as his play—and, of course, there was no legal right, since anybody could act or print his own version of a foreign piece, without regard to the original author. In short, Sheridan must be exonerated from the accusation of acting in bad faith to Schink. Papendick's only grievance was that the managers of Covent Garden did not recognize the merits of the play, as Sheridan had done.

Mr. Williams in his *Seven XVIII Century Bibliographies* is "not clear" whether *The Stranger* was issued as a separate publication, apart from its appearance in the first bound volume of Thompson's *German Theatre*. (London: Vernor and Hood, 1801.) It was, however, so issued, though copies are rare:—

The Stranger, A Drama in Five Acts, as Performed at the Theatre Royal, Drury-Lane. Translated from the German of Augustus von Kotzebue, by Benjamin Thompson, Esq., London: Printed by T. Maiden, Sherborne-Lane. For Vernor and 'Hood, No. 31, Poultry, 1800.

8vo.

Pagination. P. [i], title; p. [ii] blank; p. [iii] *Dedication*; p. [iv] *Advertisement*; pp. [v]-[vi] *Prologue by W. Linley, Esq.*; pp. [vii-viii] *Epilogue by M. G. Lewis, Esq., M.P.* and *Dramatis Personæ*; pp. [1] and 2-71 Text; p. 72 blank.

This muſt be added to the "firſt editions" of Sheridan for the reason that it contains the song "I have a Silent Sorrow here," with the note "For the Words of this Song, the Translator is indebted to R. B. Sheridan, Esq., M.P. and for the Music to Her Grace the Duchess of Devonshire." In the Advertisement Thompson acknowledged his "grateful obligations to Mr. Sheridan, who was so good as to improve its effeċt by several alterations and additions." This does not support Sheridan's claim to have written "every word" which Mr. Sichel disproved from an inspeċtion of the MSS.

But Thompson denied as "contemptible" and "prepoſterous" the charge of "another translator" (Schink) that the managers of Drury Lane had "ſtolen his play." This accusation was made in "The Stranger . . . London. Printed for C. Dilly, 1798" (8vo). The "Address to the Publick" in this Edition deserves reproduċtion because of its reference to *The Critic*:

Address to the Publick.

The following Free Translation of Kotzebue's much-admired Comedy of *Misanthropy and Repentance* is the fruit of the leisure hours of one whose pursuits are altogether distinct from the Stage. It was not undertaken with the hope of fame or emolument: but in consequence of the pleasure experienced by having seen it performed in its Native Language. When finished, it was offered, about a year and a half since, to the Managers of Drury Lane Theatre; who, after having had it in their possession eight or ten days, returned it with an answer, politely signifying "That they did not think it would succeed in representation." With this answer the Translator rested fully satisfied, the more so, as he thought it not impossible that Mr. Cumberland's very excellent and deservedly applauded Play, *The Wheel of Fortune*, might be supposed, in some measure, to have adapted one of the principal Characters to the English Stage, in manner far more interesting than any Translation could hope to do.—His surprise, therefore, was not small, when *The Stranger* was announced for representation, and when he saw it acted with scarcely any alteration from his own Manuscript, except in the names of the Characters, and with the addition of a Song and some Dancing, entirely unconnected with the subject, he could not help feeling that he had been ungenerously treated. Under these circumstances, he considered it as a point of justice due to himself, to submit his Play to the candid judgment of the Publick, as early as possible; And to endeavour to secure, at least some part of the Credit to which he was vain enough to think himself entitled. It is here printed from the Copy which was sent to the Managers; and on its merit the impartial Reader is left to decide. His indulgence is requested for such slight inaccuracies, as, it is presumed, might have been easily remedied, had there been any inclination to act with that candour and ingenuousness, which ought to characterise the conduct of those, who preside over the amusements of the Public.

That the Managers should have refused his piece was not, at first, matter either of surprise or regret to the Translator.—Had another and more perfect translation of Kotzebue's play been *previously* put into their hands, and had they signified their intention of bringing that forward, the writer of this Address would have withdrawn his claim in silence: well aware that the present Translation did, in fact, require that revisal, which appears to form almost the only, and that a very slight, difference between the play represented, and that he reprinted.—But on comparing all circumstances, he may perhaps stand excused for supposing that a Manager "who writes himself," may sometimes (as SIR FRETFUL PLAGIARY says) "serve the thoughts of others as gypsies do stolen children: disfigure them to make them pass for his own."—And though the Writer might have been well content, had "the best Thoughts in his Tragedy, been put into the Manager's own Comedy," he cannot rest altogether quiet on the undisguised appropriation of the whole of his play.

In this translation, most of the nonsense, which was hissed on the stage, is omitted. The last scene, now so admirably performed by Mr. Kemble and Mrs. Siddons, is considerably shortened from the German; in which it appears even tediously long. The Translator has also ventured to deviate from the original plot in one delicate particular. —He has not made the wife actually commit that crime which is a stain to the female character, tho' she was on the brink of ruin by eloping from her husband.

    28th March, 1798.   A. S * * * * k.

The laſt sentence shows that Schink had "in the intereſt of morality" deprived the play of its greateſt dramatic force. No further reason need have been sought for its rejeƈtion.

The Alteration of *The Tempest*, 1777

"THE representations of *The Tempest* at Drury Lane on January 4th, 1777 and March 7, 1786 were probably an arrangement by Sheridan, with music by Thomas Linley, junior," says Mr. Harold Child in his concise Stage History of *The Tempest*.[1] Mr. Sichel mentions this (definitely but erroneously) as "Dryden's version of Shakespeare's *Tempest*; with songs interspersed by Sheridan, and set by Linley—what a compound!" He adds that playgoers "acclaimed an Epilogue which Sheridan penned for this Shakespearean travesty." But the Epilogue he cites was certainly not written for this occasion; and the version of *The Tempest* had no connection whatever with Dryden's, being advertised, in *The Gazetteer* of the time, as Shakespeare's, with a full cast of characters which does not include any of Dryden's additional personages, like Dorinda[2] and Hippolyto.

The London Magazine for January, 1777, said that *The Tempest* was revived "early this month" at Drury Lane, "where it was brought out with great judgement and received with suitable applause." The account otherwise concerns only the performers —Bannister as Caliban, Bensley as Prospero, and Mrs. Schuyler as Miranda—and does not discuss the piece, but it leaves little doubt that, except for the masque, there was but little alteration from Shakespeare, or "arrangement" by Sheridan. John Bell's Edition of *The Tempest* (1778) in his *British Theatre* (12mo) which contains a portrait of Baddeley, of Drury Lane, as Trinculo, is from the collation by Theobald; but it marks "the passages omitted in representation." It appears to be the version acted at Drury Lane, except for the added songs and, of course, the customary masque.

[1] In the New Cambridge Edition of *The Tempest* (1921).
[2] Dorinda was "the" *ingénue* part of the period, and rivalled Polly in *The Beggar's Opera* as the choice of young actresses for the first appearances on the stage. To refer Mrs. Dangel's reference in *The Critic* to Dorinda in *The Beaux-Stratagem* is to misunderstand a scornful allusion.

When *The Tempest* was acted, before the Interlude of *The Storming of Fort Omoa* at the Theatre [Royal] in New Street, Birmingham, on August 30th, 1780, "by particular desire of the Noblemen and Gentlemen of the Bean Club" special mention was made of "the new songs for Ariel and Miranda, composed by Thomas Linley jun.," for which, it may be supposed, Sheridan wrote the words. But I have not succeeded in tracing these songs: it is true that in Mr. William Jaggard's *Shakespeare Bibliography* there are two entries which I cite with considerable doubt:

The Tempest . . . . . altered by R. B. Sheridan. London: 1778. 12mo.

The Tempest . . . . . altered by R. B. Sheridan. The Songs Only with Music by Linley jun. London: 1776. 8vo.[1]

The Tempest, however, was to furnish Sheridan with an opportunity for a species of raillery he delighted in, the application of a theatrical allusion to political purposes. In his contribution to the first number of the Whig periodical he exposed the inconsistency of Lord North, who had lately consented in a Committee of the whole House, to a motion which he had violently opposed in the House itself—thus "making (says Sheridan) that respectable assembly disobey its own orders, and the members reject with contempt, under the form of a Chairman, the resolutions they had imposed on themselves under the authority of a Speaker"; —He proceeds: "The burlesque of any plan, I know, is rather a a recommendation of it to Your Lordship; and the ridicule you might throw on this assembly, by continuing to support this Athanasian distinction of powers in the unity of an apparently corporate body, might in the end compensate to you for the discredit you have incurred in the attempt. A deliberate body of so

---

[1] "The Songs Only" does not read like a transcript from a title-page. Music was rarely (if ever) printed in anticipation of a performance. 8vo is an unusual size for music. As Jaggard gives no pagination, he had not seen the books, nor does he cite his usual authorities, the great Shakespeare collections in the libraries. It looks as if considerable "attribution" has taken place. The only 1778 12mo I can trace is Bell's.

uncommon a form, would probably be deemed a kind of STATE MONSTER by the ignorant and the vulgar. This might at first increase their *awe* for it, and so far counteract Your Lordship's intentions. They would probably approach it with as much reverence as Stephano does the monster in *The Tempest*: 'What, one body and two voices—a most delicate monster!' However, they would soon grow familiarized to it, and probably hold it in as little respect as they were wished to do. They would find it on many occasions 'a very shallow monster,' and particularly 'a most poor *credulous* monster,'—while Your Lordship, as keeper, would enjoy every advantage and profit that could be made of it. You would have the benefit of the *two voices*, which would be the MONSTER'S great excellencies, and would be peculiarly serviceable to Your Lordship. With 'the forward voice' you would aptly promulgate those vigorous schemes and productive resources, in which Your Lordship's fancy is so pregnant; while 'the backward voice' might be kept solely for *recantation*. The MONSTER, to maintain its character, must appear no novice in the science of flattery, or in the talents of servility,—and while it could never scruple to bear any burdens Your Lordship should please to lay on it, you would always, on the *approach of a storm*, find a shelter under its gabardine."

Robinson Crusoe (1781)

WHILE there has never been any doubt that Sheridan wrote a pantomime of *Robinson Crusoe* the fact seems to have excited no curiosity. Or perhaps it was too elusive. Mr. Allardyce Nicoll has no record of it in his copious hand-list of plays in *XVIII Century Drama*, 1750-1800. Mr. Sichel, taking refuge in a discreet statement that Sheridan "contributed some touches" to it, mentioned also that he scribbled a song for it on the back of a playbill during rehearsal. The song that he named, on the authority of Michael Kelly was "The Midnight Watch," which, however, had been sung in *Harlequin Fortunatus* (1780). Joseph Knight in the Oxford *Sheridan* says that "among dramatic works attributed to him by the *Biographica Dramatica*, is a pantomime on the subject of *Robinson Crusoe*, printed in 1797." No copy of this has yet been discovered; and (if indeed it existed) it was most likely a reprint of another publication, hitherto unrecorded, but undoubtedly printed, though still undiscovered. In a list of books "printed for T. Becket, Pall Mall," at the end of his "new Edition of *The Clandestine Marriage*" (1785) is:

"A Short Account of the Situations and Incidents in the pantomime of *Robinson Crusoe*. [Price] 6d."

After a prolonged search, I discovered, in *The Lady's Magazine* for January, 1781, "an Account of the new pantomime called *Robinson Crusoe; or, Harlequin Friday* performed at Drury Lane Theatre on January 20th." It is, in its way, a surprising document:—

"The name of this entertainment sufficiently indicates the story from whence it is taken,—or which (to speak more properly) gives origin to it, for the first part only, of the three, is founded on *Daniel Defoe's Adventures of the York Mariner, who lived so long on a deserted Island, &c. &c.* The second and third parts have no historical reference, but are pantomimical

337

in the usual ſtile, and might as well be annexed to a theatrical exhibition of *The Seven Champions of England*, or any other work of equal importance and celebrity

"The incidents introduced from the *Life and Adventures* are the anecdote of the parrot's ſtartling Crusoe with the repetition of his name: the landing of the savages with Friday, and other prisoners: Crusoe's putting them to the rout, and preserving Friday's life: the fidelity and attachment of the latter to his preserver: with the landing of another band of savages: and laſtly, of the mutinous crew of an English ship, whose captain is assiſted by Crusoe; and, being put again in possession of his command, takes all who were on the island with him to Cadiz.

"The scenes introduced are a view of the bower of Crusoe with his kid-fold; a view of his work on the two tree-trunks which he had hewn into boats; a view of the inside of Crusoe's hut; and a view of the sea in three prospeĉts,—the one, when the savages crowd to the beach in their canoes; the other, when the English ship appears in sight; and the third, when she sails for Cadiz."

So far, indeed, there is nothing remarkable about the pantomime, except its subjeĉt. But after the arrival at Cadiz, Friday is transformed into Harlequin by two witches who have been threatened by Pantaloon (a merchant who had been wrecked on Crusoe's Island) with the Inquisition. After this, "the entertainment proceeds in the usual pantomimical confusion; and we hear no more of Crusoe, nor meet with any allusion to his ſtory." Inſtead, there was a gross and ſtupid traveſty of conventual life, in which Harlequin, in love with Columbine, the daughter of Pantaloon, disguises himself successively as a Friar, a Nun, and, laſtly, succeeds in getting to his sweetheart in a nunnery "by changing place with a lovely lass, concealed in a bundle of ſtraw, which was being carried in at the portal by a holy brother as *food for the convent*." Harlequin, at laſt deteĉted, is thrown into the prison of the Inquisition, from which he emerges "among the criminals cloathed in the Sanbenito, as viĉtims of an Auto da Fé." When the torch is applied to the pile on which he has been placed, his protecting witch intervenes, and the place is transformed into "a kind of terrestial elysium." Here Pantaloon consents "to the marriage of Harlequin and Columbine, and the entertainment concludes with a dance." Among the tricks is the changing of a fat friar into a hogshead of claret. The songs included "There was a Maid and she went to a Mill." "A Lovely Lass to a Friar Came," and "The Bottle's the Sun of our Table," from, of course, *The Duenna*, all sung by the Friars. This is enough to show that the action was in the spirit of the convent-scene in *The Duenna*, to which there had been many contemporary objections—in the spirit, that is, gone mad. *The European Magazine* for February, 1782, said that *The Critic* was followed by *Robinson Crusoe*, "the last inferior to the worst performance of Mr. Messink; and a proof that even the greatest genius will sink beneath contempt, when he contends with a mechanic in his own profession."

Is it possible to deny the authorship of *Robinson Crusoe* to Sheridan? *The Thespian Dictionary* (1802) gives it among his works as "a Pantomime, with Songs," adding "it is said that one night, in the unavoidable absence of Grimaldi, the author personated Harlequin himself." Elsewhere it states that Charles Delpini "assisted in several pantomimes, particularly *Robinson Crusoe*, all the pantomimical part of which he furnished, and played the character of Robinson Crusoe himself; Friday by Mr. Grimaldi," This would seem to limit the share of Sheridan to the Songs, but there is no doubt that such was not the case: Michael Kelly names it among Sheridan's works. So does Moore, who comments: "Among other occasional trifles of this kind, to which Sheridan condescended for the advantage of the theatre, was the pantomime of *Robinson Crusoe*, brought out, I believe, in 1781, of which he is understood to have been the author. There was a practical joke in this pantomime (where, in pulling off a man's boot, the leg was pulled off with it,) which the famous Delpini laid claim to as his own, and publicly complained of Sheridan's having stolen it from him. The punsters of the day said it was claimed as literary property—being *in usum* Delpini.'

If Delpini had invented "the pantomimical part" what complaint could he have made? On this evidence alone, it would seem that he was not connected with the production; nor, if he had been, the chief "author" (there was no dialogue) would there be any point in *The European Magazine* comparing Sheridan to Messink, the "inventor of pantomime" at Covent Garden. Moreover, Grimaldi at the age of seventy cannot be supposed to have played Harlequin, but his usual part of Pantaloon.[1] Beyond this, I do not care to go, except to say that, whatever Sheridan's share in the "invention" was, there is no doubt as to his responsibility for it as manager of the Theatre Royal, Drury Lane.

Only one song from *Robinson Crusoe* (with music by Shield, who composed the overture) seems to have been printed. The words were given in a February issue of *The Whitehall Evening Post*. This song is most likely, from its obvious situation in the play, the one that Sheridan wrote hastily on a playbill, to give the carpenters time to prepare the next scene. No doubt it served its purpose:

SONG

Sung at Drury Lane Theatre by Mr. Gaudry in the new Pantomime of Robinson Crusoe

Come, come, my jolly lads, our ship's afloat:
  Brisk gales our sails shall croud;
Come bustle, bustle, bustle, boys; and haul the boat,
  The boatswain pipes aloud.
The ship's unmoor'd, All hands aboard:
The rising gale, Fills every sail,
The ship's well-mann'd and stor'd.

---

[1] *The Lady's Magazine* gives no cast. It mentions that Grimaldi had "a pantomime soul," but does not name his part—and that Robinson Crusoe "told his story very intelligibly," without stating the player: it commends Miss Collett as Columbine and "Harlequin Wright"—Woodward's successor at Drury Lane. Delpini is not mentioned. On December 14th, 1780, *Queen Mab* was played—Harlequin by Wright; Pantaloon by Johnston (but usually by Grimaldi); Columbine by Miss Collett; Clown by Delpini. I believe Delpini was a good Catholic. Is the secret—I put it as a query—that he refused to be associated with the convent scenes in *Robinson Crusoe*, just as his operatic compatriots had refused to appear in *The Duenna* (*La Governante*) unless the convent-scenes were omitted?

Chorus

Then fling the flowing bowl!
Fond hopes arise; The girls we prize.
Shall bless each jovial soul;
    The can, boys, bring
While foaming billows roll.

Then to the Spanish coaſt we're bound to float,
    We'll ſtill our rights maintain;
Then bear a hand,—be ſteady, boys;
    Soon shall we see old England once again.
From shore to shore, While cannons roar,
Our Tars will show The haughty foe
    Brittania rules the main!

Chorus

Then fling the flowing bowl, &c.[1]

---

[1] The Song was printed with Shield's Music. J. Rice, Dublin [1782]. His Overture was also printed, London, 1782.

Political Parodies

THE DUENNA (1776)

IN 1776 was issued an eighteen-penny pamphlet, which looked like a play-book, with the title of *The Duenna: A Comic Opera*. Its whole appearance was deceptive, since the title-page described it as having been performed "by His Majesty's Servants," the common term for the companies of the Theatres Royal, but in this case intended to signify the Ministers of the Crown. Its dedication to David Garrick, however, leaves no doubt that it was a catch-penny, for at a glance it would appear to be a genuine edition of *The Duenna*, whereas it is a political parody. It was thus reviewed in *The Carlisle Magazine* for November, 1776:—

Art. 6. *The Duenna*, a Comic Opera, in Three Acts, as it is performed by his Majesty's Servants. 8vo. 1s.6d. Johnston.

The Author has borrowed Sheridan's mould, in which the famous Covent-Garden *Duenna* was so successfully formed, and he has melted into it a mass of political base-metal, which resembles the original *cast* as much as a Birmingham *sand* half-penny does the genuine coin of the Tower-stamp. It is one of the most impudent court satires we have ever seen; and yet, at the same time, a very unmeaning, common-place, contemptible catch-penny. Some of the songs are, however (to give the *Grub* his due) tolerable parodies on those of Mr. Sheridan's *Duenna*.

Anderson entered it in his Bibliography without comment as "*The Duenna*: a Comic Opera. London. 1775. 8vo." as if it were a genuine edition of Sheridan. He failed to distinguish his date (there is an undated issue) as conjectural. Sichel pointed out that the edition in question was a parody. Unfortunately, however, he followed Anderson in accepting as Sheridan's another political satire "*The General Fast*: a Lyric Ode. By the Author of *The Duenna*" which was issued some four months after this travesty of *The Duenna*.

The *Dramatis Personæ* of this parody are named Don Louis, Mac Boot, Boreas, Twitcher, Minden, Mungo, and so on. No very profound knowledge of the period is required to identify them; for these political nicknames were in common use—Mac Boot is Lord Bute; Boreas, Lord North; Jemmy Twitcher, Lord Sandwich; Minden, Lord George Germaine. Don Louis is, of course, to be understood as King George III. Other nicknames are a little less obvious. Mungo, who does the "dirty work" for Lord Bute, is Jeremy Dyson: he was given his nickname, after the black servant in another comic opera, *The Padlock*, by another member of parliament, Colonel Barre. Caen-wood is Lord Mansfield, from the name of his seat; Canting John is John Wesley: Weatherbeaten I take to be Wedderburne; and Darkford was perhaps Lord Suffolk.

Among other political affairs this travesty of *The Duenna* deals with the American War of Independence. Its tone may be deduced from the soliloquy of Caen-Wood (Lord Mansfield) about Boreas (Lord North, the premier).

"Superlative blockhead! Now is his wise head full of imaginary ideas for subjugating the Americans: as if three millions of people, enthusiastic in the cause of liberty, hardy, brave, vigilant, frugal— possessing a tract of country larger than all Europe— having within themselves all the comforts and conveniences of life, and fighting for everything they hold dear to themselves and their posterity, could be conquered by any force that can be sent from this country. Ridiculous idea ... Our hopeful ministers have nothing to fight against, but the winds and the waves, the woods and swamps of an unknown country: the heats of summer, and the rigours of winter; and, above all, the unbroken spirit of a gallant, virtuous and determined people."

Another scene derives its interest from the fact that it attacks two people who were venomously treated in *The General Fast*, Lord Sandwich and his unfortunate mistress, Martha Reay, under the names of Jemmy Twitcher and Clara Raymond. It is grossly libellous, and entirely misrepresents the character of Miss Reay, who was quite an amiable woman, and by no means avaricious. But it should be noted that the law of libel worked curiously in those days: it recognized in practice the "antithesis of persons"—that is to say, the private life of a man could be attacked with impunity, but not his public character as a Minister of the Crown. Lord Sandwich had been accused by *The London Evening Post* of selling, as First Lord of the Admiralty, the place of a Commissioner in the Navy: for this he brought an action for *scandalum magnatum* in the court of King's Bench in 1773 against Miller, the printer, and was awarded £2,000 damages. But the attacks upon his private life continued without mitigation.

Who was "the author of *The Duenna*"? The Dictionary of National Biography accepts, rather doubtfully, the common attribution to Israel Pottinger. But, like everybody else, it is silent about *The General Fast* (1776) and *The Critic* (1780), a travesty, which were both printed as "by the author of *The Duenna*." (The parody of *The School for Scandal* (1779) was perhaps by the same hand.) But it seems to me that further evidence is required. To Pottinger is also attributed "*The Methodist* . . . being a Continuation and Completion of the plan of *The Minor*. 8vo [1761?]." As for Pottinger, this review from *The London Magazine* for July, 1769, will suffice:—

"*Stanzas Sacred to Liberty, &c.* By I. Pottinger. Price 1s. The author is a broken bookseller, who was for some time confined in Bedlam; and now, like the barber in the farce, is nobly solicitous for the welfare of Old England. After this account, it is not necessary to say anything of the performance."

The Town and Country Magazine was equally curt: its review ran, "We may venture to pronounce this bard the dullest as well as the lowest of her votaries."—(Liberty's, that is).

There is, however, one curious circumstance about this travesty of *The Duenna*. In Sheridan's MS. draft of the comic opera, as printed by Fraser Rae in *Sheridan's Plays as he Wrote Them*, there is one song which was never printed—not in the

Songs which were sold at the theatre, not in the *Music* of 1776, nor in any Edition. Nevertheless, it is parodied in this political travesty. How, then, did the author come by it? Was it, in despite of the various editions, sung? Or had he access to Sheridan's manuscript? With these unanswerable questions, the song and the parody may be set side by side.

THE DUENNA MS.	THE DUENNA TRAVESTY
Don Jerome.	*Mungo.*
Dominion was given	Dominion was given
To Beauty from Heav'n,	To premiers from Heaven,
Pleasing bondage to the mind:	Sweetest bondage of the mind
Will you, then, alone	But, now we're alone,
Its worship disown?	Come candidly own.
Isaac.	*Boreas.*
Never could I favour find,	Ah! no pleasure can I find,
But when, for my pain,	But when, for my pains,
I meet with disdain.	I count all my gains.
Don Jerome.	*Mungo.*
Coax her, kiss her, till she's blind.	You think—the world—is stark blind.

BIBLIOGRAPHY

The Duenna: A Comic Opera. In Three Acts: As it is performed, By His Majesty's Servants. Quid Rides? de *te* fabula narratur. London: Printed for E. Johnson, near the Obelisk, Ludgate-Hill. M.DCC.LXXVI.

Pagination. P. [i] title; p. [ii] blank; pp. [iii]–[iv] *Dedication to David Garrick Esq*. (dated *June* 18*th*, 1776); and *Dramatis Personæ*; pp. [1] + 2–43 Text; p. [44] blank.

The Duenna: A Comic Opera. The Second Edition. London. Johnson. M.DCC.LXXVI.

8vo.

[Not recorded by Anderson or Sichel. Noted by Allardyce Nicoll, *XVIII Century Drama*, 1750-1800.]

The Duenna: A Comic Opera. London. Johnson [1776].

8vo.

[Sichel's entry (giving the date as 1775) reads: "Mr. Anderson's Bibliography gives this as if it were the play, but it is another political [anti-Northite] sketch by Israel Pottinger. It was printed for E. Johnson and illustrated by a satirical vignette. Elsewhere (vol. I, p. 511) he gives the date correctly from the preface as 1776.

Allardyce Nicoll, who records all three London issues, gives the date of the third as [?1779], when it seems to me that the satire would have been obsolete. Perhaps, however, this issue should be dated 1777.]

The Duenna: A Comic Opera, in three acts; As it is performed By His Majesty's Servants ... Dublin : Printed by Spotswood For the United Company of Booksellers. MDCCLXXVI.

12mo. pp. iv + 36.

[The only copy of this Irish edition which is known to me belongs to Mr. Percival F. Hinton. It is previously unrecorded.]

THE SCHOOL FOR SCANDAL (1779)

IN 1779 was issued a piece under the title of *The School for Scandal*. "It is necessary to take notice of this political drama," said *The London Magazine* for January, 1779, "to apprize our readers of the deception which has contributed to its sale. Many persons have imagined it was the celebrated comedy under that title written by Sheridan." This piece is not strictly a parody, since it is a quite unrelated political tract preserving only Sheridan's title and the names of certain of his characters. A list of *Dramatis Personæ* followed the names of these characters by their supposed impersonators, using nicknames by which they may easily be identified. They were all, indeed, identified by a contemporary review in *The London Magazine*. These are therefore the *Dramatis Personæ* of this political tract.

CHARLES	*Mr. King*	[King George III]
JOSEPH SURFACE	*Lord Thane*	[Earl of Bute]
CRABTREE	*Lord Rubicon*	[Earl of Mansfield][1]
BACKBITE	*Lord Minden*	[Lord George Germaine]
SIR OLIVER	*Lord Sh-lb-ne*	[Lord Shelburne]
MOSES	*Lord Boreas*	[Lord North]
SNAKE	*Signor Fraserina*	[Mr. Under-Secretary Fraser][2]

Mr. James W. Tupper gave an account of this pamphlet in *The Nation* (New York) of September 25, 1913, from the copy in the Library of Harvard University. His precis is excellent, although I have corrected a few trivial errors in reprinting it:

"The Play deals with the American War of Independence and the political mismanagement and corruption in England. Charles is represented as having been completely under the influence of Joseph, but now, as determined to shake off the yoke. He

[1]Mr. Tupper says incorrectly Chancellor Thurlow.
[2]Mr. Tupper fails to identify this character. In a political squib on the Government in *The London Magazine* for December, 1777, among the Pamphlet and Political Writers pensioned is the name of W. Fraser. The review of this travesty describes him as "Mr. Under Secretary F——, who is the Gazette writer," that is, the writer of the official *London Gazette*.

has just heard of the taking of one of his 'sugar houses' in his 'western estate' by his 'perfidious foe,' the capture of Dominica by the French Governor of Martinique. But Joseph distracts his attention by showing him 'a new invented chymical paper that is proof against fire and water,' just as George III. was actually interested in the non-combustible wood of Mr. Hartley's house on Wimbledon Common. While Charles is testing the paper and expressing his admiration at the invention, more disasters are reported. 'Sir Harry Clatter (Sir Henry Clinton) is repulsed with great loss of men in his expedition up Boreas River (North or Hudson River) on a foraging party.' Since the news is not official and is only a newspaper report, Charles refuses to believe it; and as a matter of fact it was not true; for Clinton's expeditions from New York in 1778 were successful. Then comes official news of the capture of St. Petite and Mignonette (St. Pierre and Miquelon, captured by Admiral Montague, of Newfoundland, in 1778). Joseph can now easily assure Charles that what Lord and General Quomodo (Admiral Lord Howe and his brother General Howe) could not effect will be accomplished by Sir Harry Clatter and Admiral Boisterous (Byron), and that even if Occidentia (America) were never regained, it would be no great loss, since it 'fosters a nest of hypocritical cheats and wicked incendiaries.' So Charles is as much under Joseph's thumb as ever. It is 'on the eve of opening the two kennels' (the houses of Parliament) and Moses is worried to know how to silence the 'hound of opposition.' Snake [Frazer] has 'dished up for the hum' [the *Gazette*][1] reports of murderous atrocities committed by the Gasconades (the French) at the capture of the sugar house in order that the tenants may forget their loss in their renewed hatred of the Gasconades. Clatter's retreat is reported as a victory, and the importance of St. Petite and Mignonette is vastly magnified, both as a loss to the Gasconades and as a gain to the English. Snake also writes puffs of Moses for the news-

---

[1]Mr. Tupper takes "hum" to mean "debate," whereas it meant *The London Gazette,* the official means of "humbugging" the people. The capture of Dominica was reported in the newspapers from private letters on November 18th; yet no account appeared in *The London Gazette* till December 1st. Germaine was accused of concealing the defeat, while quickly announcing the victory at St. Pierre.

papers, to the disparagement of Backbite, General Flourish (Burgoyne), whose surrender will 'soon be sifted to the bottom in the lower kennell,' and of Jemmy Twitcher (Earl of Sandwich, the Lord of the Admiralty), who was blamed for the escape of the French Fleet.

"The prospects of success are not very bright, Joseph's only hope is in more troops, to be got from Mrs. Catherine (Catherine of Russia) from the German 'squires, and from home. Crabtree has lost faith in military leaders; 'little Tommy' (Gen. Thomas Gage) failed to quell the riot; General Quomodo (Howe) took a couple of towns (New York and Philadelphia), and was obliged to give one of them up (Philadelphia, as a matter of fact, was evacuated by Clinton in 1778); his brother's attempt at peace failed; Governor Insolence (Governor Johnstone) used improper means to influence the colonists to come to terms, and he was sent home in disgrace. Furthermore, there is no money, and Twitcher (Sandwich) has stirred up the kennels by fomenting the fracas between Sir Hugh Splice-rope (Sir Hugh Palisser) and Admiral Handsomely (Admiral Keppel). Moses raises a million (on paper) by taxing, among other objects, bachelors, unfaithful husbands, cats, lapdogs, gentlemen that wear their hair tied, and clergymen that have above £300 a year.

"Backbite seeks to exonerate himself from all blame for Flourish's disaster (Burgoyne's surrender at Saratoga), admits that he kept Flourish from the King's presence, and that he advised sending Flourish back to his imprisoned army, and writes a scurrilous attack on Moses. He and Twitcher are partners in a league offensive and defensive. The situation is deplorable, so corrupt and antagonistic are all of Charles's advisers. Consequently, our author seeks to anticipate history by having Charles summon Sir Oliver and offer him Moses's place. This Sir Oliver accepts after assuring the King that his advisers are a 'set of fools and knaves.' The whole junto is discarded, and the way is opened to a 'treaty with your western servants' and an immediate cessation of hostilities. The actual end was, however, different.— my last scene," says the author, "is *anticipated*."

BIBLIOGRAPHY

[i*a*]

The School for Scandal. A Comedy [quotations from Virgil and Ovid] London. Sold by S. Bladon, Pater-Noster-row; and J. Thresher, No. 38, Duke Street, Manchester Square. MDCCLXXIX. [Price One Shilling and Sixpence.] 8vo.

Pagination. P. [i] title ; p. [ii] blank; pp. [iii] & iv–v [Dedication] *To Richard Tickell Esq.*; p. [vi] blank; p. vii *Dramatis Personæ*; p. [viii] blank; pp. [1] & 2–62 Text.

[Although this pamphlet is not mentioned in Mr. Sichel's Bibliography (probably through some confusion with the "Real and Genuine School for Scandal" which appears erroneously as a political parody) the omission was accidental, since he described it in the text (vol. I, p. 284). It is not recorded by Mr. Iolo A. Williams, who, however, has since publishing his Sheridan Bibliography obtained a copy, for the loan of which I am indebted.]

[i*b*]

The School for Scandal. A Comedy. The Second Edition. 1779. 8vo.

[From Pickering and Chatto, *The Booklover's Leaflet*. No. 243. Not elsewhere recorded. Imprint as [i*a*].]

[ii]

The School for Scandal. A Comedy, 8vo. 1s. 6d. Baldwin.

[From *The Town and Country Magazine* for March, 1779, which reviews it in seven words, "A borrowed title for a political squib." Perhaps the same piece with another imprint. No other reference to it is known to me.]

[iii]

The School for Scandal. A Comedy in Five Acts. As it is performed by His Majesty's Servants. Never Before Printed. London. Printed for G. Lester. No. 46, Old Bailey. 1784.

12mo.

[Another political squib.

From Sichel, *Sheridan*, vol. I, p. 585 and vol. II, p. 452, where it is described as "to deride the Coalition." Apparently the same as that mentioned by Allardyce Nicoll, *XVIII Century Drama*, 1750-1800, as *The School for Scandal* [Political], 1784, 8vo."]

THE CRITIC (1780)

"*THE CRITIC* by the Author of *The Duenna*" (1780) appears to be a rare book. It was reviewed in *The Monthly Mirror* at the time of its publication (as being "8vo, 1s. 6d Bladon") in these terms:

"This Political Punchinello sticks as close to the skirts of Mr. Sheridan as the little black fellows did to those of Trapolin in the *Duke or No Duke*. The title of each new piece produced by the ingenious manager (and which for *Reasons of State*, he keeps unpublished), is instantly seized upon by this pilferer, and applied to his own *improper* use: to impose a state satire on the public with the appearance of a theatrical performance."

BIBLIOGRAPHY

The Critic; or, a Tragedy Rehearsed. A New Dramatic Piece in Three Acts. As it is performed by His Majesty's Servants. With the greatest applause. By the Author of the Duenna. London: Printed for S. Bladon. 1780.

[From *Book-Prices Current*, 1923, where it is described as a first edition of Sheridan's comedy. It gives this pagination: A1: recto, title; verso, blank; A2: recto, *Principal characters*; verso, blank. B1, recto, to G2 recto, text of play.
I have not discovered any further particulars.]

The General Fast (1776)

THE General Fast; A Lyric Ode: with a Form of Prayer Proper for the Occasion; and a Dedication to the King; By the Author of the Duenna. Printed for the Author, and Sold by Messrs. Fielding and Walker, Paternoster-Row; Allen, Bridges-Street, Covent-Garden; and Bowen, No. 133, and Ford, No. 263, in the Strand.

Large 4to, Pp. 16.

Pagination. P. [i] title; p. [ii] blank; pp. [iii-iv] Text of *Epistle to the King*; pp. [1] and 2-9 Text of *The General Fast*; p. [10] blank; pp. [11-12] Text of the *Form of Prayer*.

This pamphlet is not genuine, although it has been accepted by all bibliographers from Anderson to Iolo A. Williams's *Seven XVIII Century Bibliographies*. Mr. Sichel not only accepted it formally, but reprinted the entire pamphlet in his *Sheridan* (vol. I, pp. 624-626). There is no doubt that the author was not Sheridan, but the writer of the political parody of *The Duenna* (1776).

It should be sufficient to ask if Sheridan could ever have published such stanzas as these:

Shall Rigby, or shall Weymouth, drunk,
Shall ev'ry knave and ev'ry punk,
    Whom Kings shall hoist to pow'r,
Decree the empire of the seas?
Shall we submit to THINGS like these
    Nor curse the tainted hour? . . .

Sandwich, the scourge of this fair isle,
With Ray shall laugh, and joke, and smile,
    And tremble at her *rod*:
Himself the jest of human race,
Shall reach his monkey new grimace,
    To scandalize his God.

353

But they are in exactly the tone of the political travesty called *The Duenna*, in which Lord Sandwich and Martha Reay (or Ray) his mistress had been satirized as "Jemmy Twitcher" and "Clara Raymond." They had also figured in a Tête-à-tête in *The Town and Country Magazine* (1769) as Jemmy Twitcher and Miss R—y, which gave a very much more favourable (and, undoubtedly truer) view of this ill-fated young woman than that of "the author of *The Duenna*."

Mr. Sichel suggested that Sheridan composed these verses about the time when he was drafting his unpublished reply to Dr. Johnson's *Taxation no Tyranny*. As *The Duenna* was not acted till November 21st, 1775, this suggested date—which would be about April, 1775—is impossible. Indeed, there is very definite evidence that it was published some twelve months later. The Ode was dismissed, in the summary manner of the period, in two periodicals—in three words, as "an American squib" in the *Town and Country Magazine* for February, 1777; and in seven words—"ridicules the Fast and insults the Government"—in the *Monthly Review* for December, 1776.[1] The occasion of the Ode must therefore have been "the public fast and humiliation" of 1776 ordered by the King on November 28 to be observed on December 13, "for the delivery of his loyal subjects in the Colonies of North America from the violence, injustice and, tyranny of the rebels," according to the *Annual Register* of that year.

The last person in the world to expose the General Fast to public ridicule would be the manager of the Theatre-Royal, Drury Lane. In his "Dedication to the King," a truculent piece of work, this "author of *The Duenna*" declares himself "an old devotee of the Brunswick line, and a hearty detester of the Stuart race"—words which were meant to suggest a man of a senior generation. It is therefore unnecessary to say more than that "*The Critic; or, a Tragedy Rehearsed* ... By the Author of *The Duenna*," another political travesty, from the same hand, appeared in 1780.

---

[1] "This writer, like many other persons, treats the General Fast as a *political farce*."— *The London Magazine* for December, 1776.

Elopement of the Graces

THE Muses and Graces on a Visit to Grosvenor Square. Being a Collection of Original Songs Sung by the Maskers, at Mrs. Crewe's Elegant Ball, Tuesday, March 21, 1775. London: Printed for J.Bew, in Pater-noster Row, MDCCLXXV. Quarto.

Pagination. P. [i] half-title, *The Muses and Graces on a Visit to Grosvenor Square. [Price One Shilling.*]; p. [ii] blank; p. [iii] title; p. [iv] blank; pp. 1–11 Text; p. [12] blank.

Mr. Sichel attributes to Sheridan a poem called *The Elopement of the Graces* which is printed (together with four ballads, "sung by the Maskers at Mrs. Crewe's elegant ball" and some French verses "presented to the Hon. Mrs. Bouverie" on the same occasion) in *The Muses and Graces on a Visit to Grosvenor Square.* His comments are that they "seem by their style and occasion to be Sheridan's," and that they are "in the manner of Clio's Protest." It has already been noted that Sheridan's *Sylvio to Laura*, Mrs. Sheridan's reply *Laura to Sylvio* and Sheridan's *A Portrait : for Amoret* are linked together by their theme in which a prominent part is played by Mrs. Crewe and other "women of the world of fashion." Mr. Sichel traces the beginning to this celebrated fête (which, by the way, virtually introduced to the *beau-monde* the high feathers for ladies' headdresses), but the evidence as to Sheridan's authorship of this poem does not extend beyond conjecture. In its way, it is a singularly neat piece of gallantry, celebrating the charms of seven beauties of the fashionable world, who were destined to become friends of the Sheridans—the Countess of Jersey, the Duchess of Devonshire, the Countess of Sefton, the Hon. Mrs. Bouverie, the Countess of Carlisle, the Countess of Craven, and Mrs. Crewe. If the young author of *The Rivals* was the author of this poem he showed his worldly wisdom in complimenting

355

the whole seven in one graceful tribute, with a crowning gesture
to his hostess, Mrs. Crewe.

ELOPEMENT OF THE GRACES

As *Venus* one day, in a hurry for dressing,
(*Jove's* dinner-bell ringing, and time very pressing)
Call'd aloud for the GRACES—no GRACES were there;
They were gone on a visit to *Grosvenor-Square.*
Dame *Venus*, enrag'd, fell a cursing and swearing,
(Which shock'd all the Gods that stood within hearing)
Then call'd for her coachman to harness her Doves,
Vowing vengeance against the poor Girls and their Loves.
She hunted the City ten thousand times o'er,
But never could find them, till stopp'd at CREWE's door
By *Cupid*, who, just at his Mother's approach,
Was handing a Beauty from out of her coach—
She follow'd the Beauty quite up to the room;
But then what a rage did her bosom consume,
To see the fair Nymphs of *Great Britain* excel
Her, who pass'd for the Beauty of Heaven and Hell!
They had got the poor GRACES quite into the middle,
And were dancing them round to the sound of the fiddle:
The *Cyprian* Dame, who of these Three so proud is,
Found they look'd, at this Ball, like a parcel of dowdies;
For by turns they were waiting on JERSEY and DEVON,
On SEFTON and BOUVERIE, on CARLISLE and CRAVEN.
In short, the fair Goddess some time stood confounded,
And thought that she was by a Dozen surrounded:
"Which are mine of these GRACES?" she cry'd in a passion,
And scolded—like any fine Lady of Fashion:
Her scolding soon caus'd in the GRACES a flurry,
And low on their knees they dropp'd down in a hurry:
"Forgive us, good Goddess," then quickly they cry'd;
"For Beauty to Beauty so near is ally'd,
"That this house for *Jove's* Palace by us may be taken,
"And Women for *goddesses* oft' are mistaken:

"We saw one in the *Park*, whom we took for you;
"We follow'd her home—and you see it is CREWE!"
The Goddess was angry, and did not dare own it,
But thought she would e'en put a good face upon it:
"You may ſtay then," she cry'd; "for I don't dress to-day"; ⎫
Then smil'd on the Ball, and soon fled away; ⎬
But wept out of envy, as other Gods say. ⎭

An Ode to Scandal

UNTIL the publication of my edition of "*An Ode to Scandal* together with *A Portrait*. By Richard Brinsley Sheridan" (1927), no issue of that ode was known previous to that published by W. Wright of 46 Fleet Street in 1819. In my edition, however, it was reprinted *An Ode to the Genius of Scandal* from a copy, then believed to be unique, in the possession of Mr. P. F. Hinton, which was published in 1781 by G. Kearsly, at the same address as Wright's. *An Ode to the Genius of Scandal* is *An Ode to Scandal* with some verbal differences: it contains an entire episode, and also two stanzas omitted in Wright's publication, together with a Preface (or an inserted leaf) dated "Cambridge, Oct. 30, 1781." This Preface explained that the author had intended his ode "solely for the amusement of his intimate acquaintance" had printed "only the requisite number of copies," and that one of the friends "who was favoured with the poem, thought a more enlarged publication might prove beneficial to mankind, in correcting an evil of which everyone complains."

Mr. Percy Dobell in two letters to *The Times Literary Supplement* pointed out that the copy was not unique, since he possessed two others, one of which had written on it, "by Mr. Tierney," and suggesting, quite reasonably, that insufficient attention had been paid to the Preface from Cambridge. Moreover, he showed, *The Bath Chronicle* claimed it in 1819 to have been written by George Tierney and to have been printed previously in its columns as by him.

Mr. G. W. Webb, in a letter to me, pointed out that in the University Library, Cambridge, there was a copy of another edition of 1781, without the name of the author, without the printer's or publisher's name, without place of publication, and without a preface. Mr. Webb added, "on our copy in MS. is written by George Tierney, Esq., but it is not given to him in the Peterhouse lift, of which College he was a member. He was born in 1761, so it seems very unlikely that he wrote the Ode in 1781." As no other verse by George Tierney is known to me, inveftigation is difficult, but the publisher of the genuine pieces published pofthumously as *Clio's Proteft: With Other Poems* (1819) was obviously scoffing at this attribution in a footnote to his preface, which mentions *The Morning Herald* as asserting two unnamed poems to be "juvenile sallies of Mr. Tierney's."

It seems to me, however, that the authorship of *An Ode to Scandal* will not be a matter of opinion upon the relative value of attributions, but of ascertainable faƈt. For *The London Magazine* in its Appendix for 1781 (published in January, 1782) reviewed *An Ode to the Genius of Scandal* thus: "A very pretty satire againft the vice of detraƈtion, to which the female sex are so addiƈted in conversation, and in their epiftolary correspondence. We are at a loss which to admire moft, the choice of the subjeƈt, or the mafterly execution of it, and are sorry to find that the publication of it has been ftopped by an injunƈtion from the author: this circumftance will make it more valuable to those who had the happiness to obtain copies before its suppression."

This discovery came at too late a ftage to make possible a fuller enquiry. As *An Ode to the Genius of Scandal* is accessible in my edition, and *An Ode to Scandal* in Mr. Sichel's *Sheridan*, it seems unnecessary to reprint it among these apocrypha.

BIBLIOGRAPHY

An Ode to the Genius of Scandal. Qui Capit, Facit. I say Nothing! [M.DCC.LXXXI.]

4to.

Pagination. P. [1] title; p. [2] blank; pp. [3] & 4–16 Text.

[Copy in Cambridge University Library. Not previously recorded.]

An Ode to the Genius of Scandal. Qui Capit, Facit. I say Nothing! London: Printed for G. Kearsly, at No. 46, Fleet Street. M.DCC.LXXXI.

4to.

Pagination. P. [1] half-title, *An Ode to the Genius of Scandal. Price One Shilling*; p. [2] blank; p. [3] title; p. [4] blank. Inserted leaf, unnumbered; Recto, Preface dated *Cambridge, Oct.* 30, 1781: Verso, blank; pp. [5] & 6–18. Text; pp. [19–20] blank.

4to.

[Mr. Percival Hinton's copy, Reprinted in *An Ode to Scandal.* . . . By Richard Brinsley Sheridan. Edited by R. Crompton Rhodes. 1927].

An Ode to Scandal: to which are added Stanzas on Fire. By the late Right Hon. R. B. Sheridan. *The Comedy of the School for Scandal was founded on the above Ode.* London: Printed for W. Wright, 46, Fleet Street, 1814.

8vo.

[Reprinted in Sichel's *Sheridan.* vol. I, pp. 618–622. Until 1927 this was supposed to be the First Edition.]

An Ode to Scandal... The Second Edition. London: Wright, 1819.

[Copy in the British Museum.]

Addenda

"THE METRICAL MISCELLANY: consisting chiefly of poems hitherto unpublished. London: T. Cadell and W. Davies, 1802" contains three poems ascribed to Sheridan in the table of contents. They seem to have been printed from MSS. since one is not recorded elsewhere, and the others, which vary slightly from the versions I have printed, are entitled "Dried be that tear," and "Mark'd you her cheek of roseate hue?"

The third may have been one of the juvenile epigrams which Mr. Sichel records in his list of unpublished poems as being "known only by a passing mention in Halhed's letters about 1770:

ON *A HANDSOME MOTHER AND SON,*

Each Bereft of One Eye

(From the Latin)

Of his right eye young Alcon was bereft,
His mother, Lionella, of her left;
Give her thine eye, sweet boy, so shall ye prove
The Goddess she, and you the God of Love.

The three pieces thus ascribed to Sheridan are followed immediately by another which is anonymous, though it is a variant of "The Kiss."

Humid seal of soft affections,
Tenderest pledge of future bliss;
Dearest tye of young connexions,
Love's first snow-drop, Virgin kiss!

363

Sorrowing joy, adieu's laſt action
When ling'ring lips no more muſt join,
What words can ever speak affection
So thrilling, so sincere as thine!

These verses are bad enough for the bellman, and I shall not pretend to decide which is the viler phrase, "humid seal" or "hurried seal." The second verse, differing entirely from what one muſt dignify by the name of "the received text," is marked, however, by one word which haunted Sheridan throughout his verses—"ling'ring."

SONG FROM THE CRITIC

It might have been thought (if anybody had given it a moment's curiosity) that the songs by the Italian singers in *The Critic* were to be numbered as loſt for ever, with those that the Sirens sang. But one of the beſt and rareſt song-books of the period, *The Banquet of Thalia* preserves a favourite duetto in *The Critic*.

(Italian and English Words)

Lusinghiero m'ingannaſti
Mi tradiſti o Dio perche
Tu pian geſti e sospiraſti
Tu giuraſti fede ame
Traditore ingannatore
Tutto il male vien da te
Traditore ingannatore
Tutto il male vien da te.

Flatt'rer! why doſt thou deceive me?
Why betray my conſtant love?
Why, with sighs and well-feign'd sorrow,
Haſt thou sworn thy faith to prove?
False betrayer!—thou base deceiver!
Ev'ry grief I owe to thee!
False betrayer, &c., &c.

Whether Sheridan was or was not the author is of no importance, but the dramatic nature of the duet will be appreciated by
any producer. The song book was printed at least twice:

The Banquet of Thalia, or the Favourite Songsters' Pocket
Memorial, An Elegant Collection of the most admired Songs
from Ancient and Modern Authors. York, 1790. 12mo: York,
1792. 12mo.

[Compiled by F. Atkinson of York. An undated London edition (which I have not
seen) appears to be, therefore, a reprint.]

VERSES TO LAURA, 1795.

In *The Pin-Basket* by "Anthony Pasquin" (London, 1796)
occurs a line on Sheridan, "I tell you, man, his Muse is past con-
ception." To this is a footnote:

"A late copy of verses, composed by Mr. S. on Capt. N. Ogle,
who died in the West Indies, firmly persuades us that not only
will he not attempt to write any more plays, but that he is not *now*
able, however much he might desire it. We never witnessed
more scabrous lines, being exactly, including their insipidity,
what Aristophanes calls *prose on horseback*."

The poem in question is obviously *Verses to Laura*, included
in *Clio's Protest; With Other Poems* (1819) as "never before
printed." It must be assumed from "Anthony Pasquin's" reference that they had appeared in print, most probably in some
periodical, as yet untraced. "Scabrous" means, of course, no
more than crude and unpolished. The officer has been variously
identified, as "Colonel M., killed in the battle of the Helder"
(in the Preface to *Clio's Protest*) and "Captain Buller, killed in
Flanders" (in Howard's *Beauties of Sheridan*, I think). *The Pin-
Basket*, Mr. Hinton tells me, is not by the genuine "Anthony
Pasquin," John Williams, but is a spurious anticipation of his
announced poem, published 1797, 12mo. The book is :

The Pin-Basket. To the Children of Thespis. A Satire. By
Anthony Pasquin, A. London: Printed for the Author. 1796.
4to., pp. 64.